Mór Jókai, R. Nisbet (Robert Nisbet) Bain

The Lion of Janina

Or, The last Days of the Janissaries

Mór Jókai, R. Nisbet (Robert Nisbet) Bain

The Lion of Janina
Or, The last Days of the Janissaries

ISBN/EAN: 9783337241049

Printed in Europe, USA, Canada, Australia, Japan

Cover: Foto ©ninafisch / pixelio.de

More available books at **www.hansebooks.com**

Mór Jókai, R. Nisbet (Robert Nisbet) Bain

The Lion of Janina
Or, The last Days of the Janissaries

ISBN/EAN: 9783337241049

Printed in Europe, USA, Canada, Australia, Japan

Cover: Foto ©ninafisch / pixelio.de

More available books at **www.hansebooks.com**

MAURUS JOKAI

THE LION OF JANINA

OR

THE LAST DAYS OF THE JANISSARIES

A Turkish Novel

TRANSLATED BY

R. NISBET BAIN

HARPER & BROTHERS PUBLISHERS
NEW YORK AND LONDON
1898

THE LION OF JANINA

PREFACE

The first edition of *Janicsárok végnapjai* appeared forty-five years ago. It was immediately preceded by the great historical romance, *Erdély aranykora* (*The Golden Age of Transylvania*), and the still more famous novel of manners, *Egy Magyar Nábob* (*A Hungarian Nabob*), which Hungarians regard as, indisputably, Jókai's masterpiece, while only a few months separate it from *Kárpáthy Zoltán* (*Sultan Karpathy*), the brilliant sequel to the *Nabob*. Thus it belongs to the author's best literary period.

It is also one of the most striking specimens of that peculiar group of Turkish stories, such as *Törökvilag Magyarorszagon* (*Turkey in Hungary*) and *Török mozgolmak* (*Turkish Incursions*), *A kétszarvú ember* (*The Man with the Antlers*), and the extremely popular *Fehér rózsa* (*White Rose*), which form a genre apart of Jókai's own creation, in which his exuberant imagination revels in the rich colors of the gorgeous East, as in its proper element, while his ever alert humor makes the most of the sharp and strange contrasts of Oriental life and society. The hero of the strange and terrible drama, or, rather, series of dramas, unfolded with such spirit, skill, and vividness in *Janicsárok vég-*

napjai, is Ali Pasha of Janina, certainly one of the most brilliant, picturesque, and, it must be added, capable ruffians that even Turkish history can produce. Manifold and monstrous as were Ali's crimes, his astonishing ability and splendid courage lend a sort of savage sublimity even to his blood-stained career, and, indeed, the dogged valor with which the octogenarian warrior defended himself at the last in his stronghold against the whole might of the Ottoman Empire is almost without a parallel in history.

With such a hero, it is evident that the book must abound in stirring and even tremendous scenes; but, though primarily a novel of incident, it contains not a few fine studies of Oriental character, both Turkish and Greek, by an absolutely impartial observer, who can detect the worth of the Osmanli in the midst of his apathy and brutality, and who, although sympathetically inclined towards the Hellenes, is by no means blind to their craft and double-dealing, happily satirized in the comic character of Leonidas Argyrocantharides.

Finally, I have taken the liberty to alter the title of the story. *Janicsárok végnapjai* (*The Last Days of the Janissaries*) is too glaringly inapt to pass muster, inasmuch as the rebellion and annihilation of that dangerous corps is a mere inessential episode at the end of the story. I have, therefore, given the place of honor on the title-page to Ali Pasha—the Lion of Janina.

I have added a glossary of the Turkish words used by the author in these pages.

R. николаNisbet Bain.

CONTENTS

CHAPTER		PAGE
I.	THE CAVERNS OF SELEUCIA	1
II.	EMINAH	19
III.	A TURKISH PARADISE	45
IV.	GASKHO BEY	62
V.	A MAN IN THE MIDST OF DANGERS	72
VI.	THE LION IN THE FOX'S SKIN	78
VII.	THE ALBANIAN FAMILY	105
VIII.	THE PEN OF MAHMOUD	110
IX.	THE CIRCASSIAN AND HIS FAMILY	129
X.	THE AVENGER	160
XI.	THE FLOWERS OF THE GARDEN OF BEGTASH	187
XII.	THE SHIPWRECK OF LEONIDAS	198
XIII.	A BALL IN THE SERAGLIO	213
XIV.	KURSHID PASHA	238
XV.	CARETTO	244
XVI.	EMINAH	252
XVII.	THE SILVER PEDESTAL IN FRONT OF THE SERAGLIO	262
XVIII.	THE BROKEN SWORDS	275
	GLOSSARY OF TURKISH WORDS	293

THE LION OF JANINA

CHAPTER I

THE CAVERNS OF SELEUCIA

A SAVAGE, barren, inhospitable region lies before us, the cavernous valley of Seleucia—a veritable home for an anchorite, for there is nothing therein to remind one of the living world; the whole district resembles a vast ruined tomb, with its base overgrown by green weeds. Here is everything which begets gloom—the blackest religious fanaticism, the darkest monstrosities of superstition—while an eternal malediction seems to brood like a heavy mist over this region, created surely by God's left hand, scattering abroad gigantic rocky fragments, smiting the earth with unfruitfulness, and making it uninhabitable by the children of men.

Man rarely visits these parts. And, indeed, why should he come, or what should he seek there? There is absolutely nothing in the whole region that is dear to the heart of man. Even the wild beast makes no abiding lair for himself in that valley. Only now and then, in the burning days of summer, a lion of the wilderness, flying from before the sultry heat, may, perchance, come there to devour his captured prey, and then, when he is well gorged, pursue his way, wrangling as he goes with the echo of his own roar.

Solitary travellers of an enterprising turn of mind do occasionally visit this dreary wilderness; but so crushing an impression does it make on all who have the courage to gaze upon it, that they scarce wait to explore the historic ground, but hasten from it as fast as their legs can carry them.

What is there to see there, after all? A battered-down wall, as to which none can say who built it, or why it was built, or who destroyed it. A tall stone column, the column of the worthy Simon Stylites, who piled it up, stone upon stone, year after year, with his own hands, being wont to sit there for days together with arms extended in the shape of a cross, bowing himself thousands and thousands of times a day till his head touched his feet. The northern and southern sides of the valley are cut off from the rest of the world by gigantic masses of rocks as steep and solid as the bastions of a fortress; only towards their summit, at an elevation of some three to four hundred yards, is a little strip of green vegetation visible.

Darkly visible at intervals in this long and steep rocky wall are the mouths of a series of caverns, of various sizes, all close together. It looks as if some monstrous antediluvian race had cut two or three stories of doors and windows into the living rock, in order to make themselves palaces to dwell in.

The walls of these caverns are so rugged, their bases are so irregular, that it is scarcely conceivable that they could be the work of human hands, unless, indeed, the arched concavities of the chasms and the regular consecutiveness of the series may be assumed to bear witness to the wonder-working power of finite forces.

Three of the entrances to these caverns have all the loftiness of triumphal arches; nay, one of them, carved in the base of the rock, is so exceptionally vast that it rather resembles the nave of a huge church, and is said to penetrate the whole mountain to the sea beyond. It is said that if any one has the courage to attempt the journey, he will discover mysterious hieroglyphics carved on the walls. Who could have been the authors of this unknown runic language? The Chaldeans perhaps, or the worshippers of Mithra. What hidden secrets, what human memorials are enshrined in these symbols? That question must remain forever without an answer.

Most probably this valley was used as a burial-place by some long-vanished nation, whose tombs have survived them, making the whole region still more dreadful; the gaping crevices of the rocks seem to proclaim, as from a hundred open throats, that here an extinct race has found its last resting-place.

Moreover, the largest cavern of all has the unusual property of sometimes emitting whistling sounds like interrupted human voices. The shepherds on the mountain summits listen terror-stricken to this bellowing of its rocky throat. At first it resembles the buzzing of imprisoned wasps, but the din gradually gathers force and volume till it seems as if the demons of the wind had lost their way within the cavern, and were roaring tumultuously in their endeavors to find an exit. This noise is generally followed by the blast of the simoon, which no doubt penetrates into the cavern through a gap on the other side, and thus gives rise to the mysterious voices of the valley.

But not on these occasions only; at other seasons also the cavern is wont to speak. It happens now and then that a shepherd, more foolhardy than his fellows, ventures into the hollow of the cavern to light a fire, and, full of bravado, provokes the *dzhin* of the cavern to appear, till the cavern suddenly re-echoes his voice; but it does not re-echo the words he utters, but replies in a soft, low accent to the insolent youth, bidding him withdraw and cease to mock God's creatures.

On another occasion an adulterous woman and her paramour strolled towards the spot with the intent of using the deep darkness as the cloak for their sinful joys; but what terror filled the guilty lovers when their sweet whispering was interrupted by a voice which was neither near nor far, and belonged neither to man nor spirit, but whose cold sigh turned their hot blood into ice as it whispered, "Allah is everywhere present!"

Once, too, some robbers were lying in wait for their comrades, whom they intended to murder in that place, when a roaring began in the cave which seemed to make the very welkin ring, and the murderers clearly distinguished the terrible words: "The eye of Allah is upon you, and the flames of Morhut are burning for your souls!" whereupon, insane with fright, they rushed from the cave.

Every one who lived near the place knew of, and

believed in, the *dzhin* of the cavern, who, they said, harmed not the good, but persecuted evil-doers.

But it was not only terror-stricken hearts who knew of the voice of the invisible *dzhin*—crushed and bleeding hearts likewise repaired thither. And the invisible *dzhin* read their secrets; they had no need to acquaint him with their griefs, and he gave them good counsel, and, for the most part, sent them away comforted. Doubtless anybody else might have given them similar counsels; but if the advice had come from ordinary men, the suppliants would not perhaps have welcomed it with such enthusiasm, or have turned it to such good account.

And people often came thither to inquire into the future; and the invisible being, it was found, could distinguish between those who came to him in real anguish of mind and those whom only curiosity had attracted thither, or who merely wished to prove him. To the latter he made no answer, but to the former he often spoke in prophetic parables, whose deeply figurative meaning was frequently fulfilled word for word.

The superstitious common folk made a merit of sacrificing to this unknown being. The dwellers round about made a point of living on good terms with him, took care not to provoke him with vain words, did not fly to him at every trifle; nay, on one occasion, the Kadi* of Seleucia even laid by the heels a couple of wanton rascals who were caught throwing stones into the cavern.

From the mouth of the cave inward extended a

---

* For this and all other Turkish words see the glossary at the end of this book.

sort of staircase consisting of about forty steps, terminating at a point whither the light of day scarcely ever reached. Here stood a huge stone, not unlike a rude altar, in the midst of which was a slight hollow. This hollow the pious inhabitants of the district used to fill with rice or millet, and on returning next day they would see that the *dzhin* had removed it from thence, and, by way of payment, had left a small silver coin in this natural basin—a coin belonging to that old silver money which had been struck in the brilliant days of the Turkish Empire, and was worth thrice as much as the present coinage. Thus the *dzhin* would take nothing gratis, but paid for everything in ready money.

Those who wished to speak with him had to penetrate into the depths of the cave where no daylight was visible, for he was only to be found where the darkness was complete. If any one went with sword or dagger he got no answer at all. And a visitor standing alone there in the darkness was as plainly visible to the *dzhin* as if the glare of noonday were beating full upon him; not a change of countenance was hidden from this mysterious being. So they more readily believed that he who could thus see through the darkness of earth could also see through the darkness of human hearts and the darkness of the unrevealed future.

This marvel had now been notorious for fifty years, the ordinary span of human life, and princes, pashas, generals, wise men, priests, ulemas, were in the habit of visiting the abode of the *dzhin*, who seemed to know about everything that was going on in the world above. To many he prophesied death, and to those who pleased him not he foretold the Nemesis that was to come upon them as a reward for their iniquities.

In the year one thousand eight hundred and nineteen, at the season immediately following the raging of the simoon, it chanced that a pirate ship sailed into the haven of Suda, whence the magnificent ruins of the ancient Seleucia are still to be seen. The corsair carried the French flag, but her crew consisted entirely of Albanians. The deck was encumbered with wreckage, cast down upon it by the happily weathered tempest, and this the crew were energetically engaged in removing; but every one on shore was astounded to see her there at all, much more in such trim condition, for she had lost neither mast nor sail. But then, after the manner of corsairs in general, she was very much better equipped with both masts and sails than ships of ordinary tonnage are wont to be. In the same hour that the ship cast anchor the largest of her boats was lowered, and manned by four and twenty well-armed Trinariots. Every one of these stout fellows carried orders of merit on his cheek, the scars of many a battle, which accentuated the savage sternness of their weather-beaten faces.

A little old man descended after them into the boat; presently his horse was also let down by means of a crane. This was the officer in command. He was a middling-sized but very muscular old fellow, already beyond his seventieth and not very far from his eightieth year; but he was as vigorous now both in mind and body as he had been when his beard, which now swept across his breast like the wing of a swan, was as dark as the raven's plume.

His broad shoulders spoke of extraordinary strength, while the firm expression of his face, the flashing lustre of his eyes, and his calm and valiant look, testified to the fact that this strength was squandered upon no coward soul.

Some stout rowing brought the boat at last near to the shore, but not all the efforts of the men could bring her to land; the wash of the sea was so great that the foam-crested waves again and again drove the boat back from the shore.

At a sign from the old man three of the ship's crew leaped into the waves in order to drag after them the boat's hawser, but the sea tore it out of the hands of all three as easily as a wild bull would toss a pack of children.

Then the old man vaulted upon his steed, kicking the stirrups aside, and leaped among the churning waves. Twice the horse was jostled back by the assault of the foaming billows, but at the third attempt the shore was reached. The people on the shore said it was a miracle; but he, wasting no words upon any one, directed his way all alone along the shore of the haven, and leaving behind him the lofty turreted row of bastions—which crowns the edge of the rocky promontory, encircles the town, and hangs upon the shoulders of the hill like an ancient and gigantic necklace—picked his way among the lofty, scattered bowlders, and, unescorted as he was, quickly disappeared from view amid the wilderness.

He had scarcely proceeded more than half an hour among the fig and olive trees which covered the slopes of the hills, and whose scorched and withered leaves marked the passage of the burning wind, when he arrived at the place he sought. It was a crazy, tumble-down hut, whose shapeless mass was so clumsily compounded of wood, stone, and mud, that a swallow would have been ashamed to own it, let alone a beaver, whose ordinary habitation is an architectural masterpiece compared with it. Nature, however, had been gracious to this shanty, and clothed it with creeping plants, which nearly hid away all the superflous cracks and crevices which the architect had left behind him.

It was here that the new-comer dismounted from his horse, tied it to a tree, and, proceeding to the latchless door, amused himself by reading the scrawl which had been written on the outside of it, and was, as usual, one of those sacred texts which the Turks love to see over their door-posts: "Accursed be he who disturbs a singing-bird!"

The stranger fell a listening. Surely there was no singing-bird here, he thought. Then he went on reading what followed: "He who knocks at the gate of him who prays will knock in vain at the gate of Paradise."

The stranger did not take the trouble to knock; he simply kicked the door down.

Within was kneeling an anchorite of the order of Erdbuhár on a piece of matting. He was naked to the girdle, and before him stood a wooden tub full of fresh water. He was just finishing his ablutions.

He did not seem to observe the violent inroad of the stranger, but concluded his religious exercises with great fervor. First of all he washed his hands, reciting thirty times the sacred words, "Blessed be God, Who hath given to water its purifying power, and hath revealed the true faith to us!" Next he thrice conveyed water to his mouth in his right palm, and prayed, "O Lord! O Allah! refresh me with the water Thou didst give to Thy Prophet Muhammad in Paradise, which is more fragrant than balm, whiter than milk, and sweeter than honey, and satisfies eternally those who pine with thirst!" Then, with the palm of his hand, he cast water upon his nostrils, and exclaimed, fervently, "O Lord! cause me to smell the perfume of Paradise, which is sweeter than musk and ambergris, and suffer me not to inhale the accursed fumes of hell!" Then, filling both palms with water and well washing his face, he said these words, " Purify my face, O Lord, like as Thou wilt purify the faces of Thy prophets and servants on the great Day of Judgment!" But even this did not suffice, for now he put water in his right palm again, and, letting it run down his elbows, he sighed, "Lord, suffer me at the last day to hold in my right hand, which is the hand of Thine elect, the book of my good deeds, and admit me to Thy Paradise!" With that he dipped his head into the tub of water, but so as to keep his mouth clear of it, and spake in this wise, "O Lord, when I appear before Thee, encompass me with Thy mercies, and crush not my head beneath the fiery wreath of my sins, but adorn it with the golden crown of my merits!" Then came the turn of his ears, the worthy man crying the while, with unction, "Grant, O Lord, that mine ears may hear, for ever and ever, those joyous sounds which are written in the

Kuran!" This accomplished, he sprinkled his neck and throat, suitably exclaiming, "O Lord, deliver me from those fetters which will be cast upon the necks of the accursed!" After which pious ejaculation he sat down on the ground, and, reverently washing his right foot, exclaimed, "O Lord, suffer not my feet to slip on the bridge of Alserat which leads across hell to heaven!" Then he cleansed thoroughly his left foot also, and sighed, "May the Lord forgive me my trespasses and listen to my supplications!"

And the honest dervish did not utter all these pious ejaculations in a low mumble, but in an intelligible, exalted voice, as becomes an orthodox Mussulman, who does not consider it a shameful thing to pray to God in the presence of men.

After that he took up the tub and, carrying it out, sprinkled the water it contained over the wild flowers growing there, blessing them severally and collectively; then he filled it full again with fresh water from the spring, and bringing it back into the hut and turning the mat over, placed the tub full of water on it, whereupon the stranger immediately divested himself of his slippers and upper kaftan, unwound his turban, removed his red fez from his head, and proceeded to perform his ablutions also in the self-same manner.

When he had finished he kissed the hand of the dervish, and when the latter drew from his girdle a long manuscript reaching to the very ground, and began, from its eighty sections, to laud and magnify the eighty properties of Allah, the stranger repeated them after him with great unction, and, at the end of each one of them, intoned with him twice over the verse, "La illah, il Allah, Muhammad roszul Allah!"—in the chanting of which he was as practised as any muezzin.

All these pious practices were accomplished with the utmost devotion; but when the new-comer arose from his place, the expression of lowliness vanished from his features and he reassumed his former commanding look, while the dervish now humbly bowed down before him to the very earth and murmured:

"What are my lord's commands to his servant?"

The stranger let him lie there and slowly raised his sword.

"Art thou," cried he, "that dervish of Erdbuhár* to whom I despatched a fakir of the Nimetullahitas, who dwelleth in Janina?"

"Thy servant is that man."

The stranger thereupon, with his right hand, drew a dagger from his girdle, and with his left hand a purse.

"Dost thou see this dagger and this purse?" said he. "In the purse are a thousand sequins; on the blade of this sword is the blood of at least as many murdered men. I ask thee not—Dost thou recognize me? or dost thou know my name? Maybe thou dost know—for thou knowest all things—and, if so, thou dost also know that none hath ever betrayed me on whom I have not wreaked my ven-

---

* The orders of Erdbuhár and Nimetullahita are the severest of all the Turkish religious fraternities: the former fast so rigorously twice a week that they do not even swallow their saliva; the latter observe the fast only during their year of probation, after which they are free to return to the joys of this world.

geance. If, therefore, thou dost want a reward, listen; but if chastisement, speak!"

The dervish raised his hand to his ear to signify that he would prefer to listen.

"Arise, then! take my horse's bridle, and lead me to that cavern where dwelleth the *džhin* of prophecy. Dost thou know him?"

"I know him, my master, but go to him I will not, for he is wroth with me. He loves not the dervishes, because they would always be teaching. If I go to him he throws stones at me from out of the cavern, or leads me into deep pitfalls. Therefore, if thou so desire it, I will lead thee thither; but I would not go with thee if I had as many heads upon my shoulders for thy sword to sever as there are sequins in that purse."

"There is no need of that. Thou canst remain outside and hold my horse."

And with that the herculean old man flung himself haughtily on his horse, and the dervish, seizing the steed's bridle, began to lead him along the mountain path among the rugged rocks and bowlders.

The moon was already high in the heavens when they reached the mouth of the cavern.

Looking back upon the country whence they came, the region seemed more desolate than ever. In front, the savage, natural ruins; behind, the black cedar forests, where thick foliage cast night-black shadows even at noonday; on each side, the endlessly sublime masses of rocks, which stood out still vaster in the moonlight. The caverns looked still blacker at night, and the rock and ruins more sterile; but, night and day alike, the place was deserted.

On reaching the cavern of the *dzhin*, the old man dismounted from his horse and, bidding the dervish stand and hold it till he returned, disappeared in the cavern without the slightest hesitation.

He could only grope his way, step by step, through the blinding darkness; cautiously he advanced, but without fear. He tested the ground in front of him as he advanced, with one hand over his eyes and the other on the hilt of his sword. It must, indeed, be a resolutely wicked spirit that would venture to attack him.

Every now and then a bat sped rapidly past him, close to his ears, with a sound like a mocking titter; at other times he trod upon some cold, moving body. But what cared he for these? The deep silence which encircled him was far more terrible than all the voices of hell; and not even the darkness terrified him, for his powerful voice now pierced that subterranean stillness as with a sword.

"I summon thee, thou spirit, whether thou art good or evil, whom Allah permits to hold discourse with living men—I summon thee to speak with me!"

"I am even now beside thee," a voice suddenly whispered. It was low and hollow, just as if the atmosphere of the cavern were speaking.

The stranger made a clutch after the voice, as if his audacious hand would have seized the spirit; but he found nothing. It was a voice without a shape.

"Speak to me!" cried the old man, in a voice that never quavered. "Dost thou know my fate?"

"I know it," answered the invisible voice; "thou art a poor man who hast lost what thou hadst, and what thou now hast is not thine."

"Thou art a senseless spirit," growled the stranger. "Go back to thy tomb and slumber; I will inquire nothing more of thee. Thou dost not even know my present fate; how canst thou know my future? Go back to thy hole, I say, and sleep in peace."

"I know thee," continued the voice, "and I have spoken the truth. Do not they call thee Ali Tepelenti?"

The stranger was amazed. "That is indeed my name," he answered.

"Wert thou not a fugitive yesterday, and wilt thou not be dust and ashes to-morrow?"

"True; but that yesterday was eighty years ago; and who shall say when to-morrow will be?"

"Thou knowest that here there is neither morning nor evening," answered the voice. "To me yesterday was when I last saw the sun, and to-morrow will be when I see it again. Ali Tepelenti, Lord of Janina, thou art poorer than the lowliest Mussulman who girds himself with a girdle of hair, for thou hast lost everything which thou didst account precious. Thy kinsmen, who were for thy defence, thou hast slain; thy mother, who loved thee, thou hast strangled; thy right hand has pulled down the house which thou didst build up; thy glory, in which thou didst exalt thyself, has become a curse to thee; and thou hast made bitter haters of those who loved thee best."

"So it is. I know what I have done. I repent me of nothing. The hare nibbles the flower, the vulture seizes the hare, the hunter slays the vulture, the lion fells the hunter, the worm devours the lion. All of us turn to earth. Allah is mighty, and He orders it so. What am I? Only a bigger worm than the rest. Who shall strive with God? What is my fate in the future?"

"But yesterday thou wert younger than thy new-born son, to-morrow thou shalt die older than thy oldest ancestors."

"Speak more plainly. I perceive the meaning of thy words as little as I perceive thyself."

"'He who sins with the sword shall perish with the sword,' saith Allah. He who sins with love, shall perish by love. Thou hast two hands, the right and the left; thou hast two swords, one covered with gold and one with silver; thou hast three hundred wives in thy harem, but only one in thy heart; thou hast twelve sons, but only one whom thou lovest. Look, now! Take good heed of thy life, for thy death lieth in what is nearest to thee; thine own weapon, thine own child, thine own property, thine own two hands, shall one day slay thee."

"Mashallah! Death is inevitable. Tell me but one thing. Shall I one day pass in triumph through the gates of the seraglio at Stambul?"

"Thou shalt. Thou shalt stand there on a silver pedestal in the face of the rejoicing multitude."

"When?"

"That day will come when thou shalt be in two places at the same time, in Janina and in Stambul; the days to come will explain it."

"One word more. Wherefore didst thou mention that woman whom I love best?"

"She will be the first to betray thee."

"Accursed one!" roared Ali, drawing his sword and madly striking in the direction of the voice.

"Thou art a senseless spirit," growled the stranger. "Go back to thy tomb and slumber; I will inquire nothing more of thee. Thou dost not even know my present fate; how canst thou know my future? Go back to thy hole, I say, and sleep in peace."

"I know thee," continued the voice, "and I have spoken the truth. Do not they call thee Ali Tepelenti?"

The stranger was amazed. "That is indeed my name," he answered.

"Wert thou not a fugitive yesterday, and wilt thou not be dust and ashes to-morrow?"

"True; but that yesterday was eighty years ago; and who shall say when to-morrow will be?"

"Thou knowest that here there is neither morning nor evening," answered the voice. "To me yesterday was when I last saw the sun, and to-morrow will be when I see it again. Ali Tepelenti, Lord of Janina, thou art poorer than the lowliest Mussulman who girds himself with a girdle of hair, for thou hast lost everything which thou didst account precious. Thy kinsmen, who were for thy defence, thou hast slain; thy mother, who loved thee, thou hast strangled; thy right hand has pulled down the house which thou didst build up; thy glory, in which thou didst exalt thyself, has become a curse to thee; and thou hast made bitter haters of those who loved thee best."

"So it is. I know what I have done. I repent me of nothing. The hare nibbles the flower, the vulture seizes the hare, the hunter slays the vulture, the lion fells the hunter, the worm devours the lion. All of us turn to earth. Allah is mighty, and He orders it so. What am I? Only a bigger worm than the rest. Who shall strive with God? What is my fate in the future?"

"But yesterday thou wert younger than thy new-born son, to-morrow thou shalt die older than thy oldest ancestors."

"Speak more plainly. I perceive the meaning of thy words as little as I perceive thyself."

"'He who sins with the sword shall perish with the sword,' saith Allah. He who sins with love, shall perish by love. Thou hast two hands, the right and the left; thou hast two swords, one covered with gold and one with silver; thou hast three hundred wives in thy harem, but only one in thy heart; thou hast twelve sons, but only one whom thou lovest. Look, now! Take good heed of thy life, for thy death lieth in what is nearest to thee; thine own weapon, thine own child, thine own property, thine own two hands, shall one day slay thee."

"Mashallah! Death is inevitable. Tell me but one thing. Shall I one day pass in triumph through the gates of the seraglio at Stambul?"

"Thou shalt. Thou shalt stand there on a silver pedestal in the face of the rejoicing multitude."

"When?"

"That day will come when thou shalt be in two places at the same time, in Janina and in Stambul; the days to come will explain it."

"One word more. Wherefore didst thou mention that woman whom I love best?"

"She will be the first to betray thee."

"Accursed one!" roared Ali, drawing his sword and madly striking in the direction of the voice.

The sword hissed fiercely through the vacant air, and the next moment the voice replied from a respectable distance :

"It has happened already."

"This is a dream, all a dream!" moaned Ali.

"'Tis no dream; thou art wide awake," cried the mysterious voice.

"If it be no dream, give me a sign that I may know before I depart hence that I have not been dreaming."

"First put thy sword into its sheath."

"I have done so," said Ali; but he lied, for he had only slipped it into his girdle.

"Into the sheath, I say," cried the voice.

It was with a tremor that Ali felt that this being could distinguish his slightest movement in the dark.

"And now stretch forth thy hand!" cried the voice. It was now quite close to him.

Ali stretched forth his hand, and the same instant he felt a vigorous, manly hand seize his own in a grasp of steel; so strong, so cruel was the pressure that the blood started from the tips of his fingers.

At last the invisible being let go, and said in a whisper as it did so :

"Not a muscle of thy face moved under the pressure of my hand; only Tepelenti could so have endured."

"And there is but one man living who could press my hand like that," replied Ali. "His name was Behram, the son of Halil Patrona,* who, forty years

---

* The extraordinary adventures of this Mussulman reformer are recorded in another of Jókai's Turkish stories, *A feher rózsa* (*The White Rose*).

2

ago, was my companion in warfare, and has since disappeared. Who art thou?"

"Aleikum unallah!"* said the voice, instead of replying.

"Who art thou?" again cried Ali, advancing a step.

"Aleikum unallah!" was the parting salutation of the already far-distant voice.

The mighty pasha turned back in a reverie, and when he got back into the moonlight, he still saw plainly on his hand the drops of blood which that powerful grasp had caused to leap forth from the tips of his fingers.

* "God be with thee!"

CHAPTER II

EMINAH

AND now for a story, a marvellous story, that would not be out of place in a fairy tale! Away to another clime where the very sunbeams and blossoms, where the very beating of loving hearts, differ from what we are accustomed to.

In whichever direction we look around us, we shall see the land of the gods rising up before us in classical sublimity, the mountains of Hellas, the triumphal home of sun-bright heroes. There is the mountain whence Zeus cast forth his thunderbolts, the grove where the thorns of roses scratched the tender feet of Aphrodite, and perchance a whole olive grove sprung from the tree into which the nymph, favored and pursued by Apollo, was metamorphosed. The sunlit summits of snowy Œta and Ossa still sparkle there when the declining sun kindles his beacons upon them, and Olympus still has its thunderbolts; yet it is no longer Zeus who casts them, but Ali Tepelenti, Pasha of Albania and master of half the Turkish Empire, and the rose which the blood of Venus dyed crimson blooms for him, and the laurel sprung from the love of Apollo puts forth her green garlands for him also.

The poetic figures of the bright gods are seen no

more on the quiet mountain. With a long gun over his shoulder, a palikár walks hither and thither, who has built his hut in a lurking-place where Ali Pasha will not find it. The high porticos lie level with the ground; the paths of Leonidas and Themistocles are covered with sentry-boxes, that none may pass that way.

From the summit of the mighty Lithanizza you can look down upon the fairy-like city which dominates Albania. It is Janina, the historically renowned Janina.

Beside it stands the lake of Acheruz, in whose green mirror the city can regard itself; there it is in duplicate. It is as deep as it is high. The golden half-moons of the minarets sparkle in the lake and in the sky at the same time. The roofless white houses, rising one above another, seem melted into a compact mass, and they are encircled by red bastions, with exits out of eight gates.

But what have we to do with the minarets, the bazaars, the kiosks of the city? Beyond the city, where Cocytus, rippling down from the wooded mountain, forms, with the lake into which it flows, a peninsula, there, on an isthmus, stands the strong fortress of Ali Pasha, with vast, massive bastions, a heavy, iron-plated drawbridge, and a ditch in front of the walls full of solid sharp-pointed stakes in two fathoms of water. From the summits of the ramparts the throats of a hundred cannons gape down upon the town—iron dogs, whose barking can be heard four miles off. On the walls an innumerable multitude of armed men keep watch, and in front of the gate the guns look out upon each other from the port-holes of the steep bastions on both sides of it. Woe to those who should attempt to make their way into the citadel by force! The gate, fastened with a huge chain, is defended by three heavy iron gratings, and from close beneath the lofty projecting roof circular pieces of artillery shine forth, in front of which are pyramidal stacks of bombs.

The court-yard forms a huge crescent, in which nothing is visible but instruments of warfare, engines of destruction. In the lower part of the semicircular barracks stand the sentry-boxes, while in the opposite semicircle a long pavilion cuts the fortress in two, extending from the end of one semicircle to the end of the other, and here are three gates, which lead into the heart of the fortress.

In all this long building there are no windows above the court-yard, only two rows of narrow embrasures are visible therein. All the windows are on the other side overlooking the garden, and there dwell the odalisks of Ali Pasha's three sons. The three sons, Omar, Almuhán, and Zaid, inhabit the building with the three gates. The back of this building looks out upon the garden, in which the harems of the pasha's sons are wont to disport themselves.

Here again a long bastion barricades the garden, a bastion also protected by trenches full of water, across whose iron bridge you gain admission into the pasha's inmost fortress.

And what is that like? Nobody can tell. The brass gates, covered with silver arabesques, seem to be eternally closed, and none ever comes in or goes out save Ali and his dumb eunuchs, and those captives whose heads alone are sent back again. The bastion surrounding this central fortress is so high that you cannot look into it from the top of the citadel outside; but if any one could peep down upon it from the summit of the lofty Lithanizza he would perceive inside it a fairy palace, with walls of colored marble protected by silver trellis-work, with blue-painted, brazen cupolas, with golden half-moons on their pointed spires. One tower there, the largest of all, has a roof of red cast-iron, and this one roof stands out prominently from among all the other buildings of the inner fortress. The colored kiosks are everywhere wreathed with garlands of flowers, and the spectator perched aloft would plainly discern cradles for growing vines on the top of the bastion. He might also, in the dusk of the summer evenings, distinguish seductive shapes bathing in the basins of the fountains, and lose his reason while he gazed; or it might chance (which is much more likely) that Ali Pasha's patrols might come upon him unawares and cast him down from the mountain-top.

This wondrous retreat was Ali's paradise. Here he grouped together the most beautiful flowers of the round world — flowers sprung from the earth or from a human mother. For maidens also are flowers, and may be plucked and enjoyed like other flowers. But the most beautiful among so many beautiful flowers was Eminah, Tepelenti's favorite damsel, the sixteen-years-old daughter of the Pasha of Delvino, who gave her to Ali just as so many eminent Turks are wont to give their daughters. On the day of their birth they promise to give them to some powerful magnate, and by the time the *fiancée* is marriageable the *fiancé* has already one foot in his grave.

A pale, blue-eyed flower was she, looking as if she had grown up beneath the light of the moon instead of the light of the sun ; her shape, her figure, was so delicate that it reminded one of those sylphs of the fairy world that fly without wings. Her voice was sweeter, more tender, than the voices of the other damsels ; and, wiser than they, she could speak so that you felt rather than heard what she said. Ali loved to toy with her light hair, unwind the long folds of her tresses, cover his face with their silken richness, and fancy he was reposing in the shades of paradise.

And the child loved the man. Ali was a handsome old fellow. His beard was as glossy and as purely white as the wing of a swan ; the roses of his cheeks had not yet faded ; when he smiled he was no longer a tiger, but revealed a row of teeth even handsomer than her own. And, in addition to that, he was valiant—a hero. Even in old men love is no mere impotent desire when accompanied with all the vigorous passion of youth.

And Eminah knew not that there were such beings as youths in the world. Excepting her father and her husband, she had never seen a man, and therefore fancied that other men also had just such white beards and silvery eyelashes as they. Brought up from the days of her childhood in the midst of a harem, among women and eunuchs, she had not the remotest idea of the romantic visions which the hearts of love-sick girls are wont to form from the contemplation of their ideals ; to her her husband was the most perfect man for whom a woman's heart had ever beaten, and she clung to him as if he had been a supernatural being.

In her heart Eminah pictured Ali as one of those beneficent genii who in the marvellous tales of the Arabs rise up from the bowels of the earth and the depths of the sea, a hundred times greater than ordinary men, ten times younger, and a thousand times more powerful, who are wont to give talismanic rings to their earthly favorites, appearing before them when they turn this ring in order to instantly gratify their desires, their wishes; to transport them from place to place with their huge muscular hands, to make them ride a cock-horse on their middle fingers, play hide-and-seek with them in the thousand corners of their vast palaces, watch over them when they sleep, overwhelm them with heaps and heaps of gifts and treasures, and yet are gentle and complacent in spite of their immense power. They need but take one step to crush the towers and bastions of the mightiest fortress in the dust, and yet they walk so warily as not even to graze the tiny ant they meet upon their path. Why, once Ali had waded into the lake up to his waist to rescue two amorously fluttering butterflies that had fallen into it! Oh! Ali has such a sensitive soul that he weeps over the bird that has accidentally beaten itself to death against the bars of its cage; whenever he plucks a flower from its stalk he always raises it to his lips to beg its pardon; and when they told him how at the siege of Kilsura all the poor doves were burned, the tears sparkled in his eyes!

Eminah does not fully know the meaning of a siege; she only grieves for the poor doves. How they would hover above the burning town in white clusters amid the black smoke, and fall down into the fire below!

In reality the matter stood thus: Ali was besieging Kilsura, but could not take it; the besiegers fought valiantly, and the natural advantages of the place prevented him from drawing near enough to it. So he signified to the inhabitants that he would make peace with them and depart from their town, and desired them, in earnest of their pacific intentions, to send him a number of white doves. The besieged fell in with his proposal, and collecting together all the white doves in the town they could lay they hands upon, sent them to Ali. He immediately withdrew his siege artillery, with which he had already wrought no small mischief, but at night, when every one was asleep, he fastened fiery matches by long wires to the feet of the doves, and then set them free. The natural instincts of the doves made them fly back to their old homes, the familiar roofs where their nests were, and in a moment the whole town was in flames, the doves themselves carrying the combustible material from roof to roof and perishing themselves among the falling houses.

Ali wept sore as he told to Eminah the story of the doves of Kilsura; yes, Ali was certainly a sensitive soul!

The beautiful woman had everything that eye could covet or heart desire. In her apartments were mirrors as high as the ceiling, masterpieces of Venetian crystal, and the floor was covered with Persian carpets embroidered with flowers. Blossoming flowers and singing birds were in all her windows, and a hundred waiting-women were at her beck and call. From morn to eve Joy and Pleasure were her attendants, and each day presented her with a fresh delight, a fresh surprise.

Thirty rooms, opening one into another, each more magnificent than the last, were hers, and hers alone. The eye that feasted on one splendid object quickly forgot it in the contemplation of a still more splendid marvel, and by the time it had taken them all in was eager to begin again at the beginning.

But there was one thing which did not please Eminah. When one had got to the end of all the thirty rooms, it was plain that they did not end there, for then came a round brass door; and this door was always closed against her—never was she able to go through it. Now this door led into that huge tower with the red cast-iron roof, which could be seen such a distance off.

The inquisitive woman very much wanted to know what was inside this door through which she was never suffered to go, though Ali himself used it frequently, always closing it most carefully behind him, and wearing the key of it fastened to his bosom by a little cord.

Now and then she had asked Ali what was in this tower that she was not allowed to see, and what he did when he remained there all night alone? At such times Ali would reply that he went there to consort with spirits who were teaching him how to find the stone of the wise, how to become perpetually young, how to foresee the future, and make gold and other marvels—all of which it was easy to make a woman believe who did not even know that all men do not wear white beards.

After all such occasions Eminah, when she was alone again, would conjure up before her all sorts of marvellous blue and green denizens of fairyland appearing before Ali in the elements of air, fire, and water, to teach him how to make gold. And Ali always proved to Eminah that what he told her was no idle tale, for whenever he returned the next day he was followed by a whole procession of dumb eunuchs carrying baskets filled with gold and precious stones. Thus Ali not only knew how to make gold, but also those things that are made of gold —that is to say, coined money and filigreed ornaments, which he piled up before her; and to Eminah it seemed a very nice thing, and quite natural that if these peculiar spirits could manufacture gold from nothing, they should also be able to make necklaces and bracelets out of smoke, as Ali told her they did without any difficulty at all.

Now any one would have been curious to get to the bottom of such mysteries, especially if they were close at hand; how much more, then, a spoiled and pampered young woman, who frequently was not able to sleep for the joy which the presents heaped upon her by Ali excited in her breast. How much she would have loved to see these benevolent spirits who had given her so much pleasure!

Frequently she implored Ali to take her with him when he went into the red tower; but the pasha always tried to frighten her by saying that these spirits were most cruel to strangers in general, and women in particular, whom they would be ready to tear limb from limb, so that Eminah always had to abandon her desire.

But when once a woman has made up her mind to do a thing, do it she will, though a seven-headed dragon were to stand in the way; and if fear is a great power in this world, curiosity is a still greater.

One evening Eminah accompanied Ali right up to the brass door, and as he went in she dexterously thrust a little pebble between the door and the threshold. Thus the door not being completely closed, the catch of the lock, despite a double turn of the key, shot back again; so instead of closing the door behind him, as Ali fondly imagined, he left it ajar.

Eminah waited till the sound of her husband's footsteps had quite ceased. Then she softly opened the door, and at first contented herself with peeping in. Perceiving nothing to frighten her back, she ventured right in, cautiously peering around at every step lest any angry spirit should suddenly rise up before her.

Before her lay a long corridor, and she went right to the very end of it. Then she came upon a spiral staircase, which was so dark that she had to painfully grope her way along. A fatal curiosity goaded her on in spite of the darkness, and presently she found herself in a large, round room, dimly lit by a hanging lamp.

All round the walls of this room were arranged marble benches, pitchers of water, funnels, and curious instruments of iron, leather, and wood, of all shapes and sizes, looking all the more incomprehensible in the semi-darkness. These were, no doubt, the implements with which Ali was in the habit of making gold, thought Eminah to herself, and, discovering a convenient niche at the head of the staircase, she squeezed herself into it so that she could see everything from thence without being seen herself.

A few moments afterwards the door at the opposite end of the room opened, and Ali and twelve dumb eunuchs entered with torches. The room was illuminated at once, the eunuchs thrusting the torches into large iron sconces; one of them then proceeded to light the fire and pile up various instruments around it; some sort of liquid also began bubbling in a caldron. Ali meanwhile was sitting down on a camp-stool and distributing his commands in a low voice. "Now we shall see how Ali makes gold," thought Eminah.

But now at a sign from Ali two of the eunuchs entered a trap-door, and a few moments afterwards the rattling of chains was audible; the trap-door opened again, and in came two old men, peculiar-looking creatures, with long gray hair, closely cropped beards, and strange garments, the like of which Eminah had never seen before.

"Ah! no doubt these are the spirits which help Ali to make gold," thought Eminah to herself. "Well, at any rate, they are in chains, so I need not be afraid of them." And, like the timid spectator of some strange drama, she looked out from her hiding-place at the scene which followed.

The two old men were led up to Ali, who, smiling and rubbing his hands, stood up before them, and for a long time did not speak, but only smiled. At last he gently stroked the face of the younger of the two.

"Merchant of Naples, thou still dost not know, then, where thy treasures lie hidden?" said he, gently.

"My lord," replied the other, with desperate obsequiousness, " I have given up everything that was mine. I am indeed a beggar."

"Merchant of Naples! how canst thou say so? Let me refresh thy memory! Thou didst go to Toulon with a full cargo of Indian goods, and there sold it all. When we met together on thy return journey thou didst offer me a thousand ducats, which I also took. But where is the remainder? A profit of twelve thousand ducats appears entered in thy trading-books."

"Those books are false, my lord," said the merchant, in a tearful voice. "I made those totally fictitious entries simply to preserve my credit."

"Merchant of Naples, thou dost calumniate thyself. Thou dost want to make me believe that thou art not an honest man. Forgive me if I enliven thy memory a little."

With that he beckoned to the eunuchs, and they, undressing the merchant, laid him on the torturing slab and tortured him for two mortal hours. It would be too horrible to say what they did to him. Oh, that curious woman amply atoned for her curiosity! She was obliged to look upon tortures which made her limbs shake and shiver as if she were in the grip of an ague. She covered her face, but the howls of the tortured wretch penetrated to her very soul, and her sensitive nerves suffered almost as much as if she had felt these torments herself. Gradually, however, a curious sort of torpor seemed to stop the beating of her heart; her limbs ceased to tremble, she opened her eyes and, motionless as a statue, watched the hellish scene to the very end.

Ali was evidently a past-master in this horrible

science. He himself elaborately graduated the whole process, indicating briefly when and how long the thumb-screws, the Spanish boot, the boiling oil, and the water funnel were to be used. Last of all came the culminating torment. They wrapped the merchant round in a raw buffalo-skin and laid him down before the fiercely blazing fire. As the fire began to compress the raw hide, and slowly press together the tortured limbs, the limit of the poor wretch's endurance was reached, and he confessed that his treasures were concealed in an iron chest, fastened by a chain to the bottom of the ship.

Then they freed him from the torturing hide; in a state of collapse, with foaming lips, a bleeding body and dislocated limbs, he flopped down upon the cold marble.

"Thou seest now, my dear," observed Ali, gently, "what trouble thou mightest have saved thyself and me also." Then he beckoned to the eunuchs to remove the merchant.

So this was the way in which Ali made gold! A very simple sort of alchemy, certainly!

And now it was the turn of the second man. And a haughty, broad-shouldered fellow he was, who had regarded the torments of his comrade without moving a muscle of his face.

"Then thou wilt not tell me thy name, valorous warrior?" inquired Ali.

"I will tell thee thine—Devil, Belial, Satan!"

"I thank thee! Thou dost me too much honor. But it is thy name I should like to know. I suppose thou art some wealthy Venetian noble, whose whereabouts his kinsmen are rather anxious to discover, and who would not be ungrateful if any one sent thee back to them. For I value thee very highly."

"Know, then, that I *am* a rich noble, and that at home I have a palace and treasures, but not a para of my property shalt thou ever see, for I have taken poison. Dost thou not see the blue spots upon my hand? Presently thou wilt see them on my face. In five minutes' time I shall be dead."

And so indeed it fell out. The haughty noble died, while Ali, furious with passion, cursed the Prophet.

And Eminah, from her hiding-place, looked intently upon Ali's face. What must have been her thoughts at that moment?

The eunuchs removed the dead body, and Ali beckoned once more to them, whereupon they brought in through the opposite doors a wondrously beautiful damsel and a handsome youth. When the youth and the damsel beheld each other the tears gushed from their eyes. They were lovers, and lovers meet for each other.

Eminah now perceived with amazement that there were other kinds of men besides those who wore gray beards. The captive youth, with his frank and comely countenance and long black locks, so rejoiced her eyes that she could not take them off him. She had never seen anything of the sort before.

Ali approached the pair and smiled upon them both, and each of them said to him, "I curse thee!"

He said to the youth, "Renounce thy bride and thou shalt live!" and the youth replied, "I curse thee!"

He said to the damsel, "Love me, be mine, and

thy betrothed shall live!" and the girl replied, "I curse thee!"

And Eminah unconsciously murmured after them each time, "I curse thee!" without knowing what she was saying.

Then Ali forced the youth down on his knees, and the eunuchs stripped off his robe. One of them then siezed him by his beautiful long black hair, and raised him up into the air thereby, while the other stood behind him with a large sharp sword.

"Thy beloved shall die this instant," roared the infuriated Ali, "if thou dost not set him free! Embrace either me or his headless body."

Eminah turned her loathing eyes from the vile face of Ali, which, in that moment, was deformed out of all recognition.

And the young couple replied with one voice, "We curse thee!" It was as though they had taken an oath to say nothing else. The same instant the sword flashed around the youth. His beautiful head bounded into the air, then rolled along the floor to the foot of the spiral staircase, and stood still before the very niche where Eminah was concealed — at her very feet, in fact. The headless body, convulsed by a final spasm, rent its fetters in twain, and then falling prone, stretched out its hands towards the terror-stricken girl, while the severed head, which had rolled up to Eminah's feet, seemed to be murmuring something—anyhow the lips moved. Eminah bending down towards it, put her ears close to the quivering mouth and whispered, "I hear! I hear what thou sayest!" And she really believed she heard something. Perhaps it was only her heart that was speaking.

3

After that she wrapped the head in her shawl, and hastened away from the tower back into her own room, concealing the ghastly but still beautiful trophy beneath the pillows of her sofa. Then she commanded her odalisks to appear before her, that they might dance and sing.

Dawn was now not far distant, and still the entertainment was going on. Then Ali returned from the red tower—his face was gentle and smiling—and after him came two eunuchs carrying gold and treasure in large baskets; and they emptied them all at Eminah's feet. The damsel rejoiced, laughed at the sight of the treasures, and, throwing herself on Ali's neck, repaid him with kisses, and dragged him down to her on the sofa.

"Behold, the *dzhins* have sent thee treasures," said Ali. "But a strange thing hath befallen me; one of my treasures rolled away upon the floor, and, search where I will, I cannot find it."

Eminah laughed, and fell a-teasing him. "Perchance the *dzhins* have stolen it from thee," cried she. Suppose she had said, "Thou art sitting upon it, Ali Pasha?"

Ali Pasha took the damsel upon his lap, and rejoiced in her innocent, artless eyes and her childlike smile. He fancied he could look through those eyes down to the very depths of her heart. If only he *could* have seen into it!

And while he was thus toying with her, the kadunkeit-khuda entered the room of the odalisks, bringing with him a veiled damsel.

"Gracious lady," said he to Eminah, "I bring thee a Greek maiden, who hath heard the fame of thy benevolence, and hath come of her own accord to bask in the light of thy countenance, and gather fresh strength from my smiles;" and he drew the maiden forward towards Eminah, who immediately recognized the girl whose lover Ali Pasha had decapitated, and said, playfully, to the guardian of the harem:

"Lo, kadun-keit-khuda, the damsel is trembling! If thou dost not support her she will fall!"

"It is by reason of her great shyness, gracious lady."

"But how pale she is!"

"Thy beauty casteth a shadow upon her."

"But look!—she weeps!"

"They are tears of joy, lady."

Eminah gave the guardian of the harem a handful of ducats for his good answers, and allowed the bashful damsel to stand before her. Then she sent for sweetmeats, golden bread-fruits, wine with the lustre of garnets, and her opium narghily; and, cradling Ali's gray head in her bosom, seized her mandolin and sang to him Arab love-songs—hot, burning, rose-scented, dew-besprinkled love-songs—and the pasha drew over his face the long silken tresses of the damsel, as if he would envelop himself in the cool shade of Paradise, and sleep a sleep of sweet melody, intoxicating rapture, and soothing opium.

When the ivory stem of the narghily dropped from the hands of the pasha, Eminah sent from the room all the damsels; only the newly arrived Greek maiden remained behind. She made her sit down before her on a cushion, and, putting into her hands a large silk fan to fan the pasha with, she asked the damsel her name.

The damsel shook her head—she would not say.

"Why wilt thou not tell me?"

"Because I have still a sister at home."

Eminah understood the answer. "Come nearer," said she. "Last night I had a dream. Methought I was in a large tower, the interior of which was illuminated by twelve torches. Whichever way my eyes turned they lit upon horrors—strange, terrifying objects appeared before me; and, although twelve torches were burning, darkness was still all around. And it seemed to me as if this darkness was not vapor or thick smoke, but a black mass of human beings all wedged together, who raised their eyelids every now and then. After that I saw Ali Pasha sitting in a red velvet chair with golden tiger feet, and as he sat cross-legged, after the Turkish manner, it looked as if the tiger feet were his own feet. Many terrifying shapes passed before me, and at last a young man and a young woman were all who remained in the room, and to every question put to them they replied, 'I curse thee!' Ali Pasha said to the damsel, 'Love me!' and she replied, 'I curse thee!' And immediately the head of the youth began rolling from one end of the marble floor to the other, right up to my feet; and a drop of blood dripped from it on to my slipper, and, strange to say, the drop of blood was still there when I awoke. Look, is that really a drop of blood, or is it only my imagination?"

And therewith Eminah put out her pretty little foot, which hitherto she had kept hidden beneath the folds of her garment, and showed it to the Greek girl. Then the girl fell weeping at her feet and kissed the slipper. But it was not the foot of her mistress that she kissed — no, no; what she kissed was the drop of blood that had dropped upon the slipper.

"Look! that drop of blood has burned right through the morocco leather of my shoe! What will it do, then, to the soul on which it has fallen?"

And with that she withdrew her hair from the pasha's face and looked at him with loathing. Yet he slept as calmly as if he were sleeping the sleep of the just.

For nine and seventy years he had lived happily, joyously, triumphantly, beloved by angels; and all the curses, all the murders, that were upon his aged head were unable to carve one wrinkle on his forehead, or distort a feature of his face, or cut off one day of his life, or even to disturb one of his dreams; and there he lies on one and the same couch with the head of his victim, the only difference being that his head lies on the pillow, while the head of the murdered man lies beneath it.

Eminah bent over him and bared the breast of the sleeper, who slept calmly and regularly all the time.

"On that table lies an enamelled dagger," said she to the girl; "bring it hither."

The girl darted away for the dagger, and came back with it. There she stood, grasping it convulsively in her hand, as if she only awaited a signal to drive it home.

"No, not so," said Eminah. "Cut not off his life, but cut through this cord!" and, taking the key which Ali wore round his neck, she cut it from its cord with the dagger. "This key opens the red tower. When they pitched the dead bodies through the trap-door I heard the roar of falling water. It is certain, therefore, that one can get through the torture-chamber to the lake of Acheruz. We can get down to it by ropes. I can swim, and thou canst also, I am sure; for art thou not a Hydriot girl?* When we have reached the heights of Lithanizza we shall find a safe refuge in the midst of the forests. Wherever it is, it will be all one to me. Better to be among wolves and lynxes than near Ali Pasha. Will you do what I say?"

The damsel's bosom heaved violently; she hid her head on Eminah's shoulder and kissed her.

"Freedom!" she whispered, full of rapture; "freedom above all things! It is now my only joy."

"Nobody will observe us," said Eminah, spurning aside the jewels, which she loathed now that she knew whence they came. "It is the last night of the Feast of Bairam. Every one is hastening to compensate himself for the privations of the Fast of Ramadan, every one is sleeping or enjoying himself; the greater part of the garrison is making merry in the apartments of the beys; even the sons of Ali Pasha, all three of them, are feasting with Mukhtar Bey. We shall be able to escape them, and then the whole world lies before us."

The Greek girl pressed the lady's hand. "We will go together!" she cried. "My brother dwells among the mountains of Corinth; he is a valiant warrior, and will give us an asylum."

"Then go thither! I shall seek refuge with my kinsmen at Stambul. Now go into the apartments

---

* An inhabitant of the isle of Hydra. The Hydriots were remarkable for their enterprise and daring.

of the odalisks and ask for apparel. I have already hatched a good plan. If they are all asleep come softly back with thy clothes. The kadun-keit-khuda only sleeps with half an eye; beware of him! If he ask thee whither thou art going, show him the pasha's handkerchief, and he will fancy Ali awaits thee."

The face of the Greek girl blushed purple at these words; even to lie on such a subject was a horrible thought to her. But Eminah beckoned to her to be gone, and when she found herself alone she drew forth the head she had concealed beneath the pillow and placed it on a round table in front of her. For a long time she gazed at the sunken eyes, the gaping mouth, and the long black tresses which rolled over the table on both sides. The lady smoothed the raven-black tresses with her soft hand, and passed her fingers right across the noble features without a shudder at their icy coldness.

There she sat an hour long opposite the dead head; and beside her Ali Tepelenti, the terror of the whole region, lay prone in a deep, motionless slumber. It was a strange sight, this young girl alone there between these two horrors. She had resolved to quit Ali and set the Greek damsel free; but what she meant to do after that she herself could not have said.

In an hour's time the Greek damsel returned. She came so softly that nobody could have heard her; even Eminah did not perceive her till the damsel stood before the severed head and uttered a cry of terror. Only for an instant, only for the duration of a lightning-flash did this cry last; the damsel stifled it at once, and if it awoke any one in the palace he must have fancied he was dreaming or had dreamed it, and would go on sleeping again. Then the damsel, in an agony of speechless grief, bent over the head of her betrothed, and her tears flowed in streams, though not a word escaped her lips.

At last Eminah grasped the girl's hand and bade her make haste. So she dried her tears, and after placing the severed head in front of that of the sleeping pasha so that they confronted each other, and cutting off one of the locks from its temples, she covered the cold eyes with bitter, burning kisses, and then, taking up her things, rapidly followed Eminah through the long suite of rooms.

A few minutes later they were in the torture-chamber. It was quite empty; the blood stains had been washed away, there was nothing to recall the horrors of the night before.

They opened the trap-door through which the dead bodies were wont to be cast. At the bottom of the deep black void there was a roaring sound as if the lake were in a commotion. No doubt a tempest was raging outside. How were these girls to escape by way of the subterranean stream? Perhaps some of the headless corpses were also swimming down yonder amidst the foaming waves. Would those who ventured down into those depths ever see the light of day again? But to them it was all one. Better to perish in the deep void than be condemned to the embraces of Ali Pasha. How the two girls abominated him!—the one because he had murdered her love, the other because he had loved her.

"Don't be afraid," they said to each other; and

fastening their bundles to a long rope which was used in torturing, they let it down into the deep well, with a lamp at the end of it, and when the water put out the light they fastened the other end of the rope to the hinge of the door, and each in turn let herself down by it.

And whether they lived or whether they died, Ali Pasha lost on that day two talismans which he should have guarded more jealously than the light of his eyes: one was the spirit of blessing, the other the spirit of cursing, both of which he had held fast bound, and both of which had now been let loose.

At the moment when the two damsels plunged into the lake of Acheruz the slumber of tranquillity disappeared from the eyes of Ali Pasha, and he began to see spectres.

A peculiar feeling came over him. He whom phantoms avoided even when he slept, he who had never even dreamed of fear, he whom the angel of sleep had never known to be a coward, now began to experience a peculiar sensation which was worse than any sickness and more painful than any suffering. He was afraid!

He dreamed that the head of the young Suliot, which had been cut off by his order, and which had rolled away and disappeared so that nobody could find it, was now standing face to face with him on a table, staring at him fixedly with stony eyes, and repeatedly addressing the sleeper by name: "Ali Pasha! Ali Pasha!"

The limbs of the sleeper shook all over in a strange tremor.

"Ali Pasha!" he heard the head call for the third time.

Groaning, writhing, and turning himself about, he contrived to knock the head off the cushion, smearing all the bed with blood. And now he saw and heard more terrible things than ever.

"One, two," said the severed head. And Ali understood that this was the number of the years he had still to live. "Thy head hath no longer either hand or foot," continued the head; and Ali was obliged to listen to what it said. "Two severed heads now stand face to face, mine and thine. Why dost thou not reply to me? Why dost thou not look into my eyes? Two headless trunks stand before the throne of God, mine and thine. How shall the Lord recognize thee? He inquires which is Ali. For every soul there is a white garment laid up. And thou deniest thy name, with thy right hand on thy heart. Thou *art* Ali, for on thy white garment are five bloody finger-prints."

Ali writhed in his sleep, and covered with his hand that part of his caftan which lay over his heart. And all the time the head never disappeared from before his eyes and its lips never closed. Presently it went on again.

"Listen, Ali! Mene, mene, tekel, upharsin! The hand which guided thee in the performance of thy mighty deeds is also bringing thine actions to an end, and thou shalt no longer be a hero whom the world admires, but a robber whom it curses. Those whom thou lovedest will bless the day of thy death, but thine enemies will weep over thee. Moreover, God hath ordained that thou shalt be the ruin of thine own nation."

Ali tossed, sighing and groaning, upon his couch, and could not awake; a world of crime lay upon his breast. He felt the earth shake beneath him, and the sky above his head was dark with masses of black cloud, and the thought of death was a terror to him.

The head went on speaking. "Two birds quitted thy rocky citadel at the same hour, a white dove and a black crow. The white dove is Peace, which has departed from thy towers; the black crow is Vengeance, which will return in search of carcasses at the scent of thy ruin. The white dove is thy damsel, the black crow is mine; and woe to thee from them both!"

Ali, in the desperation of his rage, roared aloud in his sleep, and his violent cry tore asunder the light fetters of sleep. He sprang from his couch and opened wide his eyes—and lo! the severed head was standing before him on the table.

The pasha looked about him in consternation; he was not sufficiently master of himself at first to tell how much of all this was a dream and how much reality. He still seemed to hear the terrible words which had proceeded from those open lips, and his hand involuntarily clutched at his breast as if he would have covered there the five bloody finger-marks. Then the cut cord from which the key was missing fell across his hand, and immediately his presence of mind returned. Drawing his sword, he rushed towards the brazen door, and discovered that the fugitives had had sufficient forethought to close the door and leave the key in the lock outside, so that it could only be opened by force. He turned back and rushed to the end of the dormitories.

Some of the odalisks were awakened by the sound of his heavy footsteps, and perceiving his troubled face, plunged underneath their bedclothes in terror; in front of the doors stood the dumb eunuch sentries, leaning on their spears like so many bronze statues.

He rushed down into the garden to the end of the familiar walks, and when he came to the gate was amazed to perceive that the drawbridge which separated his palace from the dwellings of his sons had been let down and nobody was guarding it. The topidshis, the negroes, knowing that Ali always turned into his harem on the Feast of Bairam, had gone across to the palace of Mukhtar Bey, who was giving a great banquet in honor of Vely Bey and Sulaiman Bey, his brothers. All three had brought together their harems to celebrate the occasion, and while the masters were diverting themselves upstairs, their servants were making merry below. Music and the loud mirth of those who feast resounded from the house; every gate of the citadel was open; slaves and guards lying dead drunk in heaps, victims of the forbidden fluid, cumbered the streets. A whole hostile army, with drums beating and colors flying, might easily have marched into the citadel over their prostrate bodies.

Wrath and the cold night air gradually gave back to Ali his soul of steel. Wary and alert, he entered the palace of Mukhtar Bey.

CHAPTER III

A TURKISH PARADISE

ALI PASHA himself had built the whole citadel of Janina, and had been wise enough, as soon as the fortress was finished, to at once and quietly remove out of the way all the builders and architects who had had anything to do with it, so that he only knew all the secrets of the place. There were secret exits and listening-galleries in every part of the building, and each single group of redoubts which, viewed from the outside, seemed quite isolated, was really so well connected together by means of subterranean passages, that one could go backward and forward from one to the other without being observed in the least. At a later day Ali Pasha's enemies were to have very bitter experience of these architectural peculiarities.

One could go right round the palace of the three Beys, both above and below, by means of a secret corridor, and not one of the inhabitants of the building had the least idea of the existence of this corridor. It was in the midst of the fathom-thick wall between two rows of windows, and within this space invisible doors opened into every apartment, either between windows, or behind mirrors, or beneath the ceiling between two stories, and these doors could not be opened by keys, but turned upon invisible hinges set in motion by hidden screws, and they closed so hermetically as to leave not the slightest orifice behind them.

Ali Pasha stood there in the banqueting-chamber unobserved by any one. He stood beside a huge Corinthian column, and here hung a black board indicating the direction in which Mecca lay. He had no fear that any one would look thither. That place, towards which every truly believing Mussulman must turn when he prays, was carefully avoided by every eye, for fear it should encounter the golden letters which sparkle on the walls of the Kaaba.*

For now is the time for enjoyment. There is no need of a heavenly Paradise, for Paradise is already here below. There is no need to inquire of either Muhammad or the angel Izrafil concerning the wine which flows from the roots of the Tuba-tree; far more fiery, far more stimulating, is the wine which flashes in glass and goblet. The houris may hide their white bosoms and their rosy faces, for what are they compared with the earthly angels whose mundane charms intoxicate the hearts of mortals? Truly Muhammad was but an indifferent prophet, he did not understand how to arrange paradise; let him but regard the arrangements of Mukhtar Bey—they will show him how that sort of thing ought to be managed.

Muhammad imagined that the embraces of seven and seventy houris would make an enraptured Moslem eternally happy. Why, the bungler forgot the best part of it. Would it not be more satisfactory

---

* The chief sanctuary of the Mussulmans standing in the midst of the great mosque at Mecca.

if, now and then, say once in a thousand years or so, the Moslems were to exchange their own houris for those of their neighbors? In this way the aroma of brand-new kisses would prevent their raptures from growing stale, and the Paradise of Muhammad would be worth something after all. With all eternity before him, a man would scarcely mind waiting for his own wives for a paltry millennium or two while he enjoyed the wives of his neighbors, and when he returned to his seven and seventy original damsels again, what a pleasant reunion it would be!

Now the Prophet had forgotten to introduce this novelty into his own Paradise, and Mukhtar Bey was the happy man to whom the fairy Malach Taraif whispered the idea during the fast preceding the Feast of Bairam while he slept, and he immediately proceeded to discuss the matter with his kinsmen.

All three brothers lived under one roof, each of the three had his own special harem, and each of them possessed in their harems beauties far surpassing what the angels Monkar and Nakir could promise them in the next world. After the Feast of Bairam, when Mukhtar Bey had well plied his brethren with good wine, he said to them, " Let us exchange harems!"

Sulaiman Bey immediately gave his hand upon it; Vely Bey laughed at it as a good idea at first, but afterwards drew back. The other two worthies laughed uproariously at his simplicity, made fun of him, and proceeded at once to transfer to each other their respective damsels, and on the morrow and the following days aggravated Vely by extolling before him the exchanged odalisks, each of them confiding to him what novel attractions he had discovered in this or that bayadere. Thus Sulaiman could not sufficiently extol the extraordinary brilliance of the eyes of Mukhtar Bey's favorite damsel, while Mukhtar protested that the languishing Jewish maiden he had got in exchange from Sulaiman quivered in his arms like a dancing flame.

Vely laughed a good deal over the business, but still continued to shake his head, confessing at last that the reason why he did not exchange his harem was because it contained an Albanian damsel whom he had neither purchased nor captured, but who had come to him of her own accord, and whom he had promised long ago never to abandon, and her he would not give for both their harems put together; nay, he said he would not give her up for a whole world full of damsels. The two brethren thereupon assured Vely that if he loved this particular damsel so very much, he might exclude her from the others and keep her for himself, and it need make no difference. Then Vely Bey also acceded to this fraternal division of delights, and transferred his harem also, with the exception of Xelianthé.

Mukhtar Bey had fixed the last night of the great Bairam feast for the entertainment that was to rival Paradise, inviting his brethren and the Prophet Muhammad himself, in order that he might learn from them how to be happy, and might regulate heaven accordingly. To this end they had a fourth divan added to their three, with its own well-appointed table in front of it, and bade the attendant odalisks be diligent in keeping the fourth goblet well filled, and do their best to entertain the invited guest. Mockery of religious subjects was no unusual thing with Turkish magnates in those days. Blasphemy had gone so far as to become an open scandal; popular fanaticism and official orthodoxy made it all the more glaring.

So the sons of Ali Pasha invited the Prophet to be their guest, and had made up their minds that if he did appear among them he would not be bored.

All the odalisks danced and sung before them in turn, and the brethren diverted themselves by judging which of the damsels was the sweetest and loveliest.

In every song, in every dance, Rebecca, Mukhtar Bey's beautiful Jewish damsel, and the blue-eyed bayadere Lizza, who was Sulaiman Bey's favorite, equally excelled. It was impossible to decide which of the twain deserved the palm. At last they were made to dance together.

"Look!" cried Mukhtar, his eyes sparkling with delight, "look! didst ever behold a more beautiful figure? Like the flowering branch of the Ban-tree she sways to and fro. How proudly she throws her head back, and looks at thee so languishingly that thou meltest away for very rapture! Would that her light feet might dance all over me; would that she might encompass every part of me like the atmosphere!"

"She really is charming," admitted Sulaiman, "and if the other were not dancing by her side, she would be the first star in the firmament of beauty. But ah! one movement of the other one is worth all the life in her body. She is but a woman, the other is a sylph. She kills you with rapture, the other raises you from the dead."

"Thou are unjust, Sulaiman," said Mukhtar;

"thou dost judge only with thine eyes. If thou wouldst take counsel of thy lips, they would speak more truly. Taste her kisses, and then say which of them is the sweeter."

With that he beckoned to the two odalisks. Rebecca, the lovely Jewish damsel, sank full of amorous languor on Sulaiman's breast, while Lizza, with sylph-like agility, sat her down upon his knee, and the intoxicated Bey, in an access of rapture, kissed first one and then the other.

"Rebecca's lips are more ardent," he cried, "but the kisses of Lizza are sweeter. The kiss of Rebecca is like the poppy which lulls you into sweet unconsciousness, but Lizza's kiss is like sweet wine which makes you merry."

"Lizza's kiss may perchance be like sweet wine," interrupted Mukhtar, "but Rebecca's kiss is like heavenly musk which only the Blessed may partake of, and those who partake thereof *are* blessed."

And with that Mukhtar caught up both the odalisks in his arms, that he might pronounce judgment as to the sweetness of their lips. It was an enviable process. The contending parties themselves were in doubt as to which of themselves should obtain a verdict. At length they called upon Vely Bey to decide—Vely, who was now lying blissfully asleep beside them on the divan, overcome with wine, his head in Xelianthé's bosom. His two brethren awoke him that he might judge between them as to the sweetness of rival kisses.

It took a good deal of trouble to make the stupidly fuddled Bey understand what was required of him, and when he did understand, the only answer he made was, "Xelianthé's kisses are the sweetest;" and with that he embraced his favorite damsel once more and, reclining his head on her bosom, went off to sleep again.

Then cried Mukhtar, "Wherefore dost thou ask for *his* judgment, when amongst us sits the Prophet himself? Let him judge between us."

With these words he pointed to the empty place which had been left for a fourth person. Rich meats were piled up there on gold and silver plate, and wine sparkled in transparent crystal.

"Come, Muhammad!" exclaimed Mukhtar, addressing the vacant place; "thou in thy lifetime didst love many a beauteous woman, and in thy Paradise there is enough and to spare of beauty. I summon thee to appear before us. Here is a dispute between us two as to whose damsel is the sweeter and the lovelier. Thou hast seen them dance, thou hast heard them sing; now taste of their kisses!"

With that he beckoned to the two damsels, and they sat down, one on each side of the empty divan, and made as if they were embracing a shape sitting between them, and filled the air with their burning, fragrant kisses.

"Well, let us hear thy verdict, Muhammad!" cried Mukhtar, with drunken bravado; and, taking the crystal goblet from the empty place and raising it in the air, looked around him with a flushed, defiant face, and exclaimed, "Come! drink of the wine of this goblet her health to whom thou awardest the prize!"

Ali Pasha, shocked and filled with horror at the shamelessly impudent words he heard from his hiding-place, drew a pistol from his girdle and softly raised the trigger.

"Drink, Muhammad!" bellowed Mukhtar, raising the goblet on high, "drink to the health of the triumphant damsel! Which shall it be, Rebecca or Lizza?"

At that same instant a loud report rang through the room, and the upraised crystal goblet was shivered into a thousand fragments in Mukhtar's hand. Every one leaped from his place in terror. But whichever way they looked there was nothing to be seen. The only persons in the room were the three brothers and the damsels. Only at the spot from whence the shot had proceeded a little round cloud of bluish smoke was visible, which sluggishly dispersed. Nobody present carried weapons, and there was no door or window there by which any one could have got in.

From the minarets outside the muezzins proclaimed the prayer of dawn: "La illah il Allah! Muhammad razul Allah!"—"There is no God but God, and Muhammad is His Prophet!"

Ali Pasha did not pursue the fugitives. That day he was praying all the morning. He locked himself up in his inmost apartments, that nobody might see what he was doing. He now did what he had not done for seventy years—he wept. For a whole hour his inflexible soul was broken. So that woman whom he had loved better than life itself, she forsooth had given the first signal of approaching misfortune, the first sign of the coming struggle! Let it come! Let her veil be the first banner to lead an army against Janina! Tepelenti would not attempt to stay her in her flight. For one long hour he thought of her, and this hour was an hour of weeping; and then he bethought him of the approaching tempest which the prophetic voice had warned him of, and his heart turned to stone at the thought. Ali Pasha was not the man to cringe before danger; no, he was wont to meet it face to face, and ask of it why it had tarried so long. He used even to send occasionally for the *ninrethullita* dervish, who had been living a long time in the fortress, and question him concerning the future. It must not he supposed, indeed, that Tepelenti ever took advice from anybody; but he would listen to the words of lunatics and soothsayers, and liked to learn from magicians and astrologers, and their sayings were not without influence upon his actions.

The dervish was a decrepit old man. Nobody knew how old he really was; it was said that only by magic did he keep himself alive at all. Every evening they laid him down on plates of copper and rubbed invigorating balsam into his withered skeleton, and so he lived on from day to day.

Two dumb eunuchs now brought him in to Tepelenti, and, bending his legs beneath him, propped him up in front of the pasha.

"Sikham," said Ali to the dervish, "I feel the approach of evil days. My sword rusted in its sheath in a single night. My buckler, which I covered with gold, has cracked from end to end. A severed head, which hid itself away from me so that I could not find it, came forth to me at night and spoke to me of my death; and in my dreams I see my sons make free with the Prophet. I ask thee not what all these things signify. That I know. Just as surely as in winter-time the hosts of rooks and crows resort to the roofs of the mosques, so surely shall my sworn enemies fall upon me. I am old compared with them, and it is a thing unheard of among the Osmanlis that a man should reach the age of nine and seventy and still be rich and mighty. Let them come! But one thing I would know—who will be the first to attack me? Tell me his name."

The dervish thereupon caused a wooden board to be placed before him on which meats were wont to be carried; then he put upon it an empty glass goblet, and across the glass he laid a thin bamboo cane. Next he wrote upon the wooden board the twenty-nine letters of the Turkish alphabet, and then, thrice prostrating himself to the ground with wide-extended arms, he fixed his eyes steadily upon the centre of the goblet.

In about half an hour the goblet began to tinkle as if some one were rubbing his wet finger along its rim. This tinkling grew stronger and stronger, louder and louder, till at last the goblet moved up and down on the wooden board, and began revolving along with the light cane placed across it, revolving at last so rapidly that it was impossible to discern the cane upon it at all.

Then, quite suddenly, the dervish raised his fingers from the table, and the goblet immediately stopped. The point of the cane stood opposite the letter *ghain*—G.*

"That signifies the first letter of his name," said the dervish—"G!"

---

* The marvels of our modern table-turning and table-tapping spirits, and all the wonders of this sort, were known to the Arab dervishes long ago.—JÓKAI.

And then the mysterious operation was repeated, and the magic stick spelled out the name letter by letter: "G—a—s—k—h—o B—e—y." At the last letter the goblet stopped short and would move no more.

"I know no man of that name," said Ali, amazed that he whose name was so world-renowned was to tremble before one whose name he had never heard before.

"Where does the fellow live?" he inquired of the dervish.

The magic jugglery was set going again, and now the dancing goblet spelled out the name, "Stambul."

That was enough. Ali beckoned to the eunuchs to take the dervish away again.

Ali thereupon summoned forty Albanian soldiers from the garrison, and gave to each one of them twenty ducats.

"This," said he, "is only earnest money. I want a man put to death whose name and dwelling-place I know. His name is Gaskho Bey, and he lives in Stambul. This man's head is worth as many gold pieces as there are miles between him and me. He who brings the head can measure the distance and be paid for it. The first who brings but the report of his death shall receive two hundred ducats; he who slays him, a thousand."

The Albanians consulted together for a brief moment, and then intimated that if a bey of the name of Gaskho really existed, he was as good as dead already.

Towards mid-day Ali sent for his sons. He said not a word to them of the anxieties, the visions, and the apparitions of the night before, but made them, after they had respectfully kissed his hands, sit down all around him. Mukhtar Bey he invited to sit down on his left hand, Vely on his right, and Sulaiman directly opposite.

He addressed himself first of all to Sulaiman.

"Thou art the youngest and boldest," said he. "To-morrow thou must go to sea and take three ships with thee. These ships thou must take to Sicily, load them there with sulphur, and return without losing an instant."

"Oh, my father!" replied Sulaiman, "the tempest is now abroad upon the sea. Who would venture now with a ship upon the billows? All the monsters of the ocean are now running upon the surface seeking whom they may devour, and the phantom ship, with her shadowy rigging and her shadowy crew, pursues her zigzag course across the waters."

Ali Pasha said no more, but turned towards Mukhtar Bey.

"Thou art the most crafty," said he; "go then to the captains of the Suliotes and invite them to assemble with their forces at Janina with all despatch. Spare neither promises nor assurances nor fair winds."

Mukhtar Bey's face turned quite angry, and, wagging his head, still heavy from his overnight debauch, he answered, sullenly: "In the mountains the snow is now thawing; every stream is swollen into a river; naught but a bird can find a place for its foot on the dry ground; how, then, can armies move hither and thither? Wait for a week, till the inundations have subsided. Truly there is no enemy on thy borders. In thy whole realm there is not so much as a rat to nibble at thy walls. What dost thou want now with chariots and armed men?"

Ali now turned to Vely, who was sitting on his right hand. "Go thou over to Misrim," said he, "and purchase for me two thousand horses; a thousand of them shall be meet for war-chargers, and a thousand for drawing guns."

"Oh, my father!" answered Vely, who was the eldest and wisest of Ali's sons, "I will not object to thy command that the simoon has now begun in Misrim, before whose burning, suffocating breath every living creature is forced to fly. I reck little of that, but the horses, thy precious horses, will perish. And, moreover, I would ask of thee one question. Wherefore dost thou get together a host, and horses and guns, without cause, and with no danger threatening thee? Will not all these war-like preparations excite the rage of the Padishah against thee, and so thy preparing against an imagined peril will saddle thee with a real war?"

Ali Pasha laughed aloud—a very unusual habit with him.

"Well," said he, "it is for me to prove to you, I suppose, that you are all wrong in your calculations. Dine with me and be merry. After dinner you shall see that the sea is not stormy, that the rivers are not in flood, and that the simoon is not suffocating. I have a talisman which will convince you thereof."

So he entertained his sons till late in the evening, and immediately after dinner he whispered to one of the dumb eunuchs, and then he took his sons with him into the red tower, the doors of which were left wide open. He stopped short with them in one of the rooms, the solitary semicircular window of which looked out upon the lake of Acheruz. The window was guarded by an iron grating. Here he sat down with them to smoke his narghily and sip his coffee. The sons would have preferred to mount upon the roof of the tower, where the fresh air and the fine view would have made their siesta perfect; but Ali facetiously observed that in the open air cold and hot winds were just then blowing together at the same time, and he did not want the simoon to make them sweat or the trade-winds to make them shiver.

As they were sipping their coffee there the splashing of oars was audible beneath the tower, and the sons beheld three large, flat-bottomed boats propelled upon the surface of the water, in which sat the damsels of their harems; the boats were rowed by muscular eunuchs.

The faces of the three beys lighted up when they saw the damsels being rowed on the water, and Mukhtar Bey whispered roguishly in Sulaiman's ear, "Shall we make the old man also one of our party?"

Ali overheard the whisper, and replied, with a smile, "Truly your damsels are most beauteous"— here he stroked his white beard from end to end— "I am not surprised, therefore, that you like to stay at home here and call the wind hot and cold, though it is nothing but the breath of Allah, and what comes from God cannot be bad. But your damsels *are* beautiful, of that there can be no doubt. Now, last night I dreamt a dream. Before me stood the Prophet, and he told me how you had challenged him to say which of your damsels was the sweeter and the more beautiful." (Here the sons regarded each other, full of fear and amazement.) "The Prophet replied," continued Ali, "that it was not meet that he should come to your damsels; they should rather go to him. So I mean to send them to Paradise."

"What doest thou?" cried all three sons, horror-stricken.

The only answer Ali gave was to give a long shrill whistle, at which signal the eunuchs drew out the plugs from holes secretly bored at the bottom of the three boats, leaping at the same time into the water, and leaving the boats in the middle of the lake.

The damsels shrieked with terror as the water began to rush into the boats from all sides. The air was filled with cries of agony.

Mukhtar rushed madly to the door and found it locked. With impotent violence he attempted to burst it open. Sulaiman meanwhile tore away at the iron window-grating with both hands, as if he fancied himself capable of pulling down the whole of the vast building by the sheer strength of his arms. The blue-eyed Albanian girl and the languishing Jewish damsel, with the fear of death in their eyes, looked up at the closed window; the waves had already begun to swallow their beautiful limbs.

Only Vely Bey remained motionless. He, at any rate, had not sinned. He had not angered the Prophet in that orgie of amorous rivalry. He had loved one only, by her only had he been loved, and she, yes, she was perishing there among the others!

The boats sank deeper and deeper; nothing could

be heard but the cries of the drowning wretches in all the accents of despair. The two sons saw their damsels dying before their eyes, and were unable to rush out and save them; not even one could be rescued. One more shriek of woe, and then the boats sank. For a few moments the surface of the water was covered with bright gauze veils and shiny turbans and white limbs and dishevelled tresses, and then a few solitary turbans floated on the water.

Sulaiman, sobbing in despair, fell down in a heap close by the window, while Mukhtar fell madly on the door and kicked it with all his might, as if he would drown in the din the cries for help of the perishing damsels. Only Vely Bey looked in bitter silence upon the detestable waves, which within a minute had swallowed three heavens.

Far, far away on the crest of the rising waves a black object appeared to be swimming. What was it? Perhaps one of the damsels. One moment it vanished in the wave-valleys, the next it appeared again on the top of a high ridge of water. What could it be? But farther and farther it receded. Perchance some one had escaped, after all. Greek girls are good swimmers.

And now Ali Pasha arose from his place and said, with a smile, to his sons:

"Methinks that neither the storms of ocean, nor the swollen waters, nor the breath of the simoon will now appear so terrible to you as they did a few hours ago. Depart now with all speed. When you return you will find new harems here, which will make you forget the old ones." And with that he quitted them.

Sulaiman and Mukhtar immediately went their way. Woe to whomsoever shall now give them a pretext for wreaking their vengeance upon him!

But Vely Bey remained there looking out upon the water, and as the evening grew darker he thought upon Ali Pasha. His brothers had loaded their father with curses; he had not said a word. They will soon make their peace with their father —he never will.*

* It is a fact that Ali drowned the harems of his sons in the lake of Acheruz because he feared their excessive influence.—JÓKAI.

CHAPTER IV

GASKHO BEY

THE lightning strikes to the earth the man that flies from it. Ill luck is a venomous dog, which runs after him who would escape it.

Ali Pasha's band of Albanians, on arriving at Stambul, began to make inquiries about Gaskho Bey.

He turned out to be a good honest man, by profession an inspector of the ichoglanler of the Seraglio, and a particularly mild and peaceful Mussulman to boot. In temperament he was somewhat phlegmatic, with a leaning to melancholy. A palmist would have told you that the sympathetic line on the palm of his hand was so little prominent as to be scarcely visible, whereas on Tepelenti's palm there was such an abundant concourse of sympathetic lines that they even ran over on to the back of the hand. In those days the Mussulmans frequently diverted themselves with such superstitious games as palmistry.

As to his figure—well, Gaskho Bey might have stood for a perfect model of the Farnese Hercules; his huge shoulders were almost out of proportion with the rest of his body. He could stop the wing of a windmill with one hand; on the birthday of the Sultan's heir he hoisted a six-pound cannon on to his shoulders and fired it off, and he could break a hard piastre in two when he was in a good humor.

It could not be said that he had hitherto used this terrible strength to injure any one; on the contrary, he was universally known as the most forbearing of men. The pages of the court, whom he taught to fence, would sometimes in the midst of a lesson, as if by accident, but really from sheer petulance, batter him with their blunt swords till they rang again, and Gaskho Bey would always reprimand them, not for striking him but for striking so clumsily. He had never gone to war, and those who did not send him thither flattered themselves not a little on their humanity, for if it came to a serious tussle there was really no knowing what damage he might not do.

At home he was the gentlest paterfamilias conceivable. You would frequently find him on all-fours, with his little four-year-old son, Sidali, riding on his back, and persecuting his father with all sorts of barbarities. He did nothing all day but teach the pages of the Seraglio games and exercises, and at home he made paper birds for his own little boy, flew kites for and played blind man's buff with him. Whatever time he could spare from these occupations he would spend in leaning out of the window of the Summer Palace overlooking the Gökk-sü, or Sweet Waters, and looking about him a bit with a pipe in his mouth, the stem of which reached to the ground, and if any one had asked him while so engaged what he was looking at, he would assuredly have answered, " Nothing at all."

Now there were always the liveliest goings-on in

the Gökk-sü Park of an evening. The harems of the beys and pashas who dwelt on its banks took the air there under the plantain-trees, and swung and danced and sang; the wandering Persian jugglers exhibited their hocus-pocus, and the magnificent Janissaries resorted thither to fight with one another. Every Friday afternoon whole bands of these rival warriors flocked thither as if to a common battle-field, and frequently left two or three corpses on the scene of their diversions.

Gaskho Bey appeared to take very little notice of all these things, his chibook curled comfortably on the ground beneath him. At every pull at it large light-blue clouds of smoke rolled upwards from its crater, taking all manner of misty shapes and forms till they disappeared through the window, and Gaskho Bey buried himself in the contemplation of these smoky phantasms as deeply as if he were intent on writing a dissertation on the philosophy of pipe-smoking, oblivious of the fact that below the very house in which he was sitting two Albanian soldiers, in high-peaked, broad-brimmed caps and coarse black woollen mantles, who seemed to be taking the greatest possible interest in him and trying to get as near him as they could, had already strolled past for the third time, always separating and going in different directions, somewhat nervously, if they perceived any one coming towards them.

Only now and then a sly expression on Gaskho's face betrayed the fact that he was conscious of something going on behind his back. There little Sidali was amusing himself, while Gaskho Bey was leaning out of the window, by kneeling on the ottoman behind, and tickling the uplifted naked soles of his father's feet with a blunt arrow. Sometimes the arrow would slip and come plumping down on Gaskho's head, and then the bey would smile indulgently at the naughtiness of his little son.

And now the evening was falling, and the crowd beneath the plantain-trees grew thinner. The two Albanians, side by side, again came towards Gaskho Bey, who now puffed forth such clouds of smoke from his chibook that one could see neither heaven nor earth because of them. But the two Albanian mercenaries could make him out very well, and both of them standing a little way from the window drew forth their pistols, and one of them standing on the right hand and the other on the left, they both aimed at Gaskho Bey's temples at a distance of three paces.

But little Sidali was too quick for them, for he now gave his father such a poke with the arrow that the latter, provoked partly by the pain and partly by the tickling, sharply turned his head, and the same instant there was the report of two shots, and two bullets—one on the right hand and one on the left—buried themselves in the window-sill.

Gaskho's movement was so unexpected that the two Albanian braves, who had imagined that their bullets must of necessity have met each other in the middle of the bey's brain, were so terrified when they saw him still sitting there unwounded, that they stood as if nailed to the earth. Indeed, before they could make up their minds to fly, Gaskho was already outside the window, upon them with a single bound, and immediately seizing the pair of them with his terrible fists, flung them to the ground as if he were playing with a couple of dummies, and without wasting so much as a word upon them, tied them together with their own leather belts, so that on the arrival of the members of his own family, who flew to the spot, alarmed by Sidali's shrieks, the two hired assassins lay half dead and all of a heap upon the ground, for Gaskho Bey's grip had wellnigh broken all their bones.

They were conveyed at once to the Kapu-Kiaja, and Gaskho Bey went too. For a long time he was unable to contain himself, and bellowed out all along the road, "I never heard of anything like it—never!"

"It is an unheard-of case, sir," said he, on arriving at the Kapu-Kiaja's. "To furtively shoot at a peaceful Mussulman when he is smoking his pipe and amusing himself with his children, I never heard the like. If any one wants to kill me, he might at least, I think, let me know beforehand, so that I may perform my ablutions, say my prayers, and take leave of my children. But just when I am smoking my chibook!—I never heard of such a thing!"

It was plain that what he took to heart the most was that they should have tried to shoot him while he was smoking his chibook.

The Kapu-Kiaja, on the other hand, looked upon the case from another point of view. To him it was a matter of comparative indifference whether the deed was attempted before or after prayers. Why, he wanted to know, should these madmen run amuck of their fellow-men at all? He therefore asked the assassins who had set them on to murder Gaskho Bey. They, at the very first stroke of the bamboo, made a clean breast of it, and threw the blame on Tepelenti.

At first the Kapu-Kiaja regarded this confession as incredible. Why, indeed, should Tepelenti be wrath with Gaskho Bey, who knew nothing at all of Ali except by report? Nay, he greatly revered him as a valiant warrior, and had never said a single word to his discredit.

Nevertheless, the two assassins not only stuck to their confession, but maintained that besides themselves eight and thirty other soldiers had been sent to Stambul by Ali on the self-same mission.

Ciauses were immediately sent to every quarter of the city to seize the described Albanians. Five or six of them hid or escaped, but the rest were captured.

The confessions of these men were practically unanimous. Every circumstance of the affair, the amount of the promised reward, the words spoken on the occasion—everything, in fact, corresponded so exactly that no doubt could possibly remain that Tepelenti had actually sent them out to murder Gaskho Bey.

The affair made a great stir everywhere. Ali Pasha was as well known in Stambul as Gaskho Bey. The former was as famous for his power and riches, his envy and revengefulness, as was the latter for his strength and gentleness, his sympathy and tenderness.

The great men of the palace, jealous for a long time of Ali's greatness, brought the matter before the Divan, and great debates ensued as to what course should be taken against this mighty protector of hired assassins. And for a long time the opinions of the counsellors of the cupolaed chamber were divided. Some were for taking Ali by the beard and despatching him there and then. Others were for advising Gaskho Bey to be content with seeing the heads of the Arnaut assassins rolling in the dust before the Pavilion of Justice, and at the same time privately informing Ali that if he were wise he would waste neither his money nor his powder on such quiet, harmless men as Gaskho Bey, who had never done, and never meant in future to do, him any harm.

The latter alternative was the opinion of the wiser heads, and among these wiser ones was the Sultan himself.

"Ali is my sharp sword," said Mahmud. "If my sword wounds any one accidentally, and without my consent, is that any reason for snapping it in twain?"

Nevertheless, the enemies of the pasha kept goading Gaskho on to demand satisfaction of Ali personally. The worthy giant, hearing his own name on everybody's lips for weeks together, grew as wild as a baited heifer, and began to believe that he was a famous man, that he alone was ordained to clip the wings of the tyrant of Epirus, and at last was so absorbed by his dreams of greatness that when he had to give the usual lessons to the youths of the Seraglio he trounced them all, in his distraction, as severely as if they had been the soldiers of Ali Pasha.

The pacific Viziers promised him a house, a garden, beautiful horses, and still more beautiful slaves. But all would not do; what he did want, he said, was the head of Tepelenti, and he cried to Heaven against them for their procrastination.

But Sultan Mahmud was a wise man. He had no need to consult star-gazers or magicians, or even the caverns of Seleucia, as to the future, in order to discover and discern the storm whose signs were already visible in the sky.

"Ye know not Ali, and ye know not me also," he said to those who urged him to pronounce judgment against Ali. "If I were to say, 'Ali must perish!' perish he would, even if my palaces came crashing down and half the realm were destroyed in consequence. If, on the other hand, Ali said 'No!' he would assuredly never submit, and would rather turn the whole realm upsidedown, till not one stone remained upon another, than surrender himself. Therefore ye know not what ye want when ye wish to see Ali and me at war with one another."

The conspirators, however, were not content with this, but distributed some silver money among the Janissaries, and egged them on to appear before the palace of the Kapu-Kiaja and demand Ali's head.

The Kiaja, warned in good time of the approaching storm, took refuge in the interior of the Seraglio, which was speedily barricaded against the Janissaries, and the mouths of the cannons attached to the gates were exhibited for their delectation. As it did not meet the views of the Janissaries just then to approach any nearer to the cannons, they gratified their fury by setting fire to the city and burning down a whole quarter of it, for they considered it no business of theirs to put out the blazing houses.

The next day, however, the tumult having subsided as usual, when the Sultan and his suite were trotting out to inspect the scene of the conflagration, and had got as far as the fountain in front of the Seraglio, the figure of a veiled woman cast herself in front of the horse's hoofs, and with audacious hands laid hold of the bridle of the steed of the Kalif.

The Sultan backed his horse to prevent it from trampling upon the woman, and, thinking she was one of those who had been burned out the day before, ordered his treasurer—who was with him—to put a silver piece in her hand and bid her depart in the name of the Prophet.

"Not money, my lord; but blood! blood!" cried the woman; and, from the ring of her voice, there was reason to suspect that she was a young woman.

The Sultan in amazement asked the woman her name.

"I am Eminah, the daughter of the Pasha of Delvino, and the wife of Ali Tepelenti."

"And whose blood dost thou require?" asked the Sultan, scandalized to see the favorite wife of so powerful a man prostrate in the dust before his horse's feet.

"I demand death upon his head!" cried the woman, with a firm voice—"on the head of Ali Tepelenti, from whose gehenna of a fortress I have escaped on the waters of a subterranean stream in order that I might accuse him to thee; and if thou dost not condemn him, I will go to the judgment-seat of God and accuse him there!"

The Sultan was horrified.

It is a terrible thing when a woman accuses her own husband, who has loaded her with benefits. He must, indeed, be an evil-doer whom turtle-doves, the gentlest of all God's creatures, attack!

The Sultan listened, full of indignation, to the woman's accusations.

After happily escaping from the fortress of Ali Pasha with the Greek girl, she learned, during her short sojourn among the Suliotes, of all Ali's cruelties, and learned also, at the same time, that in Delvino had just died a rich Armenian lady, who had been the flame of Gaskho Bey in his younger days, and had left him all the property she owned in Albania. Of this nobody as yet knew anything. What more natural than that every one should immediately fancy he had found the key to the riddle of the mysterious attempt at assassination? Why, of course, Ali wanted to slay Gaskho Bey in order that he might take possession of his Albanian property.

CHAPTER V

A MAN IN THE MIDST OF DANGERS

The Pasha of Janina, for thirty successive days, received nothing but ill tidings; and twice within the period of two waxing moons did his own power as steadily wane.

The first Job's-messenger which reached him was the Arnaut horseman, who had escaped from Stambul, and whom the Sultan's Tartars had pursued as far as Adrianople. This man told him that the attempt on the life of Gaskho Bey had failed, and that the captured assassins had revealed the name of their employer.

"Behold, I have wounded myself with my own sword," exclaimed Ali. "The prophetic voice of Seleucia spoke the truth; yea, verily, it spoke the truth."

And still more of the prophecy was to be accomplished.

A few days later the report reached him that Eminah had cast herself at the feet of the Sultan and demanded judgment on the head of her husband.

"I knew it beforehand," sighed Ali. "The Prophet told it all to me. Nevertheless, I shall stand at the gates of the Seraglio on a silver pedestal."

Next day he heard that Gaskho Bey had been appointed Pasha of Janina.

"They act as if I were dead already," murmured the veteran, with as bitter a feeling as if he already saw his youthful supplanter standing on his threshold. "They bury me before I am dead, they divide my property before I have made my will. Nevertheless, one day I shall stand in the gates of the Seraglio on a richer pedestal."

And with that Tepelenti sent forth his ciauses to all the towns within his domains, and to all the local governors, commanding all who had sons to send their sons and all who had brothers to send their brothers to him without delay. Then he ordered that every beast of burden that could be spared should be driven into the mountains, and that every barque they could lay their hands upon should be brought from the sea-coast into the Gulf of Durazzo. The arsenal of Janina bristled with terrific rows of cannons and bombs, and the commanders of the various army corps received instructions to concentrate their forces under the walls of Janina. At any rate, he was determined not to be taken unawares. At least, he would have time to unfurl the red flag before the dread message arrived from Stambul that the Padishah demanded his head.

Ah, ha! Ali Tepelenti would not surrender his gray beard so easily. The hunters shall find out what manner of lion they are pursuing. A firman of the Grand Signior nominated the banished Pehliván Pasha, Lord of Lepanto; Sulaiman Pasha was made Governor of Trikala, and the two mountain passes guarding it; Muhammad Bey, whose father Ali had slain, was proclaimed Lieutenant-General of Durazzo. Thus they had divided his territories beforehand among his most bitter and most dangerous enemies. Ah! this will, indeed, be a magnificent chase.

Ali called together his sons, of whom Vely was Lord of Lepanto, Sulaiman of Trikala, and Mukhtar Pasha of Durazzo. He showed them on the map where their territories lay, and pointed out that if they lost them they would have nothing left. Let all three of them, therefore, gird upon their thighs the swords he intrusted to them and fight like men. The two younger sons swore fervently that they would conquer Fortune with their weapons, but Vely Bey preserved a gloomy silence.

"Art thou not my son?" asked the veteran.

"Allah hath so willed it," answered Vely, "and I also will fight, not for thee but for myself, not for life nor for what is on the other side of death, but because I have a little child in Lepanto, and the enemy is besieging that fortress. That little child is all the world to me. I will fight as only a father can fight for his son. I will rescue him if possible. Thy glory or thy ruin is alike indifferent to me. If the report reach thee that the enemy hath taken Lepanto and slain my son, then count no more upon the sword which thou hast intrusted to me."

And with these words Vely turned his back on his father and softly withdrew.

As Ali saw his son quietly pass before him, it occurred to him whether it would not be as well to draw his pistol from his belt and shoot down the waverer before he quitted Janina. It is true that he had known all this beforehand. His own wife, his own sons, his own weapons, were to turn against him; but then, on the other hand, was he not to stand at the gate of the Seraglio on a silver pedestal?

A host of more than twenty thousand men stood under arms at his disposal, Albanians and Suliotes. A gallant host, if only it would fight. But for whom would it fight?—for him or for the Sultan? And these soldiers, when they saw him besieged, would they forget their murdered kinsfolk, their plundered fields, their burned villages? Did not every man of them know that Ali Tepelenti had been amassing treasures all his life, but had never troubled himself about good deeds? And now these treasures would surely be his ruin.

Time brought the answer. While his enemies were still afar off, the Suliotes arose, under the leadership of a girl among the mountains of Bracori, where one of Ali's grandsons, Zaid, was recruiting soldiers, and massacred Ali's men to the very last one. The last one, however, they suffered to escape and convey to Ali Zaid's severed head, at the same time informing him that it was sent by that girl the head of whose betrothed he had cut off before her very eyes, and she meant to send him still more.

This was the Greek's declaration of war. There at Janina, under his very nose, the Greek captain, Zunga, deserted the Albanian camp, and when the Grand Signior's army reached Trikala, and Gaskho Bey's herald galloped between the two armies with the imperial firman hanging round his neck, and summoned the vassals to take up arms against the Pasha, the whole camp went over to Gaskho Bey. Alone, without the smallest escort, Sulaiman, Ali

Pasha's youngest son, fled without having had the opportunity of testing his father's sword, and they captured him on the road.

Still he had the other two. Mukhtar Bey, with a powerful fleet, lay in the Gulf of Durazzo, and Vely Bey, wroth though he might be with his father, was a valiant warrior, and his son was in Lepanto, and save him he must and would.

But not only his son, some one else was there also. On that cruel, murderous day when Ali Pasha drowned the harems of his sons in the lake, one person among so many escaped, and this was Xelianthé. The damsel loved Vely as much as he loved her, and contrived to let him know that she was alive. Vely Bey sent her to Lepanto, and kept her in hiding there with his little son in order that she might be far from his father.

And now the bey himself hastened to Lepanto, arrived at night in the neighborhood of the town, and perceived already from afar that the citadel in which he had concealed his darlings was in flames.

What if he had arrived too late!

With the fury of a savage wild tiger he flung himself upon the besieging Pehlivan, and in a midnight battle routed him beneath the walls of Lepanto, the Albanians fighting desperately by the side of their leader. But what was the use of it? The fortress was saved, indeed, but it was already in flames. Vely, roaring with grief and pain, flung himself on the gate, scarcely recognizing again the place he had quitted so short a time ago.

He reached the pavilion where he had concealed his wife and child. It was built entirely of wood, except the roof, which was of copper. A curious mass of molten dark-red metal gleamed among the fire-brands. Vely rushed bellowing to the spot, and his soldiers, tearing aside the charred beams and rafters, came upon two skeletons burned to cinders. A coral necklace lying there, which the fire had been unable to calcine, told him that these were the remains of his wife and son.

Not a word did Vely say to a living soul; but he plunged his sword into its sheath, and that same night he rode unarmed into the camp of the discomfited Pehliván Pasha and surrendered himself to the enemy.

His army, utterly demoralized, immediately fled back to Janina, bringing the tidings to his father that Vely Bey, immediately after his victory, had surrendered of his own accord to the Sultan.

So every one abandoned Ali. His cities opened their gates to his enemies, his best friends betrayed, his two sons forsook, him. Still the third son remained. And Mukhtar Bay was the best man of the three. He was the bravest, and he loved his father the best.

Two days later came the tidings that Mukhtar Bey with his whole fleet had surrendered before Durazzo to the Kapudan Pasha.

"The soothsayer foretold it all to me," said Ali, calmly, when the news was brought to him. "So it was written beforehand in heaven. Nevertheless, at the last, I shall stand at the gates of the Seraglio on a silver pedestal!"

CHAPTER VI

THE LION IN THE FOX'S SKIN

Blow upon blow rain down upon thee, thou veteran warrior! Thine armies go over to the enemy, thy friends leave thee desolate, thy sons betray thee, they capture thy cities without unsheathing their swords, thine allies turn their arms against thee, and with thine own artillery, of the best French manufacture, the Suliotes from the walls of Janina shoot down thine Albanian guards!

Ah, those Suliotes! How they can fight! If only now they would raise their swords on thy behalf, how thine enemies would fall in rows! But now it is thy soldiers that fall before *them!* A brother and a sister lead them on—a youth and a girl; the youth's name is Kleon, the girl's name is Artemis. Every time thou dost hear their names, it is as if a sword were being plunged into thy heart, for the girl is she whom thou wouldst have sacrificed to thy lust, and with whom thy wife didst escape; and thou never dost hear that name without hearing at the same time of the loss of thy bravest warriors!

Like the destroying angel Azrael, she fares through the din of battle, waving her white banner amidst the showers of bullets, and not one of them touches her. Before thy very eyes she plants the triumphant banner on thy bastions, and thou hast not strength of mind enough left to wish her to fall; nay, rather, when thou dost see her appear before thee, thou dost forbid thy gunners to fire upon her!

Danger approaches Janina from all sides. Thou must drain the cup, Tepelenti, to the very last drop, to the last bitter drop; and what then? Why, then thou wilt stand before the Seraglio on a silver pedestal!

One night there was a rolling of drums before the seven gates of Janina, and a bomb flying down from the heights of Lithanizza exploded in the market-place of the town. Up, up, ye Albanians! up, up, ye who have any martial blood in your veins, the enemy has seized the guns on the seven gates! Ali throws himself on his prancing steed, and in his hand is the good battle-sword which has befriended him in so many a danger. How many times has it not been the lot of Ali to lose everything but this one sword, and then to win back everything by means of it?

In a moment the army of the besieged stood in battle-array. Ali contemplated the ranks of the enemy, and a smile passed across his face. That worthy captain, Gaskho Bey, was leading his troops to the shambles. In an hour's time Ali will so completely have annihilated them that not even the rumor of them will remain behind. It will be a battle-field worthy of the veteran general. Every one who sees it will say—there is no escaping from him! Only let them advance, that is all! And again he was disappointed. At the first shot, before a sword had been drawn, his army surrendered to the enemy. If only they had fired once, the victory would have been his; but no, the army laid down its arms and the cunningly concealed gunners turned his own artillery against him.

It was all over! Only seven hundred Albanian horsemen remained with Ali, the rest either went over to the enemy or allowed themselves to be taken.

The old lion waved his sword above his head, and turning to his handful of heroes exclaimed, with a voice that rang out like a brazen trumpet, "Will ye behold Ali die?"

And with that he galloped towards the market-place of Janina, the faithful seven hundred following closely upon his heels.

The enemy poured into the town through every gate, but the market-place cut off one part of the town from the others, and the triumphant hordes came upon some very evil-looking trenches bristling with *chevaux de frise*, and the long narrow streets were swept by Ali's last twelve cannons, ably handled by the pasha's dumb eunuchs, who stood at their posts like the symbols of constancy on a tomb.

Ali Pasha put down his foot in the middle of Janina. Of his ten thousand horsemen only seven hundred remained with him. The enemy had twenty thousand men and two hundred guns, and yet all the skill of Gaskho Bey was incapable of dislodging Ali from the market-place of Janina, and although the enemy held one portion of the city, it was unable to take the other portion. If only they could have come to close quarters with him, they would have crushed him with one hand; but get at him they could not — that required skill, not strength.

At last the besiegers set the town on fire all around him, but still Ali did not budge from his place, and the wind blew the flames in the face of Gaskho Bey, who began to look about him uncomfortably when the two Suliote kinsfolk, Kleon and Artemis, at the head of their squadrons, urged him to boldly assault the market-place.

Tepelenti saw the girl with her white banner, and as her troops filled the broad space at the head of the square, he himself, at first, drew near to her. Four cannons were pointed at the Suliotes, loaded with chain-shot and broken glass. Ali looked towards them with a gloomy countenance, then stuck his sword in its sheath, bade his gunners turn the guns round, harness the horses to them, and take refuge in the citadel. He would not let a single shot be fired at the Suliotes.

The moment Ali turned his back, the besieging host captured the field of battle. They followed hard upon the heels of the retreating band all the way, and when Ali reached the bridge, the Spahis and Timariots, like two swarms of bees mingled together, gained the head of the bridge at the same time, and swarmed after him with a shout of triumph. The real struggle began on the bridge itself. Man to man they fought at close quarters with their shorter weapons (they could use no other), and clubs and dirks did bloody work in the throng which poured from two different quarters, along and over the overcrowded bridge like ants coming out of a slender reed. Six hundred of the Albanians succeeded in escaping into the citadel, and then, at Ali's command, the iron gates were clapped to, leaving the remaining hundred to perish on the bridge, where the overwhelming crowd swallowed them up. Each single Albanian fought against ten to twenty Timariots. The bridge rang with the din of combat, and trembled beneath the weight of the heavy crowd. Then suddenly the guns on both sides of the bastions which were attached to the bridge began to roar, the supports of the captured bridge collapsed, and the bridge itself, with its load of fighting Turks and Albanians, plunged down into the deep trenches below.

Down there were sharp-pointed stakes beneath the deep waters, and those of the besiegers who remained on the bank were horrified to perceive that not one of the fallen crowd reappeared on the surface of the water, while the water itself gradually grew redder and redder, till at last it was a bright crimson, painted by the blood of the corpses below.

And opposite to them stood the fast-barred gate.

Ah—ha! 'Tis not so easy to capture Tepelenti as ye thought.

Everywhere else ye have triumphed; ye have triumphed up to the very last point. And now ye *have* come to the last point, and your victories are worth nothing, for the last point is still to be won.

The fortress is unapproachable. The bastions are built in the middle of the lake, and from their dark quadrangular cavities rows of guns (each one of them a sixty-pounder) sweep the surface of the water, so that it is impossible to draw near in boats. On the land side one hundred cannons defend the bastions, and who can surmount the triple ditch?

Ye will never capture Ali there. He has sufficient muniments of war to last him for an indefinite period, and to show them how determined he was, he caused the solitary gate of the fortress to be filled with masonry and walled up. So the fortress has no longer a gate. Even desertion is now an impossibility.

There he will remain, then, walled up as in a tomb, buried alive! The only roads from thence lead to heaven or hell; the exit from the land side is guarded by the Suliotes; even if he could fly he could not escape from them.

The campaign is ended. The victorious Gaskho Bey proclaims himself Pasha of Janina. The whole of Epirus does homage to him, and deserts the fallen Vizier. In Stambul thanksgivings are offered up in the Ejub mosque and the church of St. Sophia for the accomplished victory, which is proclaimed, amidst the roaring of the cannons, by heralds in the great market-place; and all the newspapers of Europe amazedly report that the mighty and terrible adventurer, the ever-victorious veteran of seventy-nine, the party-leader who grew to such a height that it was doubtful whether he or the Sultan were the real ruler of Turkey, the man who had been the ally of the great Napoleon, who a few months before had sent as a present to England a precious dinner-service of pure gold worth 30,000 thaler, who had heaped up more treasures than any Eastern nabob—is suddenly crushed, annihilated, shut up in a fortress! It now only remains for him to die.

And not very long afterwards he did die. One night a couple of bold Albanian horsemen descended the bastions by means of a long rope, and, crossing the lake of Acheruz on a pine log, sought out Gaskho Bey in his camp that very night.

Ali Tepelenti was dead. They were the first to bear the joyful tidings to the bey. He died in his grief, in his wretchedness. Perhaps also he had taken poison. On the morrow, at three o'clock, they had arranged to bury him in the fortress. Before his death he had called together his lieutenants, and taken an oath of them that they would defend the fortress to the very last gasp of the very last man. His treasures were piled up in the red tower—more than thirty millions of piastres. He had left it all to them. But what was the use of all this treasure to them if they could not get out of this eyrie? They would not surrender themselves, for Ali had made them swear by every Turkish saint that they would defend the fortress to the death. But the rank and file were of a different opinion; they would joyfully retire from the fortress if they were assured of a free forgiveness. Gaskho Bey had only to stretch out his hand and the fortress of Janina, the impregnable fortress with its two hundred cannons and its enormous mass of treasure, would be his.

Early in the morning the gray moonless flag, the sign of death, was waving on the red tower of Janina, and the guns overlooking the water fired three and thirty volleys, whose echo proclaimed among the mountains that Ali Tepelenti was dead. Within the fortress sounded the roll of the muffled drums, and it was also possible to distinguish the dirges of the imams.

Gaskho Bey and his staff, from the top of the Lithanizza hills, watched the burial of the pasha.

There was an observatory here from whose balcony they could look down into the court-yard, and the splendid telescopes, which the sultan had got from Vienna, rendered powerful assistance to the onlookers, who through them could observe the smallest details of what was going on in the court-yard of the fortress; one telescope in particular brought the objects so near that one could read the initial letters of the verses of the Kuran which the imams held in their hands.

In the midst of a simple coffin lay Ali Pasha. It was really he; of that there could be no doubt. Let every one look for himself! There he lay—dead, cold, motionless. His lieutenants and his servants stood around him weeping. Those who walked along by his side stooped down to kiss his hands.

In the town outside the Suliotes knew of Ali's death, and by way of compliment they fired a bomb into the citadel. But the match of the bomb was too short, and it exploded in the air.

From the observatory they could see very well the fright of the crowd assembled in the court-yard at the whizzing of the bomb over their heads, and how every one looked anxiously at the little round white cloud there; only he who lay dead in the midst of them remained cold and tranquil. He will never again be disturbed by the roar of an exploding bomb.

The imams raised him on their shoulders, and, amidst the melancholy dirges of the mourners and the muffled roll of the drums, they carried him away to his open tomb, for his grave was already dug.

The Moslems do not put their dead in a closed coffin; they only half board the tomb up in order that the angels of death may have room to place the corpse in a sitting posture when they come to take an account of his actions.

They really did lower Ali Tepelenti into his tomb.

The garrison fired a triple salute, the imams thrice sang their sacred verses, and then came the grave-diggers and cast the earth upon the corpse. A large marble slab was standing there, and with it they pressed down the earth on the tomb, at the same time placing two turbaned headstones, one at each end of the tomb.

They really did bury Ali.

When the imams and the officers had departed from the covered tomb, Gaskho Bey summoned the keepers of the observatory to the summit of Lithanizza and laid this command upon them:

"Let a man stand in front of this telescope from morning to evening (and mind that he is relieved every four hours), and never withdraw his eye from that tomb. At night, when the moon goes down, a rocket is to be fired every five minutes, that the watchers may see the tomb and never leave it out of sight, and report upon it every hour."

What? Is Gaskho Bey actually afraid that old Ali, a veteran of seventy-nine, will be able to arise from his tomb and hurl away that heavy marble slab with his dead hands? There are men of whom it is impossible to believe that they are dead, and whom people are afraid of even when they are buried.

Every hour till late in the evening they reported to Gaskho Bey that the tomb remained unchanged, and all the night through not a soul approached it.

Tepelenti, then, was really dead—totally dead.

Early next morning Gaskho Bey heard a very curious story.

In the artillery barracks, where the round guns stood, a drummer had laid down his drum close beside him, with the drumsticks leaning over it, when he suddenly perceived the two drumsticks begin to move of their own accord over the tightly drawn skin of the drums as if some invisible hand wished to beat a tattoo. The drummer cried out at this marvel, and fancied that a *dzhin* was in the drum.

Gaskho Bey would not believe it till he had himself gone to the barracks and seen with his own eyes how the two drumsticks vibrated with sufficient force to tap the drum pretty loudly, moving in a spiral line backward and forward across it, tap-tap-tapping as they went.

"It is very marvellous!" cried the bey; and he immediately summoned the imams to drive the *dzhin* out of the drum.

The imams set to work at once. They fetched their fumigators and their sacred books, and they fumigated the drum with nose-offending odors and recited over it drum-expelling exorcisms in a shrill voice. And certainly if the devil was in that drum, and had anything of a nose or ears, he would have been obliged to escape from that noise and stink. So long as the drum was in any one's hand the drumsticks did not move, but when it was put down on the ground the mysterious tap-tapping began again.

The imams went on howling, and horribly they howled.

The chief of the observatory was present during

this scene. As a French renegade he was a man of some education, and therefore he did not accept the theory of the *dzhins*. When he perceived that the imams were not successful in expelling the evil spirits, he called Gaskho Bey aside and whispered in his ear:

"I know nothing about your *dzhins*, and don't understand what you are driving at with all this noise and stench, but I can tell you that this beating of the drum is a sign that invisible hands are at work here."

"What?"

"It means that we ought to get away from here, for they are digging mines beneath us, and that is why the ground trembles and the drumsticks vibrate."

Gaskho Bey began smiling. He had as little idea of sapping and mining as the French renegade had of Turkish monsters.

"How superstitious thou art, my brave moosir!" said he, shrugging his shoulders and looking down upon the Frenchman.

The latter, however, did not remain there much longer, but hastened as quickly as he could to the summit of the Lithanizza.

After about an hour and a half's more hubbub the imams succeeded in expelling the *dzhin*. The drum grew quiet, the excitement subsided, and the soldiers were instructed to lay two swords crosswise in front of the gate, so that the spirit might not be able to come back any more; and with that termination of the affair every one was satisfied.

Opposite the gate of the fortress of Janina, at the head of the collapsed bridge, stood a stone building, fenced about with redoubts and palisades, which had now fallen into the hands of the Suliotes. This building had been chosen by the two Greek kinsfolk for their dwelling-place. They wanted to get as close to Ali as possible; they would not suffer him to escape even in the shape of a bird or a spirit; their large siege-guns were pointed at the walled-up gate. Let him surrender or find his tomb in the fortress.

And lo! he *had* found his tomb without consulting them about it. In vain they had sharpened their weapons against him—the sword of Death is quicker and cuts down sooner. They had not been able to reach him on the field of battle; they had not been able to plunge their avenging swords into his heart; they had not been able to bring his gray head to the block; it had been reserved for him to pass quietly away — to die in his bed, untroubled, unmolested, to die the death of the righteous.

Kleon and Artemis were sitting sullenly in a room of the fort by the light of a flickering candle. The girl had absently divested herself of her cuirass and was walking up and down the room with folded arms. There was not a single womanly trait in her face. It was as cold as the face of a statue.

"So he is dead, then—dead!"

This phrase she repeated to herself again and again. She seemed unable to get away from it.

"Ali has died, and not by my hand."

Kleon was strikingly like his sister; indeed, his young face scarcely differed at all from hers, but in his eyes quite another sort of flame sparkled. Her face, full of dark thoughts, was much more terrible; his was free and open, and full of radiant hope.

"My triumph has lost its worth if Ali is dead," she said, with a sigh. "The old fox has dodged my steel by taking refuge in hell. Oh, would that I might follow him thither also, that I might tear his gray beard, which he has bathed in my kinsman's blood!"

"Behold! here is my gray beard!" cried a voice at that instant from the other end of the room, and the brother and sister beheld Ali Tepelenti standing before them.

The terror-stricken young people involuntarily crossed themselves. Horror nailed them to the ground and petrified all their limbs, when they saw what they imagined to be a spectre standing there before them in the self-same gray robe in which he had been buried two days before.

"Behold, here I am, Ali Tepelenti!"

With that the spectre clapped his hands, and from every corner of the room rushed forth Albanians armed to the teeth, and before the brother and sister could approach their weapons, they were overpowered and tied together.

It was really Ali Tepelenti who stood before them.

They had put him away underground, it is true, but underground there were paths and passages only too well known to him. The whole spectacle of the interment had been arranged by himself, and there was an exit from the bottom of his tomb into subterranean corridors. When the general joy and satisfaction at the victory was at its height, he was abroad and at work.

A strongly built subterranean trench had been constructed below the ditches encircling the redoubts, and its ramifications extended to the fort at the head of the bridge. Ali had so completely surprised the garrison that they had not been able to fire a shot; the Suliotes had been surprised and disarmed while in their dreams.

Up, up, Gaskho Bey! Arise, Muhammad Aga! To horse, ye captains! Seize thy sword, Pehliván Pasha! Danger is at hand! This is a bad night for sleeping!

Suddenly a frightful explosion shook the ground, just as if the earth was being wrenched from its hinges, and amidst a flame brighter than the light of day, which seemed to leap up to the very stars, huge round cannons were seen flying. The gunners in the barracks were also pitched into the air. The minarets tottered and fell before the terrific shock, every building round about crumbled into ruins. In a moment one-half of the town was reduced to a rubbish-heap, and the next moment a hail of burning beams and lacerated human limbs fell back upon the ruins from the blood and fire besmudged heavens.

It was thus that Ali Pasha signified his resurrection to his enemies! He had gone underground, and now from underground he began the war anew.

Gaskho Bey, his gigantic body half undressed (he had just leaped out of bed), rushed to the end of the street, and was so confused that he asked all whom he met where he was. The suddenly aroused soldiers, half mad with terror, rushed hither and thither in confusion, crying out, one for his horse, another for his weapons. And above their heads, more terrible than heaven's thunder-bolts, resounded the dread cry, "Ali, Ali!" There comes the entombed pasha on a white horse, with his white beard; who will dare to look him in the face? The panic-stricken throng falls in thousands beneath the swords of the Albanians, blood flows in streams in the streets of Janina, and Ali Pasha, the dead man, the buried captain, fills the hearts of their warriors with the fear of death. There is none who can stand against him.

Only Pehliván, the stalwart hero, was able to prevent the vast besieging army from being scattered altogether by a handful of Arnauts. He rallied the fugitives outside the town, and, while Ali's men-at-arms were murdering every one inside, he quickly seized all the gates, advanced in battle-array, and stayed the triumph of the veteran captain.

And enough had surely been done.

Three thousand of the besiegers lay dead, the guns were spiked or overthrown, and the leaders of the Suliote band were prisoners—and all this the result of Ali's nocturnal rally! It was time for him to return.

Pehliván thus recaptured the town and marshalled his men in the market-place, without pursuing Ali any further. But he had reckoned without Gaskho Bey, who now came rushing up and furiously accosted him:

"Why hast thou not pursued him right into the citadel?"

"It would not do to press Ali too closely," replied the practised general; "let him fly, if fly he will."

At this, Gaskho Bey, foaming with rage, tore the

sword out of Pehliván's hand (where he had left his own sword he could not have said for the life of him), and, placing himself at the head of a band of Spahis, began to pursue the retreating foe.

Ali was proceeding quite leisurely towards the fortress, as if he did not trouble himself about his pursuers, although they were six times as numerous as his forces.

When Gaskho Bey had got within ear-shot, Tepelenti shouted back to him:

"Thou hast come to a bad place, brave Bey. This ground is mine, and what is beneath it is mine also, dost thou not know that yet?"

Gaskho Bey naturally did not understand a word of this till, at a gesture from Ali, a rocket flew up into the air, at which signal those inside the fortress suddenly exploded all the mines which had been dug under all the streets of the town. Tepelenti had prepared these during his fortunate days by piercing water conduits and making subterranean vaults large enough to hold great stores of gunpowder.

Ali rallied his own bands at the head of the bridge, and when, suddenly, the explosion burst forth along the whole length of the street, and the destroying flame tossed the pursuing squadrons into the air one after the other, he amused himself by contemplating the ruin from the top of the fort, and was the last who disappeared in the hidden tunnel. For a long time those in the fortress could hear the agonized cries of the vanquished. One-third of the besieging army had been destroyed in a single night. The rest quitted the accursed town, which seemed to have been built over hell itself, and took up a position in the fields outside and on the heights of Lithanizza.

The rising sun revealed a horrible spectacle. The town of Janina no longer existed, the beautiful tall houses, the cupolaed mosques, the slender white minarets, the imposing barracks—where were they? Instead of them, all that could be seen was a shapeless mass of piled-up ruins; here and there, on a dark background, scorched by flickering flames, a huddle-muddle of broken rafters, mangled corpses, charred black or gaping hideously open, lay scattered about amongst the rubbish, and from the mouth of a conduit at the side of the bastion there trickled sadly down into the lake a dark red stream, which wound its way in and out amongst the ruins.

"Poor children, how sweetly they are sleeping!" Thus spoke Ali.

In a corner of the red tower, sleeping side by side, were the two Suliote kinsfolk, Artemis and Kleon. They slept in each other's embrace, and not even the gaze of Ali awoke them.

"Don't arouse them," said Ali to his dumb eunuchs; "let them sleep on!"

And again he regarded them with a smile—they slept so soundly. And yet they knew not when they fell asleep whether they would ever awake again.

Ali did not arouse the slumberers. Thrice he sent to see if they had awakened, but he would not have them disturbed. At last the hand of the youth made his chain clank, and both of them opened their eyes at the sound.

"I was on my way to Akro-Corinth," said he,

rubbing his large dreamy eyes with his hands, "and I saw them rebuilding the Parthenon."

"I stood at Thermopylæ," said the girl, "and the enemy fell before me by thousands."

"And now we shall go to the block," sighed Kleon, listening as the iron doors of his dungeon slowly opened.

"Be strong!" whispered the girl, pressing the hand of her brother which was enlaced in hers.

The dumb eunuchs surrounded them, and led them before Ali Pasha.

The pasha was sitting on a divan, and still wore his funeral robe; all the furniture was shrouded with cinder-colored cloth; there was nothing golden, nothing that sparkled in the room.

The brother and sister stood before him, pressing each other's hands.

"My dear children," said the pasha, in a voice that trembled with emotion, "don't look into each other's eyes, but look at me!"

At this unusual tone, at these kindly words, the brother and sister did look at him, and perceived that the old man was looking at them sadly, doubtfully, and that his eyes were full of tears.

Ali beckoned to the eunuchs, and they freed the brother and sister from their chains.

"Behold, ye are free, and may return to your homes," said Ali.

These words had the effect of an electric shock upon the youth, and his face lit up with a flush of joy.

"Why dost thou rejoice?" cried Artemis, casting a severe look upon him; "dost thou not perceive that the monster is mocking us? He only wants to excite joy within us that he may kindle our hopes, and then make death all the more bitter to us. Why dost thou make sport of us, thou old devil? Slay us quickly, or slay us with lingering torments, 'tis all one to us, but do not mock us!"

Tepelenti devoutly raised his eyes to heaven.

"My soul is an open book before you. Ye are free. Ye free Suliotes, we understand one another. I have sinned grievously against you, but ye have revenged yourself upon me. I burned your villages, ye, in return, have destroyed my fortresses. I have pillaged your lands, and ye have taken my possessions from me. I have slain your bridegroom and snatched thee from thy parent's house; thou hast cut off the head of my favorite grandson, and ravished from me my favorite wife. Now we are quits, and owe each other nothing. Go in peace!"

There was so much sincerity, so much repentant, contrite grief in the words of Ali, that the watchful maid began to regard him with curious sympathy.

"Thou art amazed at my change of countenance," said Ali, observing the impression his words had produced on Artemis. "Thou hast not seen me like this before! That other Ali is no more. He died, and was buried. A penitent kneels before thee who has a horror of his past sins, and begs thy forgiveness, kissing the hem of thy garment."

And, indeed, Ali fell down on his knees before Artemis, in order that he might kiss the border of her robe, and breaking forth into moans, shed tears at the girl's feet, so that she involuntarily bent down and raised him up.

She was a woman, after all, and could not bear to see any one weeping before her.

"Listen now to what I say," continued the pasha, "and do not fancy that Ali has gone mad. This night I saw a vision. A beauteous and radiantly majestic maiden descended at my threshold from the midst of the bright, open heavens, surrounded by a company of winged children's heads. The maiden looked at me so gently, so kindly. A divine light shone from her countenance, and, on the earth beneath, all the flowers turned their faces towards her as if she were the sun. In the arms of this heavenly maid sat a child, but what a child! At the sight of him, even I, old man as I am, trembled with joy. Round about the head of this child was a wreath of stars, and the smile upon his face was salvation itself. And when I raised my trembling hands towards her, the heavenly lady and the child extended their arms towards me, and from the lips of the maiden, in a sweet, inexpressibly sweet voice, came these words: 'Ali Tepelenti, I call thee!' And I, all trembling, fell down on my knees before her."

The brother and sister involuntarily knelt down beside Ali and stammered, full of devotion, "Blessed be the most holy Virgin!"

Ali Pasha continued the recital of his vision.

"With my face covered, I listened to the words of the bright apparition, and now she addressed me once more in a dolorous voice, which pierced my very heart, 'Ali Tepelenti, behold me!' And when I raised my face, lo! I beheld seven swords pointing towards the heart of the heavenly maid, and I felt my hand grow numb with fright. 'Ali Tepelenti,' said the lady for the third time, 'these swords *thou* hast thrust into my wounds, and my blood be upon thy head!' And I, groaning, made answer, 'How could I have done so when I do not know thee?' And she replied, 'He who persecutes mine, persecutes me, and who robs my temples, robs me; didst thou not pull down the churches of Tepelen, Turezzo, and Tripolizza?' 'I swear that I will build them up again,' I replied, raising my hand to give solemnity to my vow; and as I spoke one of the seven swords fell from the heart of the lady. 'Didst thou not rob the Suliotes of their children,' inquired the heavenly vision anew, 'in order to bring them up as Moslems?' 'I swear that I will make them Christians again!' and at these words the second sword fell out of her heart. 'Didst thou not carry off their maidens for thine own harem?' 'I swear that I will give them back to the Suliotes!' and with that the third sword fell from her heart. 'Didst thou not gather together immense treasures from the heritage of widows and orphans?' And, smiting the ground with my head, I answered: 'All my treasures shall be dedicated to thy service.' And thus she recorded my mortal sins one by one, and thus I swore to make rigorous reparation for them with an irrefragable oath, and as many times as I so swore a sword fell at my feet. Finally but one sword remained in her bleeding heart, and then she asked me, 'Hast thou not sought the death of that Suliote brother and sister who were the most faithful defenders of my altars? Hast thou not plunged them into thy dungeon, and is not their death already resolved upon in thy heart?' And, terrified, I laid my hand upon my heart, for verily that thought was in it, and not without a fierce struggle, I stammered, 'Oh, heavenly vision! these two young people are my mightiest enemies, and they have sworn to kill me; yet if thou dost command it I will lay my gray head in their hands, and I will be in their power, not they in mine.' At these words the last sword also fell from her heart, and she answered, 'Ali Tepelenti, take these swords in thy hand, and do as thou hast said.' And with that she reascended into heaven, the clouds closed behind her, and I remained alone with the seven swords in my hand, on which seven vows were written. This vision I saw in the night that has just past; and now reflect upon my words."

The minds of the brother and sister were deeply agitated. The old Moslem before them had spoken with such devotion, with such enthusiasm of his vision, that it was impossible to question its reality. The emotion visible in his countenance, the tears in his eyes, the tremor in his voice, proved that he really felt what he said. While they were standing there pondering over the old man's vision, he took them by the hand and led them into his treasure-chamber, and showed them the heaps and heaps of gold and silver, the coins piled up in vats, and the steel which had been melted into bars and stacked up there.

"My treasures are at your disposal—use them as you will." Then, selecting from amongst his choicest diamonds two stones, worth a hundred thousand sequins, he placed them in the hands of Kleon and Artemis, and said, "These I will send to the war-chest of the Hetæria!"

Why, what does Ali mean by mentioning this secret society, which had already undermined the whole Turkish Empire—just as he had undermined Janina? Perhaps he would fire these mines also!

Of a truth the arm of Ali reached as far as Stambul! aye, and as far as Bucharest also.

And now he led the brother and sister into his armory, and there they saw whole chests full of firearms from the manufactories of the best English and French makers.

"You see, I could arm a whole realm with the weapons I have in Janina."

The brother and sister sighed; one and the same thought suddenly occurred to them both.

"Tepelenti," said the girl.

"Command me!"

"Thou hast done much harm to us, we also have done much harm to thee; let us act as if we now saw each other for the first time."

"I forgive you."

"I will forget that thou didst put to death my betrothed in this room, and thou forget that we killed thy grandson. Call to mind, moreover, that not only are we captives in this fortress, but thou art also surrounded by the hosts of thine enemies."

"I alone am a captive," said Ali, humbly. "I swear by Allah, as I have promised the holy Virgin, that I will let you and all your companions free! What may happen to you after that I care not. Ali has not long to live now. But your days of combat are yet to be, and if ever the time should come when your plans need the help of arms and treasures, remember that there is enough of both at Janina."

Artemis was constrained to believe in the sincerity of Ali's words.

And now the pasha, with his own hand, selected two beautiful Damascus blades from among his store of weapons, and bound them to the girdles of the brother and sister. What a warmth of self-confidence came over them when they felt once more that they had swords by their sides!

Then he led them down to their companions, who were assembled in the court-yard of the fortress, and informed them that they were free to go whither they would. And then he put wine and pilaf before the jubilant crowd of captives, and left them to eat and drink with his own Arnauts; and, beneath the peace-making influence of the good wine, it was not very long before they fell to kissing one another and swearing eternal fellowship like brothers.

Then Ali produced his best long-range rifles, with bayonets attached, and distributed them amongst the captive Suliotes; he had not the least fear now that they would turn these arms against him. Then he kissed the brother and sister on their foreheads, and, giving them his blessing, let them through that secret tunnel which led into the town.

Meanwhile, in Gaskho Bey's camp outside curious reports began to circulate. A pair of captured Albanians, who had been surprised amongst the ruins of the town when Ali retreated, began to make the most astounding revelations before their judges; amongst other things they maintained that the Suliotes, in the camp of the bey, had a secret understanding with the Pasha of Janina—their former master. And, as a matter of fact, every one had observed that Ali had quitted the field of battle rather than fire upon the Suliotes.

But the captives confessed still more. They said that Artemis and Kleon had had secret meetings with Ali in the subterranean tunnel, and had surrendered to him voluntarily. It must have been so, argued those who had survived the last sally. Ali had made his assault from the tower at the head of the bridge, and yet the Suliotes there had not so much as fired a gun to signify his approach.

The captives also insisted that Ali was going to make another sally on the following night against the besieging army, and then all the Christians in the camp of the bey would join him.

These reports, with still more terrible variations, began to extend throughout the whole army, and here and there slight *mêlées* even took place between Christians and Moslems. The Osmanlis began to threaten the foreign soldiers, and the latter began to everywhere form themselves into independent little bands for mutual protection.

Gaskho Bey and Pehliván Pasha hastily summoned a council of war at this disquieting symptom, and it was there resolved that the Greeks should be disarmed. For this purpose they assembled them together in the midst of the camp, surrounded them with Turkish veterans, and then, pointing the guns at them, summoned them to instantly lay down their arms or they should all be shot down like dogs.

The Suliotes and Albanians listened to this summons with terror. They beheld the bloodthirsty masses around them, and reflected how many times men had lost their lives by surrendering the very weapons wherewith they might have defended themselves, and, in their hesitation, they chose out twelve youths from amongst their ranks to go to the general and ask the reason of this alarming demonstration.

Gaskho Bey was still in a towering passion, and the bold speech of the young men irritated him still further. He had them dragged into the midst of the camp, in front of the assembled battalions, and commanded that their heads should be cut off, proclaiming at the same time that any who dared to disobey this order should meet with the same fate.

The garments of the twelve young men were stripped from off them in the presence of their comrades, and the usual head severing giant stood behind them, ready to force them down upon their knees and decapitate them one by one. But he had not yet cut off a single head when a loud noise was heard coming from the direction of Janina; it was the liberated sister and brother, Artemis and Kleon, at the head of their bands. They had beheld from the tower of Janina the danger which threatened their comrades, and arrived just as the executioners were preparing to carry out Gaskho Bey's commands.

The Suliotes scattered here and there looked at each other. A tremendous roar filled the air—a roar of grief and rage and terror—breaking forth into despair. Those from before, those from behind, fell upon the ranks of the Moslems. In a moment Gaskho Bey's whole camp was converted into a chaotic mob, where Albanians and Spahis, Suliotes and Timariotes, fought together without any fixed plan, and, in utter defiance of all military science, recognizing neither friend nor foe. In vain the standard-bearers raised their banners, in vain the officers of the Spahis roared themselves hoarse, and the Sorbadzhis and the gigantic Gaskho Bey himself did the same. The army was so completely disorganized that not even the victorious enemy could make head or tail of it. Towards evening the Suliotes, under Kleon and Artemis, captured Lithanizza; while Gaskho Bey, in his despair, fled all the way to Durazzo. When he got there he discovered that of all his army only twelve ciauses remained with him. The whole host had fled higgledy-piggledy along the first road it came across, leaving behind it all its artillery, baggage, and ammunition wagons.

But Ali Pasha, sweetly smiling, calmly looked on from the red tower of Janina, while the enemy worried itself to death, and the besieging thousands scattered in every direction without his having to waste a single cannon-shot upon them.

But as I have already said, Ali was often so reduced as to possess nothing but his sword, and with this same sword he would win everything back again.

CHAPTER VII

THE ALBANIAN FAMILY

AND now we will let the rumor of great deeds rest a while; we will close our eyes to the wars that followed upon the siege of Janina; we will shut our ears against the echoes of the names of a Ulysses, Tepelenti, a Kolokotrini, those heroes who shook the throne of the Sultan, and all of whom the Pasha of Janina called his very dear friends. While these bloody wars are raging we will turn into the grove of Dodona, where formerly the ambiguous utterances of sacred prophecies were always resounding in the ears of contemplative dreamers. Let us go back eighty years! Let us seek out that quiet little glen whither neither good report nor evil report ever comes flying, whose inhabitants know of nothing but what happens amongst their own fir-trees; why, even the tax-collecting Spahi only light down amongst them to levy contributions once in a century!

The house of Halil Patrona's consort no longer stands beside the rippling stream. Nobody even knows the tomb in which the beautiful, the elfin Gül-Bejáze now lies; Gül-Bejáze, the White Rose,*

* The heroine of another Turkish tale of Jókai's, *A feher rózsa* (*The White Rose*).

blooms no longer anywhere in that valley. Nobody knows the name even; only the oldest old grandmother in the circle of the spinning maidens can tell them tales, which she also has heard from her mother or her grandmother, of a mad lady who used to dwell in this valley and lay a table every evening and prepare a couch every night for an invisible spirit, whom she called her husband, and whom nobody saw but herself.

This old woman had a son called Behram, a brave, honest, worthy youth; many a time with his comrades he would pursue the Epirot bandits, who swooped down upon their valley and carried off their cattle.

Near to him dwelt the widow Khamko, whose husband had been shot at Tepelen, and who, with her son, little Ali, in her bosom, had sought refuge amongst these mountains.

Formerly Khamko was a gentle creature, but when they began to talk to her about the mad lady she also grew as crazy as ever the other was. She was ready to destroy the whole world, and over and over again she would utter the wildest things; she would like, she said, to see the whole four corners of the world set on fire so that the flames might shoot up on all four sides of it, and every living man within it, good as well as bad, might be burned. Listen not to such words, O Allah!

Behram was a very quiet fellow, not more than six and twenty years old; little Ali was scarce sixteen. But this wild, restless lad was already wont to wander for days together amongst the glens and mountains, and whenever he came home he invariably brought his mother money or jewels. And nobody knew whence he got them save Behram, to whom the youth confessed everything, for he loved him dearly.

Ali joined the company of the Epirot adventurers, and with them he would go sacking villages, waylaying rich merchants, and shared with them the easily gotten booty.

And whenever he returned home without money, his mother, Khamko, would rail upon and chide him, and let him have no peace until he had engaged in fresh and more lucrative robberies.

Behram looked askance at the perilous ways of his young comrade, and as often as he was alone with him did his best to fill his mind with honest, noble ideas, which also seemed to make some impression on Ali, for he gradually began to abandon his marauding ways, and in order that he might still be able to get money for his mother, he fell to selling his sheep and his goats, and even parted with his long, silver-mounted musket. At last he had nothing left but his sword. Dame Khamko, meanwhile, scolded Ali unmercifully. If he wanted to eat, let him go seek his bread, she said. And the lad wandered through the woods and thickets, and lived for a long time on the berries of the forest. At last, one day, when he was wellnigh famished and in the depths of misery, he came upon an Armenian innkeeper standing in the doorway of his lonely little tavern. Ali rushed upon him, sword in hand, like a wolf perishing with hunger. The Armenian was a worthy old fellow, and when he saw Ali he said to him:

"What dost thou want, my son?"

The honest, open look of the old man shamed Ali, and casting down his eyes, he replied: "I want to give thee this sword." Yet the moment before he had determined to slay him with it.

The Armenian took the sword from him, and gave him ten sequins in exchange for it, besides meat and drink. So Ali returned home without his sword.

When Dame Khamko saw her son return home disarmed she was greatly incensed and exclaimed:

"What hast thou done with thy sword?"

"I have sold it," answered Ali, resolutely.

At this the mother flew into a violent rage, and catching up a bludgeon, belabored Ali with it until she was tired. The big, muscular lad allowed himself to be beaten, and neither wept nor said a word, nor even tried to defend himself.

"And now dost see that spindle?" cried Dame Khamko. "Learn to spin the thread and turn the bobbins quickly; thou shalt not eat idle bread at home, I can tell thee. A man who can sell his sword is fit for nothing but to sit beside a distaff."

So Ali sat down to spin.

For a couple of days he endured the insults which his mother heaped upon him, and on the third day he returned to the Armenian, to whom he had sold his sword, robbed him of and slew of him with it, plundered and burned down his house, and from thenceforth became such a famous robber that the whole countryside lived in mortal terror of him.

Dame Khamko lived a long time after this event, and ruined her son's soul altogether by urging him to kill and slay without mercy, till one fine day her son murdered her likewise, and thus added her blood also to the blood of those whom, at his mother's instigation, he had cruelly murdered.

And this lad became the Pasha of Janina, Ali Tepelenti!

Through what an ocean of treachery, perjury, robbery, and homicide he had to wade before he attained to that eminence! How often was he not so reduced as to have nothing left but his sword and his crafty brain? But many a time, in the midst of his most brilliant successes, in the very plenitude of his power, he would bethink him of the two quiet little huts where he and Behram had been wont to dwell. He never heard of Behram now, but he used frequently to think in those days and wonder what would have become of himself if he had listened to Behram's words and lived a quiet, contented life. 'Tis true he would not have been so mighty a man as he was now, but would he not have been a much happier one?

Once, when he was a very great potentate, he had visited the little village in the glen in which they had hidden away together. But nobody would tell him anything of Behram. He had disappeared none knew whither. Perhaps he had died since then!

CHAPTER VIII

THE PEN OF MAHMOUD

When, during the reign of Mahmoud II., the caravan of Meccan pilgrims was plundered by the Vechabites, lying in ambush, the Sultan ordered the rulers of Meccao and Medina to immediately send to the lair of the Vechabites and buy back the dervishes with ready money.

The Vechabites gave up the captives in exchange for the ransom sent them, but they adhered so rigidly to the terms of the bargain whereby they were to surrender the captives only, that they even kept for themselves the garments that happened to be on the captives, and let nothing go but their bare bodies, on which account Mahmoud was obliged to give his rescued subjects raiment as well as freedom.

Amongst those who were so liberated was a dervish of the Nimetullahita order, who, after this incident was over, arose, sought out the Sultan and said to him, "Thou art a poor potentate. Thou art the most sorry of all the caliphs. Thou art the greatest son of suffering* among all the sultans who have gone before thee, or shall come after thee. I thank thee for delivering me from the hands of

* *I.e.*, patient of insult.

the Vechabites,* and as a reward, therefore, I bring thee a gift which, even when they left me without any raiment, I was still able to conceal from them."

And with that he produced a writing-reed and gave it to the Sultan, and when Mahmoud asked him in what way he had concealed it from the eyes of the robbers, he explained how he had cunningly thrust it into his thick black beard, where nobody had perceived it.

Mahmoud accepted the gift of the dervish, and put it where he put his other curiosities; but he did not think of it for very long, and gradually it escaped his memory altogether.

One day, however, when one of his favorite damsels, moved by curiosity, had induced him to show her the treasures of his palace, and they came to the spot where lay the pen of the dervish, the damsel suddenly cried out, and said that she had seen the pen move.

The Sultan looked in that direction, and, observing nothing, treated the whole affair as a joke, and went on showing the damsel the accumulated relics and curiosities of centuries which thirteen successive Sultans had stored up in the khazné or treasury, and then gave the damsel permission to choose for herself whichever of these treasures might please her most.

Many costly things were there covered with gems, and worth, each one of them, half a kingdom; there were also rare and precious relics, and antiquities rich in historical associations. But the Sul-

---

* The Vechabites are accounted heretics by the orthodox Mussulmans.

tan's pet damsel chose for herself none of these things; to the amazement of the Padishah, she only asked for this simple black pen.

Mahmoud was astonished, but he granted the damsel her wish, and making light of it, he gave her the writing-reed which was fashioned out of a simple bamboo cane, and was nothing very remarkable even at that.

The odalisk took the pen away with her to her room, and waited from morning to night to see it move. But the pen calmly rested where she had placed it all day long and all night too, and the odalisk began to be sorry that she had not rather selected for herself some other more precious thing instead of the object of her curiosity; but one evening, when the Sultan was visiting her in her flowery chamber, and they were holding sweet converse together, they suddenly heard in the room, where nobody was present but themselves, a faint sound as if some one were writing in great haste, the scratching of a pen on the extended parchment was distinctly audible.

They both looked in the direction of the sound, and words failed them in their astonishment, for behold! the writing-reed was half raised in the air, just as when one is holding it in his hand, and it seemed to be writing of its own accord on the parchment extended beneath it.

The damsel trembled for terror, while the Sultan, who was a stranger alike to fear or superstition, imagining that perhaps a spider had got into the upper part of the reed, and consequently made it move up and down, and anxious to convince his favorite thereof, approached the table, and took up the pen in order to shake the spider out of it. But there was nothing at all there, and the pen went on writing of its own accord.

The Sultan himself began to be astonished at this phenomenon. What the pen seemed to be so diligently writing remained a hidden script, however, for its point had not been dipped in ink. Wishing, therefore, to put it to the test, the Sultan dipped the point of the reed in a little box full of that red balsamic salve with which Turkish girls are wont to paint their lips, and then placed it on a smooth, clean sheet of parchment, whereupon it again arose, and wrote in bright, plainly intelligible letters these words, "Mahmoud! Mahmoud!"

The Sultan's own heart began to beat when he saw his own name written before his eyes, and he inquired with something like consternation, "What dost thou want of me?"

The pen immediately wrote down again these two words, "Mahmoud! Mahmoud!" and then lay still.

"That is my name," said the Sultan; "but who then art thou, O invisible spirit?"

The pen again arose and wrote beneath the name of Mahmoud this name also, "Halil Patrona!"

Mahmoud trembled at this name. It was the name of a man who had been murdered by one of his ancestors, and if the apparition of a spirit be terrible in itself, how much more the spirit of a murdered man!

"What dost thou want here?" exclaimed the terrified Sultan.

The pen answered, "To warn thee!"

"Perchance a danger threatens me, eh?" inquired the Sultan.

"'Tis near thee!" wrote the pen.

"Whence comes this danger?"

And now the pen wrote a long row of letters, and this was the purport thereof, "A great danger from the East, a greater from the West, a greater still from the North, and here at home the greatest of all."

"Where will the Faithful fight?" asked the Sultan.

"In the whole realm!" was the reply.

"Near which towns?"

"Near every town and within every town."

"How long will the war last?"

"Nine years."

It was now the year eighteen hundred and twenty, and there was not a sign of danger at any point of the vast boundaries of the Turkish empire.

The Sultan permitted himself one more question: "Tell me, shall I triumph in these wars?"

The pen replied, "Thou wilt not."

"Who will be my enemies?"

There the pen stopped short, as if it were reflecting on something; at last it wrote down, "Another time."

The Sultan did not understand this answer, so he repeated his question, and now the pen wrote, "Ask in another place!"

"Where?"

"Alone."

Evidently it would not answer the question in the presence of the Sultan's favorite. It did not trust her.

The Sultan almost believed that he was dreaming, but now his favorite damsel also drew near and, leaning on Mahmoud's shoulder, stammered forth, "Prithee, mighty spirit, wilt thou answer me?"

And the pen replied, "I will."

The woman asked, "Tell me, will Mahmoud love me to the death?"

The Sultan was somewhat offended. "By the prophet!" cried he, "that thou shouldst put such a question!"

But what is not a living woman capable of asking?

The pen quivered gently as it wrote down the words, "He will love thee till thou diest."

"And when *shall* I die?"

To this the pen gave no answer.

In vain the favorite pressed her question. How many years, how many months, how many days had she to live? The spirit answered nothing.

"And how shall I die?" asked the woman.

The Sultan shivered at this senseless question, and would have made the girl withdraw; but, in an instant, the pen had written out the answer, "Thou shalt be killed."

The woman grew as pale as a wax figure, and stammered, "Who will kill me?"

Both of them awaited in terror and with baited breath what the pen would answer, and the pen, taking good care not to form a single illegible letter, wrote on the parchment, "Mahmoud!"

The favorite fell unconscious into the arms of the Sultan, who, carrying her away, laid her on the divan, watching over her till she came to herself again, and then comforting her with wise saws.

An evil, mocking spirit dwelt in the reed, he said,

consolingly, who only uttered its forebodings to agitate their hearts. "Did it not say also that I should love thee to the death? How then could I slay thee? A lying spirit dwelleth in that reed!"

And yet the Sultan himself was trembling all the time.

That night no sleep visited his eyes, and early in the morning he took the reed from his favorite by force, telling her that he was going to throw it into the fire.

But he did *not* throw it into the fire. On the contrary, the Sultan frequently produced it, and, inasmuch as he sometimes convicted the spirit of a false prophecy, he began to regard the whole thing as a sort of magic hocus-pocus, invented by the kindly Fates to amuse mankind by its oddity, and he frequently made it serve as a plaything for the whole harem, gathering the odalisks together and compelling the enchanted pen to answer all sorts of petty questions, as, for instance, "How old is the old kadun-keit-khuda?" "How many sequins are in the purse of the Kizlar-Agasi?" "At what o'clock did the Sultan awake?" "When will the Sultan's tulips arrive?" "How many heads were thrown to-day into the sea?" "Is Sadi, the poet, still alive?" etc., etc. Or they forced the pen to translate the verses of Victor Hugo into Turkish, Arabic, and Persian. And the pen patiently accomplished everything. At last it became quite a pet plaything with the odalisks, and the favorite Sultana altogether forgot the evil prophecy which it had written down for her.

Now it chanced one day that the famous filibusterer Microconchalys, who had for a long time disturbed the archipelago with his cruisers, and defied the whole fleet of the Sultan, encountered in the open sea, off Candia, a British man-of-war, which he was mad enough to attack with three galleys. In less than an hour all three galleys were blown to the bottom of the sea, nothing of them remaining on the surface of the water but their well-known flags, which Morrison, the victorious English captain, conveyed to Stambul, and there presented them to the Divan.

Boundless was the joy of the Sultan at the death of the vexatious filibusterer, and there was joy in the harem also, for a feast of lamps was to be held there the same night, and Morrison was to be presented to the Divan on the following day to be loaded with gifts and favors.

At night, therefore, there was great mirth among the odalisks. The Sultan himself was drunk with joy, wine, and love, and the hilarious Sultana brought forth the magic pen to make them mirth, and compelled it to answer the drollest questions, as, for instance, "How many hairs are there in Mahmoud's head?" "How many horses are there in the stable?" and "How many soldiers are there on the sea?" And, finally, laughing aloud, she commanded it to tell her how many hours she had to live.

Ah, surely a life full of joy lay before her! But the Sultan shook his head; one ought not to tempt God with such questions.

The pen would not write.

Then the favorite cried angrily, "Answer! or I will compel thee to count all the drops of water in the Black Sea, from here to Jenikale in the Crimea!"

At these words the pen, with a quivering movement, arose, and scratching the paper with a shrill sound, as if it would weep and moan, wrote down some utterly unintelligible characters, with the number "8" beneath them, and surrounded the whole writing with a circle to signify that there was nothing more to come.

Everybody laughed. It was plain that the spirit also loved its little joke, and was angry with the Sultana for torturing it with so many silly questions.

It was then the third hour after midnight, all the clocks in the room had at that moment struck the hour. After that the odalisks fell a-dancing again, and the eunuch-buffoons exhibited a puppet show on a curtained stage, which greatly diverted the ladies of the harem. But the number "8" would not go out of the head of the favorite, and as all the clocks in the room, one after the other, struck four, she took out the pen, and with an incredulous, mocking smile on her face, but with horror in her heart, she asked, "Come, tell me again, if thou hast not forgotten, how many hours have I got to live?"

The pen wrote down the number "7."

Those who stood around now began to tremble. But Mahmoud treated the whole affair as a joke, and assured them that the pen was only making them sport. And again they went on diverting themselves.

An hour later the clocks, in the usual sequence, struck the hour of five. And now the favorite stole aside, and placing the reed on a table repeated her former question. And the pen wrote down the number "6."

Thus, with each hour, the number indicated was lesser by one than the previous number. The Sultan observed the gloom of his favorite, and to drive away her sad thoughts, compelled her to retire to her bedchamber, where she enjoyed two hours of sweet repose, leaning on the Sultan's breast; whereupon the Sultan arose and went into his dressing-room, for he had to hold a divan, or council.

The first thing the favorite did on awaking was to look at the time, and she perceived that it was now seven o'clock. She immediately hastened to interrogate the pen, and asked the question of it with fear and trembling; and now the pen wrote down the number "4."

The Sultan himself sent for Morrison.

The English sailor was proudly conscious of owning no master but the sea. During his long roamings in the East and South he had always made it a point of visiting all the barbarous chiefs and princes who came in his way. He regarded them simply as freaks of nature, whose absurd rites and customs he meant to thoroughly investigate in order that he might make a note of them in his diary, and he even went the length of adopting for a time their manners and customs, if he could not get what he wanted in any other way.

A summons to appear before the divan was scarcely of more importance in his eyes than an invitation to a wild elephant hunt, or initiation into the mysteries of Mumbo Jumbo, or an ascent in the perilous aërial ship of Montgolfier. He donned a dark-blue-colored garment and a plumed three-cornered hat, and condescended to allow himself to be conducted by the ichoglanler specially told off to do him honor to the splendid canopied, six-oared pinnace, which was to take him to the palace.

They escorted him first to the Gate of Fountains, and left him waiting for a few moments in the Chamber of Lions, allowing him in the meanwhile to draw a pocket-book from his breast-pocket and make a rapid sketch of all the objects around him. They then relieved him of his short sword, as none may approach the Sultan with arms, and threw across his shoulders an ample caftan trimmed with ermine. He did not reflect for the moment what a distinction this was. His only feeling was a slight surprise that he should be dressed in green down to his very heels, as, with the dragoman on his left hand, he was conducted into the Hall of the Seven Viziers, where the Sultan sat in the midst of his grandees.

Morrison greeted the Padishah very handsomely, just as he would have greeted King George IV. or King Charles X., perhaps.

"Bow to the ground—right down to the ground, milord!" whispered the dragoman in his ears.

"I'll be damned if I do!" replied Morrison. "It is not my habit to go down on my knees in uniform!"

"But that was why they put the caftan on you," whispered the dragoman, half in joke. "'Tis the custom here."

"And a deuced bad custom, too," growled Morrison; and, after reflecting for a moment or two, he hit upon the idea of letting his hat fall to the ground, and then bent down as if to pick it up again. But, by way of compensation, immediately after righting himself he stood as stiff and straight as if he were determined never to bend his head again, though the roof were to fall upon him in consequence.

The Sultan addressed a couple of brief words to the sailor, metamorphosed by the dragoman into a floridly adulatory rigmarole, which he represented to be a faithful version of the Sultan's ineffable salutation. In effect he told the sailor that he was a terrible hippopotamus, an oceanic elephant, who had ground to death countless crocodiles with his glorious grinders, trampled them to pieces with his mighty hoofs, and torn them limb from limb with his trunk, and had therefore merited that the sublime Sultan should cover him with the wings of his mantle. Let him, therefore, ask as a reward whatever he chose, even to the half of the Padishah's kingdom. I may add that if any one had in those days actually asked for half of the Sultan's kingdom, he would probably have got that part of it which lies underground.

Morrison thanked the Sultan for his liberal offer, and asked that he might see the favorite wife of the Grand Signior.

At these words the dragoman turned pale, but the Sultan turned still paler. The convulsive twitching of the muscles of his face betrayed his strong revulsion of feeling, and, lowering his heavy, shaggy eyebrows, he dashed at the sailor a look of deadly rage, while a heavy sigh escaped from his deep chest.

The Englishman only regretted that he could not acquit himself as creditably in this play of eyebrows.

His own were small, of a bright blonde color, and somewhat pointed.

The dragoman, however, could read an ominous meaning in this deep silence.

"O glorious giaour, rosebud of thy nation!" whispered he, "fleet water-spider of the ocean, ask not so senseless a thing from the Grand Signior! Behold his wrathful eyes, and ask for something else; ask for his most precious treasure; ask for all his damsels, if thou wilt, but ask not to see the face of his favorite. Thou knowest not the meaning thereof."

Morrison shrugged his shoulders. "I want neither his treasure nor his damsels. I only want to see his favorite wife."

Mahmoud trembled, but not a word did he speak. Two tear-drops twinkled in his dark eyes and ran down his handsome, manly face.

At this the Viziers leaped to their feet, and it was evident from their agitated cries that they expected the Sultan to order the presumptuous infidel to be cut down there and then.

The dragoman, in despair, flung himself at the seaman's feet.

"O prince of all whales!" he cried. "O unbelieving dog! Thou seest me, a true believer, lying at thy feet, O wine-drinking giaour! Why wilt thou entangle me with the words which the Sultan said to thee through me? Art thou not ashamed to place thy foot on the neck of the lord of princes? Ask some other thing!"

In vain. The sailor changed not a muscle of his face. He simply repeated, with imperturbable *sang-froid*, the words:

"I want to see his favorite wife."

The Viziers rushed at him with a howl of fury, but Morrison merely threw back the caftan which had been folded across his breast, revealing his dreaded uniform and the decorations appended thereto — memorials of his services at Alexandria and Trafalgar. That, he thought, would quite suffice to preserve him from any violence.

But the Sultan leaped down from his throne, beckoned with his hand to the Viziers, and whispered some words in the ear of the Kislar-Agasi, who thereupon withdrew. This whispered word went the round of the Viziers, who straightway did obeisance and disappeared in three different directions through the three doors of the room, their places being taken by two black slaves in red fezes and white robes, with broad-bladed, crooked swords in their hands. Only the Sultan remained behind there with the sailor.

The clocks in the rooms of the Seraglio struck a quarter to ten. The pen of the dervish in reply to the question of the favorite as to how many hours she had to live now wrote down "$\frac{1}{4}$."

At that moment the Kislar-Agasi entered. The favorite went to meet him, trembling like a lost lamb coming face to face with a wolf.

The Kislar-Agasi bowed deeply, and beckoned to the serving-women of the Seraglio standing behind him to come forward.

"Has the Sultana accomplished the prescribed ablutions?" said he.

"Yes, my lord!"

"Gird her round the body with a triple row of

pearls; fasten on her turban the bird of paradise with the diamond clasp. Put on her gold embroidered caftan."

The favorite let them do what they would with her without saying a word.

The waiting-woman, covering the favorite's face with a light fan, thickly sewn with tiny gold stars, conducted her to the door which led to the Procelain Chamber, and there the Kislar-Agasi left her, after indicating whither they had to go next.

Guards stood in couples before each one of the doors; the last door they came to was only protected by a curtain. This was the door of the cupola chamber where the Sultan had received the sailor.

The favorite could not see the sailor because of the lofty projecting wings of the throne; she only saw the Sultan sitting on a divan. She hastened up to him, and when she stood before him she suddenly caught sight of the stranger regarding her with coldly curious eyes. Shrinking away with terror, she screamed out "Giaour!" and, wrapping her veil more closely around her, turned to the Sultan for protection. Then Mahmoud seized the damsel's trembling hand with one of his, and with the other raised the veil from the face of his dearest wife in the presence of the stranger.

The girl shrieked as if her face had been bitten by a serpent; then she fell at the knees of the Sultan, and looked at the face of the Grand Signior with an appealing glance for mercy. In the eyes of the caliph of caliphs the moisture of human compassion sparkled. Poor Sultana! who would not have pitied her?

Morrison made a courtly bow, and the dragoman

not being present, he expressed his thanks by using the well-known Turkish salutation, "Salám aláküm!" The extraordinary charms of the damsel made no more impression upon him than the sight of any ordinarily pretty lady at a court presentation at home would have done.

The damsel meanwhile writhed in torments at the feet of the Sultan, who, having had enough of it himself, covered her with her veil, and beckoned to the Kislar-Agasi. He raised the damsel, and carried her behind the curtains that surrounded the throne; the same instant the two eunuch guards standing beside the throne also disappeared.

The Sultan listened and covered his eyes.

After a few moments of deep silence, it seemed to the sailor as if he heard a long sigh behind the curtains. The Sultan shivered in every limb, and immediately afterwards the clocks in the Seraglio began to strike; they struck eleven.

Then the Sultan arose from his place and said, with a deep sigh:

"'Twas the will of Allah!" Then he descended from the divan and said to Morrison in the purest Italian, "Thou didst see her; was she not beautiful?"

Morrison, astonished to hear Italian spoken by the Sultan, who, as a rule, never spoke a word save through an interpreter, in his amazement could not find an answer to this question quick enough.

"Come now and see her once more," continued the Grand Signior, and with these words he went towards the curtains.

Morrison fell back confounded. The rosy-red damsel of a few moments before lay there pale, lifeless, at full length, her lips and eyes closed, her bosom motionless. A thin red line was visible round her beautiful white neck—the mark of the silken cord!

"But this is brutal!" exclaimed the sailor, beside himself with indignation.

The Sultan coldly replied, "Whenever a Christian man beholds the face of one of our women, that woman must die." He then signified to the sailor that he was dismissed.

Morrison hastened from the room, immediately hoisted his anchor, and the same night sailed out of the Golden Horn, everywhere pursued by the memory of the beautiful Sultana, whom he had killed with a glance of his eyes.

"Behold, behold!" cried the Sultan, pressing the cold, murdered limbs to his bosom; "the *dzhin* told the truth. Mahmoud loved thee to the death, and yet Mahmoud slew thee!"

These words he repeated two or three times to the dead woman, and then, descending the steps of the throne, rent his garments across his breast, and looking up to heaven with tearful eyes, exclaimed:

"And now let the rest come too!"

And the rest did come. It came from the east and from the west, from the north and from the south—four empire-subverting tempests, which shook the strong trunk of Osman to its very roots, and scattered its leaves afar.

Ali Pasha of Janina was the first to kindle the blood-red flames of war in the west, and soon they spread from the Morea to Smyrna. In the north the crusading banners of Yprilanti raised up a fresh foe against Mahmoud, and the cries of "the sacred army" re-echoed from the walls of Athens and the banks of the Danube and the summits of Olympus. In Stambul the unbridled hosts of the Janissaries shed torrents of blood among the Greeks of the city on the tidings of every defeat from outside. And when the peril from every quarter had reached its height, the Shah of Persia fell upon the crumbling realm from the east, and captured the rich city of Bagdad.

And still Mahmoud had the desire to live — to live and rule. A pettier spirit would have fled from the Imperial palace and taken refuge among the palm-trees of Arabia Felix when it recognized that an endless war encompassed it on every side, that to conquer was impossible, and that the nearest enemy was the most dangerous. A mine of gunpowder had been dug beneath the throne, and around the throne a mob of madmen were hurrying aimlessly to and fro with lighted torches. And yet it was Mahmoud's pleasure to remain sitting on that throne.

Frequently he would steal furtively at night from his harem. Alone, unattended, he would contemplate the flight of the stars from the roof of the Seraglio, and would listen to the nocturnal massacres and the shrieks of the dying in the streets of Stambul. He would watch how the conflagrations burned forth in two or three places at once, both in Pera and Galata their lordships the Janissaries were working their will. And he felt that cruelly cold piercing wind which began to blow from the north, so that in the rooms of the Seraglio the shivering odalisks began to draw rugs and other warm coverings over their tender limbs. Never had any one in Stambul felt that cold wind before. Whence came it, and what did it signify?

Mahmoud knew whence it came and what it signified, and he had the courage to look steadily in the face of the future, in which he discerned not a single ray of hope.

CHAPTER IX

THE CIRCASSIAN AND HIS FAMILY

In those days Kasi Mollah did not go by the name of Murstud—*i.e.*, a pillar of the faith. He was a simple sheik at Himri, in the northern part of the land of Circassia, a remote little place, where the Muscovite was no more than a rumor from afar.

Nature herself had fashioned a strong fortress around Himri. Immense mountain-chains enclosed it within massive walls on both sides, rising bleak, interminable, and ever upwards into the dim distance.

In the midst of this valley of eternal shadows arose a third rocky mass, forming—on both sides—a steep, ladder-like wall; and, after extending far among the other mountains, terminating in a ragged-looking, concave hill, defended by the junction of the impetuous mountain streams, which dug a deep hollow among the excavated rocks. Along this channel, running like a spinal cord throughout the backbone of the mountain, extended some few thousands of acres of luxuriant corn—a long but narrow strip.

At the head of an opening in the chain a rocky scaffolding was visible, about one hundred feet in height, as regularly disposed as if a number of gigantic dice had been designedly placed there one on the top of another. By a marvellous freak of Nature, this rocky conglomeration was provided apparently with towers, bastions, and buttresses; so that, viewed from afar, it looked like a gigantic fortress, and, on the very first glance at it, the thought involuntarily occurs to one that if but four guns were planted on those summits a few hundred men might defend themselves against an army-corps. At the rear of the hill, moreover, where the cataracts make any approach impossible, the flocks and herds of the defending army could go on contentedly browsing for years together.

A foolish idea! To whom would it ever occur to attack Himri, that tiny Circassian village with scarcely five hundred inhabitants, who have nothing in the world but their kine, their goats, and their pretty girls? Who would ever come against Himri with guns and an army—against those most worthy men who all their life long have never done anything but make cheese and tan hides, who only exercise their valor against the devastating bands of bears, and only extirpate with their long, far-reaching muskets the wild goats of the rocks?

They do not even build their houses on the summit of this wondrous fortress of Nature, but among the rocks below, constructing them prettily of regularly disposed logs, with roofs like dove-cots, surrounding them with linden-trees and flower-gardens. And so far from keeping a visitor at bay with cannon-shots, they go forth to meet him, conduct him into their villages, hospitably entertain him, insist on his tarrying long with them; and if the visitor be a handsome young fellow, the loveliest eyes that ever smiled and wept grow moist at his departure. Who amongst those who have been lulled to sleep in Himri by the songs of the lovely and bewitching Circassian girls could ever have dreamed that the time would come when these mountain walls all round about would be dyed red with the blood of thousands and thousands of strangers, who came thither to seek death, and found what they sought?

The house of the meritorious sheik differed in no respect from the dwellings of the other inhabitants. It also was entirely built of timber, consisted of four rooms leading one out of another, and two venerable nut-trees stood in front of it.

Kasi Mollah sits outside, leaning tranquilly against the door-post beneath the projecting eaves, both sides of which are covered by large scarlet-runners, plaiting with great care and solemnity a whip out of twelve fine thongs of kid-skin hanging on a crooked nail.

Squatting on the ground beside him on a bear-skin sits a peculiar-looking stranger. Even if you had not seen it in his features and clothing, his mules standing before the door would have told you that he did not belong to these parts. He was, indeed, a Greek merchant from Smyrna, who visited Circassia every year to purchase kid-skins—or, so he said. He had three palaces in Smyrna; but it is scarcely credible that he could have acquired them by his kid-skins only. At any rate, his mules were laden now with whole bundles of furs and pelts, and the merchant was toasting his host in a sour beverage, made by the Circassian from horse's milk, the evil odor of which he was striving to dispel with the smoke of good Latakia tobacco.

It was for him also that the Circassian was making that long mule-driving whip of thongs of twelve different colors, serpentine in shape, and plaited at the ends with beautiful white horse-hair; and when it was ready he smacked it so vigorously, by way of showing it off, that the merchant could scarce save his eyes from it.

"A pretty whip, and a good whip," he said, at last, in order that its owner might leave off cracking it.

"I'll very soon prove whether it is a good whip or not," said the Circassian, without moving a muscle of his brown, oval-shaped, apathetic face; and with that he began to make the handle of the whip out of fine copper wire of a fantastically ornate pattern nicely studded with leaden stars.

"How will you prove that it is a good whip?" asked the merchant.

"Stop till my children come home."

"Your *children?*"

"Yes, naturally. I should not think of proving it on other people's children."

"You are surely not going to prove the whip on your own?"

"On whom else, then? Children should be whipped in order that they may be good, that they may be kept in order, and that they may not get nonsense into their heads. 'Tis also a good thing to train them betimes to endure greater sorrow by giving them a foretaste of lesser ones, so that when they grow up to man's estate, and real misfortune overtakes them, they may be able to bear it. My father used always to beat me, and now I bless him for it, for it made a man of me. Children are always full of evil dispositions, and you do well to drive such things out of them with the whip."

A peculiar smile passed across the long, olive-colored face of the Greek at these words; he seemed to be only smiling to himself. Then he fixed his sly, coal-black eyes on the sheik, and inquired, sceptically:

"But surely you don't beat your children without cause?"

"Oh, there's always cause. Children are always doing something wrong; you have only to keep an eye on them to see that, and whoever neglects to punish them acts like him who should forbear to pull up the weeds in his garden."

"Kasi Mollah," said the Greek, puffing two long clouds of smoke through his nostrils, "I tell you, children are not your speciality, for you do not understand how to bring them up. In the whole land of Circassia there is none who knows how to bring up children."

"Then how comes it that our girls are the fairest and our youths the bravest on the face of the earth?"

"Your girls would be still more beautiful and your lads still more valiant if you brought them up in the land where dwell the descendants of white-bosomed Briseis and quick-footed Achilles. O Hellas!"

The Greek began to grow rapturous at the pronunciation of these classical names, and in his excitement blew sufficient smoke out of his chibook to have clouded all Olympus.

"I tell you, Kasi Mollah," continued he, "that children are the gifts of God, and he who beats a child lifts his whip, so to speak, against God Himself, for

His hands defend their little bodies. You do but sin against your children. Give them to me!"

"You are a Christian; I am a Mussulman. How, then, shall you bring up my children?"

"Fear nothing. I do not want to keep them for myself; I mean rather to get them such positions as will enable them to rise to the utmost distinction. I would place them with some leading pasha, perhaps with the Padishah himself, or, at any rate, with one of his Viziers, all of whom have a great respect for Circassians."

"Thank you, Midas, thank you; but I don't mean to give them up."

"Prithee, prithee, call me not Midas; that is an ominous name which I do not understand. You might have learned any time these ten years, when I first came to buy pelts from you, that my name is Leonidas Argyrocantharides, and that I am a direct descendant of the hero Leonidas, who fell at Thermopylæ with his three hundred valiant Spartans. One of my great-great-grandfathers, moreover, fell at Issus, by the side of the great Alexander, from a mortal blow dealt to him by a Persian satrap. If you do not believe me, look at this ancient coin, and at these others, and at this whole handful which are in my purse, all of which were struck under Philip of Macedon, or else under Michel Kantakuzenos or Constantine Porphyrogenitus, all of whom were powerful Greek emperors in Constantinople, which now they call Stambul, and built the church of St. Sophia, where now the dervishes say their prayers; and then look at the figures which are stamped on these coins, and tell me if they do not resemble me to a hair. It is so. No, you need not give me back the money; give me rather the two little children."

The Circassian, who had taken the purse with the simple intention of comparing the figures on the coins with the face of the merchant, drew the strings of the purse tight again at this offer, and thrust it back into the merchant's bosom.

"Thank you," said he, dryly. "I deal in the skins of goats, not in the skins of men."

The face of the merchant showed surprise in all its features. Not every man possesses the art of controlling his countenance so quickly, especially when his self-command is put to so sudden and severe a test. The Georgians, more to the south, were a much more manageable race of men. With them one could readily drive a bargain for their daughters and give them a good big sum on account for their smallest children. One could purchasé of them children from two to three years of age at from ten to twenty golden denarii a head, and sell them in ten years' time for just as many thousands of piastres to some illustrious pasha. This was how Leonidas was able to build himself palaces at Smyrna.

"You talk nonsense, my worthy Chorbadzhi," said the merchant, when he had somewhat recovered himself. "Shall I prove it to you? Well, then, in the first place, you do not sell your children, and, in the second place, why shouldn't you sell them? If a Circassian wrapped in a bear-skin comes to you and asks you for your daughter, would you not give her to him? And at the very outside he would only give you a dozen cows for her, and as many asses. I, on the other hand, offer you a thousand piastres for them from good, worthy, influential beys, or perhaps from the Sultan himself, and yet you haggle about it."

The sheik's face began to show wrath and irritation. He was well aware that the merchant was now dealing in sophisms, though his simple intellect could not quite get at the root of their fallacy. It was plain that there was a great difference between a Circassian dressed in bear-skin, who carries off a girl in exchange for a dozen cows, and the Captain-General of Rumelia, who is ready to give a thousand ducats for her—and yet he preferred the gentleman in bear-skins.

The Greek, meanwhile, appeared to be studying the features of the Circassian with an attentive eye, watching what impression his words had produced, like the experimenting doctor who tries the effects of his medicaments *in anima vili.*

"But I know that you will give them, Kasi Mollah," he resumed, filling up his chibook. "No doubt you have promised them to another trader. Well, well! you are a cunning rogue. Merchants of Dirbend or Bagdad have no doubt offered you more for them. They can afford it, they do such a roaring business. Those perfidious Armenians! They buy the children for a mere song, and sell them when they are eight or nine years old to the pashas, so that not one of them lives to see his twentieth year, but all die miserably in the mean time. I don't do such things. I am an honest man, with whom business is but a labor of love, and who is just to all men. It is sufficient for me to say that I was born where Aristides used to live. Numbers and numbers of my ancestors were in the Areopagus, and one of my great-great-uncles was an archon. Do not imagine, therefore, that I would do for every foolish fellow what I offer to do for you. I only do kindnesses to my chosen friends; the ties of friendship are sacred to me. Castor and Pollux, Theseus and Pirithous are to me majestic examples of that excellent brotherhood of kindred spirits which I constantly set before me. Wherever I have gone people have always blessed me; nay, did I but let them, they would kiss my feet. The daughter of a Georgian peasant whose father trusted me is now the first waiting-woman of the wife of the Governor of Egypt. Is that glory enough for you! The daughter of a poor goatherd, whom I picked up from the mire, is now the premier pipe-filler of the Pasha of Salonica. A high office that, if you like! What Ganymede was to Jove in those classical ages— Ah! the tears gush from my eyes at the sound of that word. O Hellas!"

The Circassian allowed his good friend to weep on, considering it a sufficient answer to let his dark bushy eyebrows frown still more fiercely, if possible, over his downcast eyes. Then he caught up a hammer and hammered away with great fury at the handle he had prepared for the whip, riveting the wire with copper studs.

"Kasi Mollah, hitherto I have only been joking, but now I am going to speak in earnest," resumed Leonidas Argyrocantharides, raising his voice that he might be heard through the hammering. "You should bethink you seriously of your children's destiny. I am your old friend, your old acquaintance; my sole wish is for your welfare. I love your children as much as if they were my own, and the tears gush from my eyes whenever I part from them. What will become of them when they grow up? I know that while you are alive it will be well with them, but how about afterwards? You may die to-morrow, or the next day; who can tell? We are all in the hands of God. Now I'll tell you something. Mind, I'm not joking or making it all up. I know for certain that Topal Pasha has been informed that you have two lovely children. Some flighty traders of Erzeroum revealed the fact to him. They are wont to trade with you here, and he has paid them half the stipulated sum down on condition that they bring the children to him. Now this pasha is a filthy, brutal, rake-hell sort of fellow, the pressure of whose foot is no laughing matter, I can tell you; a horrible, hideous, cruel man. I can give you proofs of it. And these merchants have made a contract with him, and have engaged, under the penalty of losing their heads, to deliver your children to him within a twelvemonth. What do you say? You'll throw them down into the abyss, eh? Ah! they are not as foolish as I am. They will not openly profess that they have come here for your children, as I do, but they will lie in wait for them when they go to the forest, and when nobody perceives it they will clap them on the back of a horse and off they'll go with them, so that nobody will know under what sky to look for them. Or, perhaps, when you yourself are going along the road with them, they'll lay a trap for you, shoot you neatly through the head, and bolt with your children. Well, that will be a pretty thing, won't it? You had better not throw me over."

The Circassian did not know what to answer—words were precious things to him—but he thought all the more. While the merchant was speaking to him, his reflections carried him far. He saw his children in the detested marble halls, he saw them standing in shamefully gorgeous garments, waiting upon the smiling despot, who stroked their tender faces with his hands, and the blood rushed to his face as he saw his children blush and tremble beneath that smile. Ah, at that thought he began to lash about him so vigorously with the whip that was in his hand, that the Greek rolled about on the bear-skin in terror, holding his hands to his ears.

"Do not crack that whip so loudly, my dear son," said he, "or you'll drive away all my mules. I really believe your whip is a very good one, but you need not test it to the uttermost. I thank you for making it; but now, pray, put it down. I must go. It is a good thing you have not knocked out one of my eyes. You certainly have a vigorous way of enjoying yourself. But let us speak sensibly. Do you believe that I am an honest man, or not?"

At this the Circassian did *not* nod his head.

"Very well, then. It is natural that you should believe, you ought to believe it. Since Pausanias there has not been a sharper among my nation. He was the last faithless Greek, and they walled him up in the temple. I am a man without guile, as you are well aware. But I am more than that, more than you suspect. Oho! in this shabby, worn-out caftan of mine dwells something which you do not dream of. Oho! I know what I really am. I am on friendly terms with great men, with many great men, standing high in the empire, whose fame has never reached your ears. In the palm of this hand I hold Hellas, in the other the realm of Osman. I shake the whole world when I move. Why do I take all this trouble? Oh, for the sake of your holy shades, Miltiades, Themistocles, Lysippus, and Demosthenes! for the sake of your shades, O Solon, O Lycurgus, O Pythagoras, and a time is coming in which I will prove it! It is thy memory, Athene, which inspires me to heap up treasures for the future! Thou, O holy Goddess of Liberty, hath whispered in my ear that thou canst make use of the lowly as well as of the mighty to promote thy cause!" Here the merchant leaped to his feet in his enthusiasm, and, extending his hand towards the Circassian exclaimed, "Kasi Mollah, you groan beneath the yoke just as much as we do; let us join hands against our oppressors, and let us gradually melt the hearts of their leaders by the strongest of fires, by the fire of the eyes of the Greek and Circassian maidens, and we shall catch them in a flowery net!"

Kasi Mollah did not clasp the hand of the enthusiastic Greek; and, without turning towards him, replied, coldly, "I do not grudge you the drink which I put before you, worthy merchant, but I perceive that it has begun to mount into your head, or else you would not talk such rubbish as selling free people to your enemies from motives of freedom. Nor do you say well in saying that we are under the yoke, for that is not true. Nobody has ever made the Circassian do homage, nor would any try to conquer us for the sake of the eyes of our poor damsels. Say no more about my children. I will not give them up. If any one comes to visit me, I'll send him about his business; if any one tries to deceive me, I'll cudgel him; and if any one tries to rob me, I'll slay him. And tell that to the merchants of Erzeroum also. And now say no more about it."

At these words the face of the merchant grew very long indeed. In his spite he began pulling at the stem of his chibook with such force that his face was furrowed right down the middle, and his eyebrows ascended to the middle of his forehead. From time to time he kept on wagging his head, and his scarlet, mortar-shaped fez along with it, and burned the tips of his fingers by absently poking the red-hot bowl of his pipe. But his indignation did not go beyond a shaking of the head, and there he wisely let the matter rest.

"Very well, Kasi Mollah. You are an honest fellow. We shall see—we shall see."

The sun was now setting, and from among the hills the bells of the home-returning cattle resounded across the level plain which extended in front of the rocky heights of Himri. Fifteen head of snow-white kine strolled leisurely towards the house of Kasi Mollah, passing one by one through the gate of their enclosure; behind the last of them came the children of the sheik, who guarded the herd in the forest.

The boy appeared to be about twelve, and the girl a year younger, and so closely did they resemble each other that, viewed in profile, it was impossible to distinguish one from the other. Both had the same long, black hair, which flowed in wondrous ringlets down their shoulders, the same soft complexion of a naïve maturity, and as smooth as velvet, just as if they never walked in the sunlight, and yet they had no head-coverings. The youth's face revealed so much girlish tenderness, and the girl's so much vigor and expression, that by changing their clothes it would have been possible to substitute one for the other; and, but for the well-known, tight-fitting corset, peculiar to the Circassian maidens, which caused her figure, slender as a delicate flower-stalk, to bend somewhat backwards, throwing into relief the contours of her childlike breasts, it would have been scarcely possible to have distinguished her from her brother, especially when, as now, they walked side by side, half embracing. The snow-white arm of the girl was round her brother's neck, and her humidly glittering black eyes seemed to be sucking the virile courage from his face; the boy held the slim figure of his sister encircled by one of his arms, tapping her, from time to time, caressingly on the shoulder, while his eyes rested, full of tenderness, on her beloved face.

"What a majestic pair of children!" exclaimed Leonidas Argyrocantharides, in his enthusiasm. "What a shame it is to lock them up in this corner of the world! But what the deuce is the lad dragging along with his left hand while he embraces his sister with his right? What *is* it, my pretty children? Nay, don't bring it here. What sort of unclean animal is it?"

The lad, with a triumphant smile, stood before the merchant while his sister ran to her father, climbed on to his knees, and throwing her arms shamefacedly round his neck hid her face from the stranger.

"Do you not recognize the bear-skin?" cried the youth, in a strong, clear voice; and as he spoke you became aware of the light black down which shaded his upper lip and revealed the man, and with one of his hands he raised up the beast he was dragging after him on to its hind legs. It was a young bear, about a year and a half old, whose head was battered and smashed in a good many places, thus showing what a severe struggle it had cost to bring it down.

"Where did you find that monster? Who gave it to you?" cried Leonidas, holding his hand before him as if he believed that the hideous monster, even when dead, could clutch hold of his thin drumsticks of legs.

"Where did I find it? Who gave it me?" cried the youth, proudly, and with that he pointed to his sister, and, as if ashamed to speak of his heroic deed himself, he said, "Tell him, Milieva!"

The old Circassian looked attentively at the two children. Neither of them perceived that their father was angry.

"We were in the forest," began the girl—her voice was like a silvery bell. "Thomar was carving a fife, and I was twining a garland for his head, because he pipes so prettily, when all at once a little kid with its mother came running towards us, and the little kid hid itself close to me—it trembled so, poor little thing! but its mother only bleated and kept running round and round, just as if it wanted to speak. Thomar looked all about, and not far from us perceived two young bears running off, and one of them had another little white kid on its back, which was certainly the young one of the little she-goat that was trying to talk to us. 'Thomar,' said I, 'if I were a boy, I would go after that young bear and take away the poor little kid from it.' 'And dost thou think I will not do it?' replied Thomar, and with that he caught up his club and went after the two young bears. One of them perceived him and quickly ran up a tree, but the other would not give up his prey, but turned to face Thomar. Ah! you should have seen how Thomar banged the wild beast on the head with his club till the blood ran down its shoulders, and suddenly it let go the white kid, which ran bleating after its mother."

The child clapped her little hands for joy, while her father softly stroked her long hair.

"But now the young bear, gnashing its teeth, rushed upon Thomar and seized the club in Thomar's hands with its teeth and claws. 'Thomar, don't let him have it!' cried I. But, indeed, he had no fear of the wild beast, for he drew his knife from his girdle and thrust it with all his might into the head of the furiously charging wild beast."

"Oho!" interrupted Thomar, "don't forget that you also rushed upon it, and gave me time to draw out my knife by seizing the ears of the bear in both hands and dragging it off me."

The father looked at the two children with an ever-darkening face, but the merchant solemnly shook his head and raised his hands aloft with an expression of horror. "O foolish—O mad children!" cried he.

"The bear had now had enough," continued Milieva, trying to give her talkative little mouth an

earnest expression befitting her serious narration;
"it tore itself out of our hands, and with a great
roar took refuge from us in a subterranean cave,
taking along with it Thomar's knife, buried in its
head. Now this knife we had got from Hassan
Beg, so we could not afford to lose it. So what do
you think Thomar did? He dived into the narrow
hole after the bear, and, seizing it there by the
throat, throttled it, and dragged it out."

Cold drops of perspiration trickled down the foreheads of the two men.

"Then he caught the young bear by the foot,
and as it was heavy we both dragged it along together. We had to make haste, for the old bear
had scented our trail and was after us, and pursued us as far as the herds, where the herd-keepers
shot it down, but its young one we brought along
with us."

"O ye senseless children!" cried the merchant in
his terror. "O blockheads! Suppose the bear had
clawed your faces, you would have been disfigured
forevermore. It would really serve you right if
your father gave you a good thrashing with this
new whip."

And that is what really did happen.

In his wrath Kasi Mollah seized the freshly made,
mule-driving whip, and cannot one imagine the
fury, begotten of fear, which would take possession
of a father's heart on hearing such a hair-bristling
narrative from the lips of his children? To poke
their noses into a bear's den, forsooth! The old
bear would have torn the pair of them to pieces
had she been able to catch them! They had certainly well deserved a thrashing, and a good thrash-

ing too! Thomar would not have wept or groaned however many stripes he might have got; he only clinched his teeth, and, standing upright, bore with tearless eyes the lashing of the whip on his back and shoulders without a cry, without a sob.

But Milieva cast herself, shrieking, on her father's breast, and the tears began to pour abundantly from her radiantly bright eyes. She caught hold of the Circassian's chastising right arm with both her hands, and begged so sweetly, "Do not hurt Thomar; do not hurt him, father! It was indeed not his fault. I assure you I set him on. I told him to go after them. Thomar only went because I asked him."

Kasi Mollah tried to push the child aside, whereupon she flung her arms round Thomar's neck and protected her brother's body, exclaiming, her face all aglow, "'Tis my fault, beat me, but don't hurt Thomar!"

The lad would have disengaged her arms, and, clinching his teeth for pain, said:

"'Tis not true! Milieva did not urge me to do it. Milieva was looking on from a distance. Milieva was not there. Don't hit Milieva."

But the girl threw her arms so tightly round her father that he was not able to tear himself loose. At last, in sheer desperation, he was obliged to lift the paternal instrument of admonition against the girl also. But now the youth snatched at the whip, and exclaimed, with sparkling eyes:

"Strike her not, for she has done no wrong! Beat me as much as you like, but do not strike Milieva. If you do I will leave your house, and you shall never see me more!"

"What, you ragged cub, you!" cried the old Circassian, infuriated by the opposition of his son, and forcibly tearing away the whip from his hand, he struck the girl a violent blow across the shoulders with it.

Milieva ceased to weep, she only pressed her lips together, as her brother had already taught her to do, and cast down her eyes; but Thomar perceived a tremor run through her tender, maidenly bosom at the torture.

The old Circassian himself felt sorry for the poor thing, though he was too proud to show it; but it was plain he had put his wrath behind him from the fact that he now began to wind the whip round its handle.

Thomar bent over the girl's shoulder, and wherever he saw one of the painful bruises which she had got on his account he kissed it softly, and after that he kissed the girl's face, and those kisses were parting kisses.

He said not a word to anybody in the house, but taking up his shepherd's staff and his rustic flute, he went forth from his father's dwelling without once looking behind him.

"Father," cried the girl, sobbing, "Thomar is going away forever!"

The old Circassian made no reply. His son did not look back at him, and he did not cast a glance after his son, and yet they were both heart-broken on each other's account.

"He'll soon be back," thought the father to himself. "Hunger and want will bring him back."

It was late evening, and still the youth had not returned. The sun had set long ago. A violent storm with thunder and lightning arose. The wind roared among the trees of the distant woods, and the wolves howled in the mountains.

"Father, let me go and bring back Thomar," pleaded the girl, gazing sorrowfully into the dark night through the window.

"He will come back of his own accord," replied the Circassian, and he would not let the girl go.

"Listen, how the rain pours, and how the wild beasts are howling! Thomar is all alone there in the tempest, and it is so dark."

"'Tis a good night for a son who forsakes his father," replied the sheik. But within himself he thought, "Some neighbor is sure to take the lad in and give him shelter."

At midnight the tempest abated, and the moon shone forth brightly. From the distant woods came floating back to the village the notes of a rustic flute. Neither father nor daughter had had any sleep.

"Listen, father!" said Milieva. "Thomar is piping in the wood; let me go and bring him back!"

"That is not a flute, but a nightingale," replied the stony-hearted Circassian. "Lie down and sleep!"

Yet he himself could not sleep.

In the morning both the tempest and the song had ceased. The old Circassian pretended to be asleep. Milieva softly raised her head and looked at her father, and seeing that his eyes were closed, stealthily put on her clothes and went out of the house on tiptoe. Her father did not tell her not to go. He had already forgiven his son, and resolved never to be angry with him any more. After all, it had only been an ebullition of fatherly affection that had made him punish his son for jeopardizing his life so blindly.

Shortly afterwards the jingling of the asses' bells told him that the Greek, who slept on the floor outside, was getting ready to depart. The merchant seemed to be in great haste. He piled his boxes on the backs of his beasts higgledy-piggledy, even overlooking a parcel or two here and there, and all the time he kept talking to himself, stopping short suddenly when he caught sight of the Circassian.

"I was just going to take leave of you, Chorbadzhi. Why do you get up so early? Go to sleep! What a nice day it is after the storm! Salám aláküm! Peace be with you! Greet my kinsmen, your sweet children. No, I will speak no more of your children. I will do as you desire, I promise you, and what I have once promised— So our business is at an end? You are a worthy man, Kasi Mollah! ... You are a good father—a very good father. I only wish every man was like you. The only thing that grieves me is that you cannot join our holy covenant. The Hellene and the Circassian groan together beneath the yoke of a common tyrant. And then you don't reflect who are on our side. Our northern neighbor is always ready to liberate us. I say no more. To a wise man a hint is a revelation. But do you not long for glory? You have no glorious ancestors. With you there are no memories of a Marathon, a Platäa. ... God bless you, Kasi Mollah! Go on shooting lots of antelopes, and I'll come back and buy the hides from you; mind you let me have them cheap! Take this kiss for yourself, this for your son, and this third one for your daughter. Then you won't give them to me, eh? Well, God bless you, Kasi Mollah!"

The sheik felt as if a great stone had rolled off his breast when at last he saw his guest depart, though even from afar the Greek turned back and shouted all manner of things about Leonidas and the other heroes. But the Circassian did not listen to him. He went back into his house again, lest he should seem to be moping for his children.

Leonidas Argyrocantharides, on the other hand, whistling merrily, proceeded with his asses on his way to the forest, and, when he found himself quite alone there, began to sing in a loud voice the song of freedom of the Hetairea, which put him into such a good humor that he even began to flourish his weapon in the most warlike manner, though, unfortunately, there was nobody at hand whom he could smite.

It would be doing a great injustice to the worthy merchant, however, to suppose that he was fatiguing his precious lungs without rhyme or reason, for during this melodious song he kept on looking continually about him, now to the right and now to the left. He knew what he was about.

Yes, he had calculated well. Any one who might happen to be hidden in the forest was bound to hear the great blood-stirring song. He had not advanced more than a hundred yards or so when a well-known suppliant voice struck his ear. It came from among the thick trees.

"Oh, please! listen, please!"

At first he pretended not to know who it was, and, shading his eyes with his hand, made a great pretence of looking hard.

"Oho, my little girl! so 'tis you, eh? Little Milieva, by all that's holy! Come nearer, child."

The girl was not alone. She had found her brother, and was shoving and pushing the lad on in front of her, who, sulkily and with downcast eyes, was skulking about among the trees as if he were ashamed to appear before the Greek, who had been a witness of his flogging.

Milieva had insisted on his returning home and begging his father's pardon, and the lad had consented, not for his own sake, but for his sister's.

"What a good job I've met you! Come here, little girl. Don't be afraid of me. I want to whisper something in your ear that your brother must not hear."

And he bent down towards the girl from the back of the ass and whispered in her ear, it is true, but quite loud enough for her brother to hear also:

"My dear child, don't take your brother home now, for your father is furious with the pair of you, and is coming after you straightway. That is why I have been singing so loudly, for I thought you had come hither and might hear; and let me tell you that it will be just as well for Thomar to hide himself for a time, for your father, when I left him, had shouldered his musket, and he swore in his wrath that he would hunt his runaway son with the dogs, and shoot him down wherever he found him."

"Let him shoot me down!" cried the lad, defiantly. He had heard the whole of the whisper.

The good-hearted merchant shook his head reprovingly.

"Keep your temper, my son; anger is mischievous. It would be much better if you left these parts for a little while, and Milieva can go back in the mean time and pacify her father. I should mention, however, that Kasi Mollah is preparing a rope in salt-water, with which he intends to beat her."

"What!" cried Thomar, with flashing eyes. "He would whip her again, and with a rope?"

He could say no more. The two children fell upon each other's necks and wept bitterly.

"Poor children! orphans worthy of compassion!" cried the sympathetic Leonidas, stroking their pretty heads. "It is plain that they have no mother. Willingly would I shed my blood for you. But it is vain to speak to that savage madman. The last thing he said was that your mother had been faithless to him, and that was why he was so furious against you."

"Then he shall never see us again," said the lad, tenderly embracing his sister. "I will go away, and I will take you with me."

"Where?" said his sister, trembling.

"The world is wide," said the lad. "I have often seen from the summits of the mountains how far it stretches away. I will go away as far as ever I can."

"But what provision have you got?" inquired the worthy merchant.

At this idea the lad seemed to hesitate, and for a moment his face flushed red; but he soon recovered his *sang-froid*.

"You complained the other day that your ass-driver had run away, and that you had all the trouble of looking after the beasts yourself. Take me for your ass-driver. I will do all your work for you, and I will ask nothing except that Milieva may come with me without doing any hard work. I will work extra in her stead."

The merchant was quite overcome by these words.

"O children, what words must I hear! Thou art the pearl of youths, my son. What a pity thou wast not born in Samos, the isle of heroes! Thou shalt be no ass-driver of mine; no, thou shalt be my own son, and thy sister shall be my own daughter, and ye shall both sit on my asses, not follow after them. In the neighboring village I shall get ass-drivers and to spare. I will share my last crumb with you, and ye shall dwell at home within my palace as if ye were my own children." And with that he embraced them both.

As for the children, they were overpowered by so much unexpected goodness, and did not hesitate to accept the offer, although Milieva said, somewhat tremulously:

"But you will take us back afterwards to our father, wont you?"

"Certainly; is he not my good friend? When we get to my house I will let him know that you are with me, and he will be very glad. But first we will go from here to splendid cities by the sea, where edifices three stories high float on the surface of the water. There my great palaces are—you could put the whole of your father's house inside the hall of any one of them—and my gardens are full of those beautiful fruits which I have so often brought for you in my sack. Thomar shall have a beautiful steed. You would like to ride a horse, my son, eh? Well, don't be afraid, and it shall fly away with you like the wind. And it shall have a mane as white as a swan's—or perhaps you'd like a black one? I have got both, and you shall sit on which you like, with a sword dangling at your side. And when you draw that sword? Ah, ha! It shall be a bright Damascus blade, and you will be able to make it span your body right round without breaking. I will bet anything that among five hundred Turkish youths you will carry off the wreath of pearls in the sports. How nicely that wreath of pearls will become Milieva's head! How beautifully the folds of the silken robe embroidered with flowers will sweep around her slim figure! And then the palm-leaf shawl when she dances! Eh, children?"

"When will you take us back to our father?" inquired the girl, sorrowfully.

"Why, at once, of course. As soon as Thomar has become a famous man; as soon as half the world recognizes him as a valiant bey, and the fame of him spreads to the huts of Himri likewise. Then will Thomar go with you to your father. He will sit on a proudly prancing horse, tossing its head impatiently beneath its gold trappings. A grand retinue will come riding behind him—valiant heroes, all of them, with glittering shields and lances. And after them will follow a litter on two white asses, with curtains of cloth of gold, and in this litter will sit a wondrously bright and beautiful maiden, and men will stand at all the gates and cry, 'Make way for the valiant lord and the majestic lady!'

"But, meanwhile, old Kasi Mollah will be sitting at his door, and, perceiving the splendid magnates, will do obeisance to them ; then you will leap from your horse, assist Milieva to descend from her litter, and will go to meet him. He, however, will not recognize you. Milieva will be so much rosier, and her figure so much more lovely ; and as for you, you will be wearing a beard and mustache, and without doubt you will be scarred with wounds received upon the field of glory. So Kasi Mollah will conduct you into his house with the utmost respect and make you sit down ; but you will have victuals and sherbet brought from your carriages, and will constrain him to eat and drink with you. Then you will fall a-talking, and you will ask him whether he has any children, and thereupon the tears will start to his eyes."

"Oh," sighed the girl, melting at the thought.

"No, no ; it would not do at all to make yourself known all at once. The joy would be too much for him ; he might even have a stroke. You, little Milieva, would be content to sit and listen, leaving Thomar to speak. And Thomar will say that he has heard tidings of Kasi Mollah's lost children, gradually leading him on from hope to joy, and at last you will throw yourselves on his neck, and say to him, 'I am thy son Thomar ! I am thy daughter Milieva ?' How beautiful that will be !"

The heads of the children were completely turned by this conversation, and they followed the merchant joyfully all the way to the next village. There Leonidas Argyrocantharides rested for a little while, and made the children dismount and have some lunch in a hut. Then he produced a gourd full of strong, sweet wine, and the children drank of it. The wine removed whatever of sadness was still in their hearts, and they then resumed their journey. The asses he left behind, but two well-saddled horses were awaiting them in front of the hut. On these the children mounted, and leaving the asses to stroll leisurely on by one road, under the charge of the hired ass-drivers, they themselves took another. How delighted the children were with their fine steeds!

The sheik, meantime, was still awaiting the return of his children, and as they did not come back by the evening he began to make inquiries about them. Some of his neighbors, who had been in the forest, informed him that they had seen the children with the Greek merchant; they were riding on his asses. At this Kasi Mollah began roaring like a wild beast.

"He has stolen my children!" he groaned in his despair, and flew back home for his horse and his weapons, not even waiting for his comrades to take horse also. One by one they galloped after him, but could not easily overtake him.

Riding helter-skelter he soon reached the neighboring village, but here the track of the asses led him off on a false scent, for only when he overtook them did he realize that the merchant with his children had gone far away in another direction.

With the rage of despair in his heart he galloped back again. Not till evening did he dismount from his horse; then he watered his horse in a brook and rushed on again. Through the whole moonlit night he pursued the Greek, and as towards dawn Argyrocantharides looked behind him he saw a great cloud of dust on the road rapidly approaching him, and the bright points of lances were in the midst of it.

"Well, children," said he, "here we must all die

together, for your father is coming and will slay the three of us. But whip up your horses."

Then, full of terror, they bent over their horses' necks, and the desperate race began.

The Circassian perceived the merchant and the children, and rushed after them with a savage howl. They had better horses, but the Circassian's horses were more accustomed to mountainous paths and had better riders.

The distance between the two companies was visibly diminishing. The merchant flogged with his whip the horses on which the children were riding. They dared not look back.

Their father shouted to them to turn their horses' reins. He called Thomar by name, and bade him tear the merchant from his saddle. The son heard his father's voice, he heard his own name mentioned; but he fancied his father was threatening him, and clung to his horse still more tightly.

A steep mountain torrent ran across the road in front of them. If only the Greek could succeed in getting across it with but two minutes to spare, so that he might pitch the little wooden bridge over it down into the abyss below, he would be saved, for the space between the two steep mountain-sides was much too wide for a horse to leap, and a ford was not to be found within an hour's ride.

By the time they came to the bridge the pursuing Circassians were scarcely distant more than three gunshots, and Kasi Mollah was riding well in advance of the rest. He must needs overtake them before the Greek could push the bridge over.

At that instant the horse on which Milieva sat

slightly stumbled, and plunging forward on to its knees, fractured its leg.

"Hah!" cried the sheik, with wild delight, "I have got back one of my children, at any rate."

But how amazed was he when he saw Milieva, instead of running to him or even remaining in the road, cry out in terror to her brother and raise her arms towards him, and Thomar, never expecting to save her, bent down from his horse, and grasping his sister round the waist with a swift hand, placed her in the saddle in front of him, casting a wild look behind him, and then galloping on farther.

Kasi Mollah suddenly reined in his flying horse and stopped short, allowing them to escape. Not a step farther did he pursue them. By the time his comrades had joined him the Greek was well on the other side of the bridge, and they could all see Thomar helping the merchant to cast it down.

Two burning tear-drops stood in Kasi Mollah's eyes. They really burned, and he felt the pain. And yet—and yet, when the two children sat in the saddle again, Milieva extended her hands towards her father as if in most ardent supplication. What was the meaning of it?

The good Greek shortly afterwards arrived safely in Smyrna with the children, and had them taught singing, riding, and how to walk about in nice clothes, and some years after he sold them to the Seraglio of the Grand Vizier for two thousand sequins.

And all that he had said at random to the children during the journey, to cheer their spirits, actually came to pass, as we shall presently see.

When Sultan Mahmoud lost his favorite damsel

so strangely, Milieva was brought into the Seraglio instead. The girl was then about fourteen years old. The Circassian girls at that age are fully mature, and the bloom of their beauty is at its prime. Milieva, from the very first day when she entered the harem, became the Sultan's favorite damsel.

Thomar joined the ranks of the ichoglanler, a band of youths who are brought up in the outer court and form the Sultan's body-guard.

It was in this year that Mahmoud instituted the Akinji corps, selecting its members from amongst the Janissaries, and formed them into a small regular army. Thomar very soon won for himself the command of a company, and continued to rise higher and higher till at length he reached the eminence which the merchant had foretold to him; and when the course of time brought with it the day on which he was to see Kasi Mollah again, he had become Derbend Aga, one of the Sultan's very highest officials, and his name was mentioned respectfully by all true believers. And in the village of Himri his name was also mentioned. Kasi Mollah often heard it attached to the title of "bey," and Thomar also heard a good deal of the village of Himri and of Kasi Mollah, for they now called his father "murshid," and the name "murshid" is full of mournful recollections for both Moscow and Petersburg.

But of all these things we shall know more at another time.

CHAPTER X

THE AVENGER

AND what now is old Ali Tepelenti about in his nest at Janina? Is he content with a state of things which results in this—that he must either perish or pass the brief remainder of his days in constant fighting? Is he satisfied with this sea of blood over which the tempest rages, and whose shores he cannot see?

Not yet has he surrendered to fate. His country has declared war against him, the Sultan has pronounced his death-sentence, his family have abandoned and turned against him; but Ali has not suffered his sword to be broken in twain. For eight and seventy years he has been the scourge of his enemies, the defence of his country, the Sultan's right hand, the patriarch of his family, and in his nine and seventieth year the Sultan and his relations say to him, "Die! thou hast lived long enough!" And he, by way of reply, set his country in flames, shook the throne of the Sultan, and extirpated his own kinsfolk.

The Greeks, whose tyrant he once was, are now his allies. Tepelenti provides them with arms and money, and with good and bad counsel, whichever they want most.

Three armies were sent out against him, and he has annihilated all these.

His enemy, Gaskho Bey, has lost his army in a battle against the rebels without anything to show for it, and now only holds the fortresses round about Janina, to wit: Arta, Prevesa, Lepanto, Tripolizza, and La Gullia. The Hellenes are besieging every one of them day by day. One day Ali proclaims that in Tripolizza there are five hundred eminent Greeks whom the Turks compel to fight along with them. At this report the besiegers attack the fortress with redoubled fury. Now these five hundred Greeks Ali himself got together while Tripolizza was still in his possession. When he was obliged to leave the fortress, he cast these Greeks down into a well, placed three loads of stones upon them, and covered the spot with grass. This he did himself.

Exhausted by furiously fighting against superior numbers, the Turks surrendered in three days to Kleon, who conducted the siege, simply stipulating that they might be allowed to go free, and this was promised them. When, however, the fortress was surrendered to the Greeks, their first question was, "Where are the hostages, our brethren?" The Turks were amazed. They knew not what to reply, for they had no hostages in their hands.

Then a Suliote warrior discovered the pit which had been sown over with grass, and what a sight presented itself when they broke it open!

Thirsting for blood and vengeance, the Greeks flung themselves forthwith on the disarmed garrison, and despatched them to the very last man, nay, they did not leave a living woman or child remaining in the fortress—they threw them all down headlong from the bastions.

But Ali Pasha smiled to himself in the fortress of Janina.

He himself had destroyed more Turks than the whole Greek host had done.

When Demetrius Yprilanti captured Lepanto, he allowed the garrison a free exit from the citadel. Demetrius himself signed the terms of the surrender. But when the Turks emerged from the fortress, Ali Pasha's Suliotes rushed upon them and cut them all to pieces. Yprilanti, full of indignation, threw himself in the midst of them, exhibiting the document in which he had promised the Turks their lives. But Kleon only laughed—he had learned that brutal, scornful laugh from Ali.

"Don't trouble yourself about them," cried he. "We are only killing those whose names are not written in the agreement."

Yprilanti turned from the butchery in disgust, and immediately embarking his army, set sail for Chios again.

Ah, the Greeks had learned a great deal from Ali. Woe to those Mussulmans who fall alive into their hands, or who are not so brave or so cunning as they themselves are! The Turkish general, Omar Vrione, along his whole line of advance, marched between rows of high gibbets on which bleached the bones to horribly tortured Turks. Here and there, by way of variety, nailed by the hands to upright planks, were the bodies of dead Jews, half flayed and singed—a ghastly spectacle.

Verily the descendants of the heroes of Marathon have diverged very far indeed from their forefathers, and the experienced Turkish commander knew right well that he is a bad soldier who even descends to cutting off the head of his slain foe on the battle-field.

At Puló, Omar Vrione encountered the army of Odysseus. Now Omar was at one time one of the best of Ali Pasha's lieutenants. Ali promoted him to the rank or general, and he had begun life as a shepherd-boy. Ali had taught him how to use his weapons, and now he turned them against his master.

The Sultan had intrusted to him a fine army with which he had assisted Gaskho Bey to beleaguer Ali. It consisted of eight thousand gallant Asiatic infantry, two thousand Spahis, and eight guns. The leader of the Spahis was Zaid, the Bey of Kastorid, Ali's favorite grandson, whom, twenty years before, he had rocked upon his knee, and whom, while still a child, he had carried in front of him on his saddle, and taught him to ride. Zaid himself had asked, as a favor, that he might lead a division of cavalry against his grandfather. He had promised his mother to seize that sinful old head by its gray beard and bring it home to her.

A precious grandson, truly!

So Omar Vrione reached Puló. Looking down from the hill-tops there, he discerned the army of Odysseus. He saw him planting his white banners in rows upon the heights, and without giving his forces a moment's rest, he set his own martial chimneys a-smoking and attacked the Greeks with all his might.

After an hour's combat, in which they fought man to man, the Greeks were driven from their intrenchments, and began slowly descending into the valley.

The Timariotes remained behind, and Zaid began to send forward his Spahis to attack the retreating army in the rear. Odysseus slowly retraced his steps till he came to Puló. There his war-path stopped. His banner was no longer white, but red; it was sprinkled with the blood of the many heroes who had died in its defence.

Suddenly, from the heights of Pindus above them resounded the tempestuous melody of the "Marseillaise," which the Greeks had adopted as their war-song, and rapid as a storm-swollen mountain torrent the Suliotes, with Kleon and Artemis in the van, hurled themselves upon the Turks.

Omar Vrione was caught between two fires. It was too late to turn back, too late to reform his order of battle. His guns were useless, his cavalry could not move forward, and his infantry columns were so completely isolated that they could not render each other any assistance.

The general saw that he could not save his army, but he was at least determined not to save himself, so he hastened to where the fight was raging most furiously.

A wild, merciless *mêlée* was proceeding between the inextricably intermingled foes. Forcing his way along, Omar Vrione suddenly encountered, in the midst of reeking powder and streaming blood, a tall youth with a blackened face, whom he at once recognized as Kleon. There, then, they stood, face to face. Three years before, when Ali had sent Omar Vrione to threaten the Suliotes, Kleon fled before him, and then he had called after the fugitive, "Stand, I would send thy head to Ali Tepelenti!"

And there, indeed, Omar Vrione fell, combating, and Kleon cut off his head.

How strange is fate!

The fall of Omar Vrione sealed the fate of his army. The Turks fled wherever they saw the chance, leaving all their guns, all their flags, and all their officers in the lurch. The cavalry had no chance of escaping. Half of it fell, the other half surrendered.

Zaid, in the moment of extremest danger, took his silver aigrette out of his turban and threw it away; then he changed caftans with his servant, and mingled with the rank-and-file, so that none might recognize him. It would have been much better for a child like him to have remained at home than to have gone hunting that old lion, his aged grandfather.

The Suliotes surrounded Zaid's company. "Dismount from your horses!" exclaimed the clear voice of Kleon.

The Spahis, full of shame, dismounted.

"Which is your leader, Zaid?" cried Kleon, advancing. The edge of his sword was dripping with blood.

"I am," said the servant who had changed clothes with Zaid, and he approached Kleon.

"Bow down before me, thou slave!" cried Kleon, kicking him.

The servant bowed his head before the victor, and he never raised it again, for Kleon chopped it off with his bloody sword, and sticking it on the point thereof, raised it on high and cried to his bloodthirsty comrades: "Here is their second general, Zaid, who came to subdue us! Hallelujah!"

and the victorious host repeated after him, "Hallelujah! Hallelujah!"

And then they stuck the heads of the two generals on the points of two lances, and carried them through the streets of Puló in the sight of the crowds of women and children on the housetops, bellowing, "We have conquered! We have conquered! These are the heads of the enemy's leaders: one of them is Omar Vrione, and the other is Zaid Bey! Kyrie eleison?"

And what face was ever so pale as Zaid's when he heard his name called out and saw how they mocked and jeered at the head they took for his?

The Suliotes returned to Janina with the captives and the emblems of victory. Tepelenti, hearing that they had decapitated Zaid, went down into the camp and demanded his head.

Kleon was sitting in front of his tent *en déshabillé*. He was not disposed to part with the symbol of victory, but wanted it to dazzle the eyes of the host for some little time longer.

But Ali was ready at once with a good idea: "Cut off the head of another prisoner," said he, "in its stead; none will notice the difference."

Kleon acted upon the advice, and immediately sent forth his men-at-arms to take the exhibited head to Ali. But Ali shook his own head when he saw it, and wagging his finger at Kleon, he said: "Thou art over-young, my son, to try and impose upon Ali. Thou wouldst turn my counsel to my own hurt, and give me the head of another instead of Zaid's!"

Kleon leaped to his feet. "Do you mean to say that is not Zaid's head?"

"Of a truth it is not. Dost thou suppose I do not know the youth—I who used to dandle him on my knee ever since he was a child, and was the first to place a sword in his hand?"

"But, indeed, he himself told me," cried Kleon, pointing at the head, "that he was Zaid, and he was wearing a general's uniform."

"'Tis a slave," said Tepelenti, regarding the head more closely. "Dost thou not see? His ears have been cropped, so that he may not wear ear-rings in them, which only great lords may do."

"Then Zaid has gone free!"

"Zaid will be among the captives," said Tepelenti. "I would recognize him amongst a thousand. He was my favorite grandson. His image even now is engraved in my heart."

Then they went down amongst the captives. Ali had scarce cast a glance at them when he pointed with his finger.

"There he is! Dost thou not perceive how much paler his face is than the faces of the others?"

Kleon wrathfully drew his sword and would have rushed upon the person indicated, but Ali held his hand.

"What doest thou? Wouldst thou slay my grandson before my very eyes?"

"Thou didst ask for his head, and it shall be thine."

"But now I ask for his life, Kleon. Zaid is my favorite grandson. I brought him up. I loved him better than his dear mother—better than all my children. Look now, I share with thee all the booty, and all I ask of thee is mine own—flesh of my flesh."

The unhappy youth, hearing these words, fell at Ali's feet and embraced his knees, wept, covered his hands with kisses, and implored him to release him —he would be a good and dutiful son to him ever afterwards.

"Thou seest, too, how much he loves me," said Ali, looking with tearful eyes at Zaid and covering the cowering fugitive with his long gray beard. "Well, Zaid," said he, "so thou dost now fly for refuge beneath the shadow of that same gray beard, by grasping which thou wert minded to take Ali's head to thy mother, eh?"

Kleon looked at Ali Pasha with a contemptuous smile. Then Ali was tender, Ali had a heart, Ali's heart ached at the slaying of his kinsfolk! The Greek felt a cruel satisfaction in tormenting the pasha.

"If thou dost not wish to see Zaid die," said he, "depart from hence. Alive thou shalt not have him!"

"What!" cried Ali, and, standing erect, he drew his sword. "Because my beard is long dost thou think thou canst trample upon me? I will defend my blood with my blood, and will perish myself rather than let him be slain. Let us see, mad youth, wouldst thou lop off thine own right hand?"

Kleon was so surprised that he did not know what to do. It was in his power to slay Ali; but then that would be a greater triumph for Stambul than all the victories of the campaign.

At that moment a herald arrived from Odysseus with a command for Kleon to send all the Turkish officers captured at the battle of Puló to Prevesa, that they might be exchanged against the youths of the sacred army who had been captured in Moldavia.

Kleon's pride was wounded by this direct command. He considered himself just as good a general as Odysseus or Yprilanti, and did not recognize orders sent from them.

Turning from the herald to Tepelenti, he thus replied:

"Tell Odysseus that I and my soldiers are in the habit of killing the enemy's officers on the battle-field. Only one of them, and he in disguise, remains. He, however, is Tepelenti's grandson, who has recognized him and ransomed him from me for a hundred thousand piastres, which he has engaged to pay me within an hour. Is it not so, Tepelenti?"

"It is so," said Ali; "within an hour the hundred thousand piastres shall be in thy hands."

Zaid, with a shriek of joy, kissed the hem of his grandfather's robe, and Kleon gave his hand upon the bargain. An hour later the money arrived in little hogsheads, and he had it weighed in the presence of his captains. Ali, however, binding his grandson by the left arm, and giving him his own caftan, had him conducted into the fortress of Janina.

Kleon looked contemptuously after him. So the old man had become soft-hearted! How he had wept and supplicated and paid for this youth, who was his favorite grandson!

An hour later the roll of drums was heard on the bastions of Janina, and when the Greeks looked in that direction they saw the stake of execution erected there. Four black executioners were carrying Zaid, who had his hands tied behind his back, and was wearing the self-same caftan which Ali had given him. Ali himself, mounted on a black horse, rode right up to the stake. At a signal from him the executioners hoisted Zaid into the air, and a moment later Tepelenti's favorite grandson, whom he had dandled so often on his knee, was done to death by the most excruciating torments!

Ali watched his death-agony with the utmost *sang-froid*, and, when all was over, he shouted down from the bastions with a strong, firm voice, "So perish all those of Tepelenti's kinsfolk who draw the sword against him! For them there is no mercy!"

Kleon felt his heart's blood grow cold. Ah! he had much, very much to learn from the agonized cries of the dying before he could overtake Ali, that old man who weeps, prays, and pays, in order to rescue his favorite grandson for the sole purpose of killing him himself with refined tortures!

Of all Ali's large family only two sons now remained, Sulaiman and Mukhtar. They were the first who had betrayed their father, and it was their treachery that had wounded him most. For a whole year Ali carried that wound about in his heart. During that time nobody was allowed to mention the names of his sons in his presence. Everything, absolutely everything, which reminded him of them was removed from the fortress. If any one was weary of life, he had only to mention the name of Mukhtar before Ali, and death was a certainty.

Meanwhile the two apostate sons were living in great misery at Adrianople; for the Sultan, though he paid them for their treachery, would have nothing more to do with them. The first instalment of the money which they were to receive as the price of their father's blood melted away very rapidly in merry banquets, pretty female slaves, fine steeds, and precious gems; and when it was all gone the second instalment never made its appearance. Far different and far more important personages had still stronger claims upon the Sultan's purse. Tepelenti's vigorous resistance, the innumerable losses suffered by the Sultan's armies, buried in forgetfulness the services of the good sons whose betrayal of their father had profited the Sultan nothing. They were already beginning to bitterly repent their overhasty step when the rumor of Ali's victories reached them; and as the days of necessity began to weigh heavily upon them, as money and wine began to fail them, as they found themselves obliged to sell, one by one, their horses, their jewels, and, at last, even their beautiful slave-girls, it became quite plain to them that no help could be looked for from any quarter, unless perhaps it was from wonder-working fairies, or from the genii of the *Thousand and One Nights*.

But let none say that, in the regions of the merry Orient, fairies and wonders do not still make their home among men.

Just when the beys had consumed the price of the last slave they had to sell, such wealth poured in upon them, in heaps, in floods, as we only hear of in old fairy tales; and fairy tales, as we all know very well, have no truth in them at all.

One day, as Ali Pasha was walking to and fro on the bastions of Janina, he perceived among the garden-beds in the court-yard below a gardener engaged in planting tulips.

Tepelenti knew all the servants in the fortress thoroughly, down to the very lowest. He not only knew them by name, but he knew what they had to do and how they did it.

The name of this gardening slave was Dirham, and he was so named because, many years before, Mukhtar had purchased him when a child from a slave-dealer for a dirham, and although his master often plagued him, he nevertheless cared for him well, and brought him up and provided him with all manner of good things. Thus Dirham, whenever his master's name was mentioned, bethought him how little he was worth when Mukhtar Bey bought him, and how many more dirhams he was worth now, and for all this he could not thank Mukhtar enough.

Ali Pasha for a long time watched from the bastions this man planting his tulips. Some of them he pressed down into the ground very carefully, strewing them with loose powdery earth, preparing a proper place for the bulbs beforehand, and moistening them gently with watery spray; others he plumped down into the earth anyhow, covering them up very perfunctorily, and never looking to see whether he watered them too much or too little.

Ali carefully noted those bulbs which Dirham had bestowed the greatest pains upon, and then went down and entered into conversation with him.

"What are the names of these tulips?"

Dirham ticked them all off: King George, Trafalgar, Admiral Gruithuysen, Belle Alliance, etc., etc. But at the same time he skipped over one or two here and there, and these were the very ones which he had covered up with the greatest care.

"Then thou dost not know the names of those others?" inquired Ali.

"I have lost my memoranda, my lord, and I cannot remember all the names among so many."

"Look, now, I know the names of these flowers. This is Sulaiman, that over there is Mukhtar Bey."

Dirham cast himself on his face before the pasha. Ali had guessed well. Dirham remembered the two gentlemen just as a good dog remembers his master—they were ever in his mind.

The wretched man fully expected that Ali would immediately tear these bulbs out of the ground and plant his own head there in their place.

Instead of that Ali graciously raised him from the ground and said to him in a tender, sympathetic voice, "Fear not, Dirham! Thou hast no need to be ashamed of such noble sentiments. Thou art thinking of my sons. And dost thou suppose that I never think of them? I have forbidden every one in the fortress to even mention their names; but what does that avail me if I cannot prevent myself from thinking of them? What avails it to never hear their names if I see their faces constantly before me? The world says they have betrayed me; but I do not believe, I cannot believe it. What says Dirham? Is it possible that children can betray their own father?"

Dirham took his courage in both hands and ventured to reply:

"Strike off my head if you will, my lord, but this

I say—they were not traitors, but were themselves betrayed; for even if it were possible for sons to betray their father, Tepelenti's children would not betray Tepelenti."

Ali Pasha gave Dirham a purse of gold for these words, commanding him, at the same time, to appear before him in the palace that evening, and to bring with him, carefully transplanted into pots, those tulips which bore the names of Sulaiman and Mukhtar.

Dirham could scarcely wait for the evening to come, and the moment he appeared in Ali's halls he was admitted into the pasha's presence. Then Ali bade every one withdraw from the room, that they twain might remain together, and began to talk with him confidentially.

"I hear that my sons are living in great poverty at Adrianople. As to their poverty, I say nothing; but, worse still, they are living in great humiliation also. Nobody will have anything to do with them. The wretched Spahis, who once on a time mentioned their names with chattering teeth, now mock at them when they meet them in the street, and when they go on foot to the bazaar to buy their bread, the women cry with a loud voice, 'Are these, then, the heroes at whom Stambul used to tremble?' Verily it is shameful, and Ali Pasha blushes thereat. I know that if once I ever place in their hands those good swords which I bound upon their thighs they would not surrender them so readily to the enemies of Ali Pasha. What says Dirham?"

Dirham was only able to express his approval of Ali's words by a very audible sigh.

"Hearken, Dirham! I have known for a long time a secret, which I will venture to confide to thee."

"'Twill be as though you buried it under the earth, my master."

"In the Gulf of Durazzo there lies at anchor an English vessel, under the command of Captain Morrison. On that ship I have deposited five millions of piastres in gold—not less than five millions. A large amount, eh! At any moment I like I can blow the fortress of Janina into the air, embark on board that ship, and sail away to England or Spain, and there I can live in a lordly fashion without care, just as I please. But to what purpose? My remaining days are but few. Why should I try to save them? Here I must perish. Here, where I have grown great, it becomes me to die, and it is not for me to retreat before the advancing sword. This money must serve another design of mine, which has been in my mind long since, but I seek a man capable of executing it.

"Thou shalt be that man. Falter not. Fate does great things with little ones. Thou shalt go from Janina and pass through Gaskho Bey's army. When thou dost arrive at Durazzo, show Morrison this ring. When he sees it he will do everything thou sayest to him, for he will know that these are my commands. Thou wilt have the anchor raised and sail with the first favorable wind to Stambul. Sail not into the Golden Horn, for it will be more difficult to get out of it again, but cast thy anchor hard by Anadoli Hissar. There thou wilt land, and, taking with thee a hundred thousand piastres, thou wilt put them in sacks of chaff, the chaff being on the top, and lading sundry asses with the sacks, thou wilt take them to Adrianople. There thou wilt seek out my sons, and, humbly kissing the hem of their garments, give them to understand that I have sent thee. Then thou wilt tell them of the warfare waged around Janina, all that thou thyself hast seen and heard. If from their faces thou seest that they receive thy words coldly, and show no ardor of soul, then measure out to them the hundred thousand piastres, and bid them buy and keep shop therewith, start a large wholesale business if they feel any disposition that way, and apply themselves diligently to heap up riches upon riches, as it becomes honest men to do who have long years to live. But if thou seest their face aflame and the heroes' love of glory sparkle in their eyes; if they listen to thy words with parted lips and throbbing hearts; if they press thy hand warmly and frequently clutch the hilts of their swords; if they ask thee to tell them again and again what thou hast told them already — then tell them that the path of glory and Tepelenti's arms are always open before them, that those one hundred thousand piastres are only for buying horses and weapons. I have five times as much on board the English ship, and five hundred times as much in the red tower of Janina. With the five millions of piastres they must get ships, and these ships they must fully equip in secret. And this will not be difficult, for all the Greek seamen have deserted the Turkish fleet. These Greeks will offer their services gratis. When the ships are ready, let them, through thee, inform thereof Bublinia, the heroic Greek amazon, who is cruising off Crete with thirty vessels to divert the attention of the Turkish fleet, and then row out to Beikos. With favorable weather thou shouldst get to Durazzo in ten days. Simultaneously, I from one quarter, Kleon from a second, and Odysseus from a third will attack the army of Gaskho Bey, and if my sons are victorious at sea, in the evening of the same day we shall be able to rest in one another's arms."

Dirham wept like a child.

The pasha continued his directions:

"At every step be cautious. Accomplish everything amidst the greatest secrecy. Don't let my sons scatter their money right and left, lest their wealth be suspected and give rise to envy and jealousy. It would be better if they left the bulk of it on board ship, and only drew from it whatever may be necessary for the time being. When thou dost communicate with Bublinia, write on the parchment all sorts of different things higgledy-piggledy. Say, for instance, that thou art disembarking wool in Crete, and will consign it to Argyrocantharides, who is friendly with the Sultan and all the pashas, and, at the same time, an intermediary between us and the Greeks. But in the empty spaces between the lines let Mukhtar write the message for Bublinia in special characters with oil of vitriol; then, when thou dost hand over the documents, moisten these special rows of letters with a piece of citron. But stay, I will give thee a still better counsel. Melt some lunar caustic in water, and write therewith thy message on the shell of hard-boiled eggs. Then boil the eggs again; and when thou dost break them open thou wilt find the writing visible on the white membrane inside. Do that. Eggs are the least suspicious of cargoes."

Dirham made a careful mental note of all that was told him, secretly amazed that Ali Pasha should have extended his attention to the smallest details.

"One thing more," said Ali, and his voice trembled with emotion. "I know right well that I am giving my sons dangerous parts to play, and the issue thereof is uncertain. Take, therefore, this ring; the stone set in it contains a talisman. Give it to Mukhtar. Let him wear it on his finger, and if ever he finds himself environed by a great danger, a very great danger—which Allah forfend!—then let him open the stone of the ring and read the talisman engraved therein. But this he is only to do if a great danger be at hand, when he trembles for his life, when the lowest slave would not change heads with him; for when once it has been read the talisman loses all its virtue. And now depart, and bethink thee of all I have told thee."

Dirham kissed the hem of the pasha's garment and promised that he would carefully perform everything. Ali accompanied him down into the garden. On their way back to the place they had to cross the spot where Zaid was buried. As the hollow earth resounded beneath Ali's feet, he stopped for a moment and murmured to himself, "H'm! thou shalt not be the only one!"

Two weeks later Dirham met the sons of Ali in Adrianople. Morrison's ship had taken him on the way thither, and during the voyage Dirham had countless opportunities of convincing himself that the money deposited by Ali was safely guarded in the hold of the vessel. There he said everything which Ali had confided to him, and as it seemed to the poor servant, through the medium of his tearful eyes, as if the beys grew enthusiastic at the tidings of the war which their aged father was waging, he told them, in this persuasion, that Ali had sent them five million piastres, that they might buy ships and collect arms and unite their forces to his.

The beys rejoiced greatly at the tidings of the five millions, and embraced Dirham, who did his best to attribute all the merit of the deed to Tepelenti for sending the money so magnanimously.

"The old man might have sent us still more," said Sulaiman. "What does he want with it in Janina? Sooner or later it will become the prey of his enemies."

"Pardon me, my lord!" objected Dirham. "It will become nobody's prey if only you unite with him."

"Ugh!" said Sulaiman; and at that moment the two brothers caught each other's eye, and it was as though the same thought suddenly occurred to them both.

When Dirham delivered the ring to Mukhtar, the latter asked, suspiciously:

"Is there any poison in this ring?"

"What are you thinking of, my lord? I wore it on my finger the whole way hither. There is a talisman in it."

At this both the brothers burst out laughing. They had often ridiculed Ali for his absurd superstition. Nevertheless, Mukhtar kept the ring, for there was a splendid emerald in it.

But the secret of the eggs completely won the favor of the brothers. That was really a capital idea of Ali's. In this way the pashas could send secret messages even in their harems. Who would ever suspect an egg? They would put it to the proof at once. They would send a declaration of love to the odalisks of the Seraskier, written in an egg.

Dirham shook his head and spoke seriously, and entreated the beys to first of all enter into a league with Bublinia, the amazon of Chios, who was even bold enough on occasions to make a dash at the Dardanelles; for if they did not hasten, the money that had been sent to them would be of no use. It would be dangerous, he urged, to show the people of Adrianople that they had received money. The English captain, moreover, was not disposed to render any other service than that of keeping safe custody of the money confided to him; but if any harm happened to them because of it, he would neither defend them nor even convey them out of Turkish waters.

These wise remonstrances made some impression upon the beys. Just as if their thoughts were pursuing the same course, they both hastened to beg Dirham to let them have at once the eggs, the lunar caustic, writing materials, and all other indispensable things. Moreover, they forgot to give him money for these purchases, so the poor fellow had to buy them out of his own purse.

Dirham's foot was scarcely out of the house when the two brothers looked at each other and smiled.

"I have a good idea," began Sulaiman.

"And I also," said the other.

"I don't mean to return to Ali."

"Nor I. I bear in mind what happened to Zaid."

"I propose we buy a ship, on which we may hide our money."

"And we'll man her with a Greek crew."

"Then we will send Dirham with the messages written in the eggs to Bublinia, and we'll write great things therein. We'll tell her that we stand ready here with our fleets, and if she will attack the Kapudan Pasha in front we will attack him in the rear. The woman is mad. She will come forth from the Archipelago and fall upon the Turkish fleet. Then the Kapudan Pasha will assemble his forces against her, and she will engage all his attention till we have nicely set sail, nor will we stop till we reach Cadiz."

"Admirable! for that is the land of good wine and fair women."

"And then Ali Pasha may wait for us till the angel Izrafīl blows his trumpet on the last day!"

"And Bublinia as well—not forgetting the Sultan! Let them worry each other."

"Mashallah! Life is sweet!"

And so it chanced that the sons of Ali, like the princes in a fairy tale, suddenly and marvellously came into the possession of great riches, and were wise enough to profit by these riches in the merriest manner in the world. The money was given to them for blood and weapons. They were going to lavish it on love and wine. And is not life lovelier so?

When Dirham came back they immediately boiled the eggs hard, and wrote upon them every sort of magnificent message that occurred to their minds. They promised to hasten to the assistance of the

Greeks, both by land and by sea; to cut their way through the fleets with their fire-ships and blow the Turkish flag-ship into the air; to incite the Janissaries to rise against the Sultan and the Greeks to rise against the Janissaries; in all of which there was not a single word of truth. Only worthy Dirham believed these things, and trembled in body and soul at the bare thought of the sublime deeds that his masters had determined to perform.

He himself hired a barge, loaded it with wool, and, hiding the eggs full of secrets in a basket, set out for the Archipelago.

The good youths meanwhile laughed to their hearts' content. They laughed at worthy Dirham; they laughed at the worthy Bublinia, and at the wise Kapudan Pasha; they laughed at this amusing piece of good fortune which brought them riches in heaps. But at nobody did they laugh so much as at old Tepelenti, who was believing all along that his sons were collecting war-ships for him.

But did he really believe it?

On the same day that Dirham quitted Adrianople, a fakir of the Nimetullahita Order penetrated into the Seraglio and demanded an audience of the Sultan. It was the self-same old soothsayer who had exhibited his enchantments to Ali.

On being admitted to the presence of Mahmoud, he stood audaciously upright before him, bending his head no lower than it was already crooked by the weight of years.

"Allah hath sent me to thee," said the dervish, in a deep, hollow voice, which had lost all its sonorousness. "A great danger is approaching thee. The storm hanging over thy head is at this moment compressed within the skin of an egg, and thou couldst crush it in the palm of thy hand; but if thou dost suffer it to come forth from the egg, thy whole realm will not be sufficient to contain it. This, therefore, is the word of Allah unto thee: This day and this night, and to-morrow and to-morrow night, stop every vessel which sails up the narrow waters of the Golden Horn and search them, and whenever thy guards come upon an egg, let them seize it and bring it to thee; for amongst them are diverse cockatrice eggs which, if once they be hatched, will swallow up both thee and thy realm."

Having said these words, the dervish turned him about, and without so much as saluting the Padishah, without even taking off his slippers before him, he withdrew, not even asking for a reward.

The Sultan was profoundly impressed by this audacity. He immediately sent orders to the wardens of the two watch-towers at the entrance of the Golden Horn to board and search thoroughly every vessel that passed between them, seize every egg they found on board and bring them to him, at the same time detaining all the crews of such vessels.

Fate so willed it that Dirham's was the first vessel that fell into the hands of the searchers.

When the unfortunate servant perceived that the guards seized the eggs, he leaped into the sea, and although he was a good swimmer, he allowed himself to be suffocated in the water lest he should be compelled to betray his masters.

The eggs they carried to the Sultan, and when he had opened them and had read the writing written on their inner skins, he was horrified. Treachery and rebellion! The conspiracy was spreading from one end of the empire to the other. The complicated intrigue, one of whose threads was in Janina and the other in the islands of the Archipelago, had its third in the very capital. This called for terrible reprisals.

The beys were seized the same night in the midst of their joys, and dragged from the paradise of their hopes to be thrown into a dungeon.

Who could have betrayed the secret of the eggs? they asked themselves. Why, who else but Tepelenti?

Fools! to fancy that they could make a fool of Tepelenti!

Sulaiman fainted when they informed him that the secret of the eggs was discovered. Mukhtar felt that the moment had come of which Ali had said that the lowest slave would not then exchange heads with his two sons, and in that hour of peril he bethought him of the talismanic ring which had been sent to him. Hastily he removed the emerald, believing that at least a quickly operative poison was contained therein, by which he might be saved from a shameful death. There was, however, no poison inside the ring, but these words were engraved thereon, "Ye have fallen into the hands of Ali!"

Mukhtar dropped the ring; he was annihilated.

The hand of Ali, that implacable hand which reached from one end of the world to the other, which clutched at him even out of the tomb—he now felt all its weight upon his head.

Die he must, and his brother also.

The Reis-Effendi examined them, and both of them doggedly denied all knowledge of what was written on the eggs. But there was one thing they could not deny — the five million piastres on the English ship; this was the most damaging piece of evidence against them, and proved to be their ruin.

The Sultan demanded from Morrison the money of the beys, and Morrison himself appeared before the Reis-Effendi to defend his consignment, which he maintained he was only bound to deliver to its lawful owner.

The Reis-Effendi replied that in the Ottoman Empire there was only one lawful owner of every sort of property, and that was the Sultan. The property of every deceased person fell to the Grand Signior, and nobody could make a will without his permission.

Morrison objected, very pertinently, that as the beys were not deceased the Sultan could scarcely be looked upon as their heir.

Instead of making any answer, the Reis-Effendi sent out his officers with a little piece of parchment which he had previously subscribed, and a few moments later the severed heads of the beys stood in front of Morrison on a silver trencher.

"If their not being dead was the sole impediment," remarked the Minister of Foreign Affairs, "you perceive that it has now been removed."

Morrison thereupon handed over all the gold and silver in his possession as rapidly as possible, and quitted Constantinople that very hour; he had no great love of a place where every word cost the life of a man.

But the heads of the beys were stuck on the gates of the Seraglio for three days and three nights in the sight of all the people, and mounted heralds proclaimed, at intervals of an hour, "Behold the heads of the sons of the rebellious Ali Tepelenti, who would have devastated Stambul!"

And the people loaded the heads with curses each time the proclamation was made.

A few days later the news reached Janina that Sulaiman Bey and Mukhtar Bey had been beheaded at Stambul.

Ali Pasha thrice bowed his face to the ground and gave thanks to Allah for His mercies. And he caused to be proclaimed on the ramparts, amidst a flourish of trumpets, that his sons, the treacherous beys, had been decapitated at Stambul. Such is the reward of traitors!

After that, for three days and three nights—just as long a time as the heads of the beys had been exposed on the gates of the Seraglio—a banquet, with music and dancing, was given in the fortress of Janina, and every morning a hundred and one volleys were fired from the bastions—the usual ceremony after great triumphs.

And when in the evening Ali took a promenade in his garden, and walked up and down among his flowers, he would now and then trample the earth beneath his feet. It was the grave of Zaid that he was trampling upon. There stood an old dahlia, the sole survivor of its extirpated family, and, levelling it to the ground with his foot, he trod it into the grave, murmuring to himself, "No longer art thou alone—no longer alone!"

CHAPTER XI

THE FLOWERS OF THE GARDEN OF BEGTASH

At the end of the fifteenth century, when the Turkish crescent had won an abiding-place among the constellations of Europe, there dwelt in the Turkish dominions a worthy dervish, Haji Begtash by name.

As the overflowing armies of the newly founded empire submerged the surrounding Christian kingdoms, Haji Begtash went everywhere with the conquering hosts, but in the intervals of peace he begged his way about the empire, and scraped together a little money from the Turkish grandees or from the extravagant, booty-laden Turkish soldiers.

Now wherefore did this worthy dervish make it a point to collect so much money and wear himself out by travelling from the Adriatic to the Euxine, when he might have sat all day long at the gate of the Kaaba, as they call the stone on the tomb of the Prophet, and recited from his long bead-string the nine properties of Allah (no very exhausting labor, by-the-way), and received therefor, from the pilgrims to the shrine, meat, drink, and abundance of alms?

Well, Haji Begtash had taken up a great work. When he accompanied the Turkish armies, and they, on entering a Christian village, began to cut down the inhabitants and tie the captives together with ropes, the dervish would force his way through the bloodthirsty soldiery, and if he beheld any wild Bashkir or Kurdish desperado about to dash out the brains of a forsaken, weeping orphan child against a wall, he would lay his hand upon them, take away the child, cover it with his mantle, caress it, and take it away with him. And thus he would keep on doing till he had with him a whole group of children, all of whom were concealed beneath the folds of his ample cloak, where nobody could hurt them; nay, frequently he would carry babies in swaddling-clothes in his bosom, till people began to wonder what on earth he meant to do with them.

Subsequently he announced that any captive who brought him his children should receive a silver denarius per head for each one of them. This was not much, it is true; but then there was little demand for children. In the slave-market only the adult human animal had its price-current. And so it came about that innumerable children were brought to the worthy dervish.

He took them away with him to a mosque at Adrianople. Folks laughed at him, and asked him mockingly if he was going to plant a garden with them.

Haji Begtash accepted the jest in real earnest, and called his children the flowers of Begtash's garden; and this name they preserved in the coming centuries.

These saplings (amongst them were some of the loveliest little creatures of six and seven years of age) were brought up by the indefatigable Haji year after year. He instructed them in the Kuran; he told them everything concerning the innumerable and ineffable joys which the Prophet promises to those who fall in the defence of the true Faith; and at the same time accustomed them to endure all the hardships and privations of this earthly life.

Most of these children had never known father or mother, and those who had quickly forgot all about them as they grew up. No love of home or kindred bound them to this world, and therefore they were all the more attached to one another. Their comrades were the only beings they learned to love, and every one of them treated old Begtash as a father. His words were sacred to them.

Their days were passed in hard work, in perpetual martial exercises, fighting, and swimming. A youth of twelve among them was capable of coping with full-grown men elsewhere, and each one of them at maturity was a veritable Samson.

In those days the Ottoman armies suffered many defeats from the Christian arms. Their strength lay for the most part in their cavalry, but their innumerable infantry was a mere mob, two of their foot-soldiers not being equal to one of the well-disciplined European men-at-arms who advanced irresistibly against them in huge compact masses; and they were of no use at all in sieges, except to fill up the ditches and trenches with their dead bodies, and thus make a road for the more valiant warriors that came after them.

And now, as if by magic, a little band of infantry suddenly appeared on the theatre of the war. These new soldiers were dressed quite differently from the others. On their heads they wore a high hat bulging outward in front, with a black, floating cock's plume on the top of it; their dolmans were of embroidered blue cloth; their hose only reached down to their knees, below that the whole leg was bare; their only weapon was a short, broad, roundish sword, in marked contrast to the other Turkish soldiers, who loaded themselves with as many weapons as if they were going to fight with ten hands.

None recognized the youths—and youths they all were. They did not mingle with the other squadrons, nor place themselves under any captain, nor did they ask for pay from any one.

But in the very first engagement they showed what they were made of. A fortress had to be besieged which was defended in front by a broad stream of water. The strange youths clinched their broad swords between their teeth, swam across the water, scaled the bastions amidst fire and flames, and planted the first horse-tail crescent on the tower.

These were the flowers of Begtash's garden.

The first battle established the fame of the youthful band that had been brought up by the old dervish, and by the time the second campaign began, Haji Begtash was already the chief of innumerable monasteries whose inmates were called the Brethren of the Order of Begtash. Consisting, as they did, of captive Christian children, and standing under the immediate command of the Sultan, they composed a new army of infantry, the fame of whose valor filled the whole world.

These were the "jeni-cheri" (new soldiers), which name was subsequently altered into Janichary or Janissary. But for long ages to come, if any Janissary warrior had a mind to speak haughtily, he would call himself "a flower from Begtash's garden."

Many a glorious name bloomed in this garden in the course of the ages. The power of the Sultan rested on their shoulders, and if they shook the Sultan from off their shoulders, down he had to go.

If they were powerful servants, they were also powerful tyrants. Their valor often reaped a harvest of victories, but their obstinacy again and again imperilled their triumphs. With the increase of their power their self-assurance increased likewise. It was not so much the Sultans and Viziers who commanded them as they who commanded the Sultans and Viziers. And if the rebellious Janissaries hoisted on the Atmeidan a kettle, the signal of revolt, it was always with fear and trembling that the Seraglio asked them what were their demands; and the whole Divan breathed more freely when the answer came that it was gold they wanted, and not blood—the blood of their officers. And when, after the great Feast of Bairam, there was the usual distribution of pilaf, and the dangerous kettles were filled full with this savory mess of rice and sheep's flesh, the Sultan, all trembling, would anxiously watch to see how the majestic Janissaries partook of their pottage. If they devoured it voraciously, that was a sign of their satisfaction; but if they only touched it in a finiking sort of way, then the Sultan would fly into the Seraglio, and lock himself up among the damsels of the harem, for it was now certain that their lordships the Janissaries were displeased, and it was well if their displeasure only expressed itself by reducing a whole quarter or so of the city to ashes.

Two Sultans had tried to break in two this dangerous double-edged weapon, which inflicted as many wounds in the heart of the realm as ever it dealt outside; but the Janissaries' magic influence was so interwoven with, so ingrafted in, the mind of the nation that public feeling was on their side, and both rulers perished in the bold attempt. They dragged Sultan Osman forth from the Seraglio, and set him on the back of an ass with his face to its tail, carried him in derision from one end of the town to the other, and then flung him into the fatal Seven Towers, where the Turkish rulers and their relatives are wont to be buried alive and die forgotten. Mahmoud II.'s father, Selim, on the other hand, expired beneath the sword-thrusts of the rebels, and those swords were still sharp and those hands were still strong when the son of the man whom they had slain sat on the throne, and under no other Sultan did the throne tremble so much as under him.

In these days the mighty corps of the Janissaries lived only to commit crimes or gigantic mistakes; its ancient glory was not renewed. During the last century their arms had constantly been shattered whenever they came into collision with the progressive military science of Europe. In the course of the ages the flowers in Begtash's garden had sadly faded. The flowery petals of their glory had fallen from them, and only the thorns remained; and even these were no longer the thorns of the brave thick-set hedge which defends the borders of the garden against would-be invaders, but the stings of the nettle which hurts the hand of the gardener as he hoes.

Neither life nor property was any longer safe from them. The Sultan himself, when he sat upon the throne, was in the most dangerous place of all, and the Viziers—the chief officials of the realm—trembled every day for their lives. The turbulence of the Janissaries was a perpetually recurring disease, running through all the arteries of the realm, and covering the once mighty empire with poisonous ulcers.

These seditious outbreaks occurred even during the deliberations of the Divan, and fear on such occasions was a more urgent counsellor than conviction to the palace magnates who sat in the cupolaed chamber.

The threats of the Janissaries had compelled Mahmoud to take up arms against Ali Pasha; and now, when Ali had kindled the flames of war all over the empire, and the Sultan bade the Janissaries hasten against the enemy and subdue him, they replied that they would not fight unless the Sultan led them in person.

Instead of that, they waged war within the very walls of Stambul, for whenever the news of a defeat reached the capital, the Janissaries would fall upon the defenceless Greeks and massacre them by thousands.

From distant Asia, from the most savage parts of the empire, Begtash's priests appeared and proclaimed in the mosques death and destruction on the heads of all the Greeks. It was they who, with torches in their hands, headed the rush of the fanatical Janissaries against Buyukdere, Pera, and Galata, the quarters of the city where the Greeks resided, and every day they thundered with their bludgeons at the gates of the Seraglio, demanding ever more and more sentences of death against the

Greek captives who were shut up in the Seven Towers. The Sultan's officials, trembling with fear, wrote out the sentences demanded of them, and the victims fell in hundreds; and when the Russian ambassador, Stroganov, protested against this butchery, the Janissaries attacked his palace and riddled all the doors and windows with bullets, which was the subsequent pretext for the long war which shook the empire to its base, though the Janissaries never lived to feel it.

Mahmoud watched from the summit of the imperial palace the devastation of Stambul and the devastation of his empire, and he saw no help anywhere. He saw nothing but the melancholy examples of his ancestors and the disappearance of his dominions; and as he stroked the head of his first-born, Abdul Mejid, a child of nine, he thought to himself, "This lad will not sit on the throne, he will not be a ruler as his forefathers were; he will not dictate laws to half the world like the other descendants of Omar; but he will be a fugitive on the face of the earth, the slave of strange people, as was the fugitive Dzhem, whom they cast forth ages ago."

How miserable was the life of the Sultan! What avails it though an earthly paradise be open to him if life itself be closed against him? What avails it to be a god if he cannot be a man? The Sultan never knows what it is to have relatives. Very early, while they are still children, the latest born are shut up in the Seven Towers. The first-born son can never meet them, unless it be on the steps of the throne, when the rebellious Janissaries drag one of them from his dungeon to raise him to the throne, and lock up the first-born in his stead. The Sultan cannot be said to possess a wife; all that he has are favorite concubines, in hundreds, in thousands, as many as he chooses to have, and there is no difference between them except differences of feminine loveliness and the blind chance which blesses some of them with children. And he makes no more account of one than he does of another. Not one of them feels it her duty to love her husband; it is enough if she be the slave of his desires. If the Padishah be troubled or sorrowful, there is none about him to whom he can open his heart. He may go from one end of the harem to the other, like one who wanders through a conservatory whose flowers are all so beautiful, so radiantly smiling; but in vain will he tell them of his grief and trouble, for they do not understand him, they do not trouble their heads about his thoughts; and if, perchance, he tells them that from all four corners of the world mighty foes are marching against Stambul, here and there, perchance, he may hear a sigh of longing from some captive maiden, who cannot conceal her secret joy at the thought of the happy hour when the hand of deliverance will thunder at the harem door and break its bolts and give freedom, beautiful sunbright freedom, to the captives.

It is slavish obsequiousness and nothing else which bends its knee before the Padishah; it is fear, not love, which obeys him. And to whom shall he turn when his heart is held fast in the iron grip of that numbing sensation which makes the mightiest feel they are but men—fear?

Mahmoud's sole joy was his nine-year-old son.

The child was brought up by his grandmother, the Sultana Valideh, herself scarce forty years of age. This dowager Sultana had civilized, European tastes. She had been educated in France; the young prince was passionately attached to her, and she inspired him with all those desires and noble instincts under whose influence, thirty years later, new life was to be poured into the decrepit Turkish Empire.

The Sultana Valideh wished to so educate her grandson that one day he might occupy a worthy position among the other rulers of Europe. She sowed betimes in his heart the seeds of high principles and enlightened tastes, and the Sultan would frequently listen to the wise sentences of his little lad, and, while rocking him on his knee, with a smile upon his face, his heart would beat in an agony of fear, "What if anybody got word of this?"

For the old Turkish party lay in wait for every word that fell from the Sultan's mouth, and the pointing of the little finger of one of Begtash's fakirs was more to be feared than the armed hand of the most valiant of the Greek heroes. If any one of the Ulemas should chance to discover that the young heir to the throne listened to any other bookish lore than what was contained within the covers of the Kuran, which comprised within itself (so they taught) all the wisdom of the world, they were capable of hounding on the Janissaries against the Seraglio, and slaying both sovereign and child.

The recollection of Achmed Sidi was still fresh in the memory of men. Sidi had been one of the Chief Ulemas, and the Imam of the Mosque of Sophia; and when, a few years ago, the warriors and the diplomatists of the Tsaritsa Catherine had won victory after victory over the Ottomans, not only on every battle-field, but also in every political arena, the unfortunate imam advised the Divan that, in view of the indisputable superiority of the Christians, it was necessary to teach the Turkish diplomatists the Bible, the inference being that just as the Moslem sages derived all their military science and all their administrative wisdom from the Kuran, so also the Christians must needs learn all these things from their Bible, thereby tacitly acknowledging the capacity of the Christians for appropriating all knowledge. But the well-meaning Ulema paid dearly for this good counsel. They banished him to the Isle of Chios, and there, for a very trivial offence, he was first degraded from his office (for it is not lawful to kill a Ulema with weapons), and then handed over to the pasha of the place, who pounded him to death in a stone mortar —a deterrent example for future reformers. Let them beware, therefore, of moving a single stone in the ancient fabric of the Ottoman constitution!

CHAPTER XII

THE SHIPWRECK OF LEONIDAS

Now, one fine day, when the worthy Leonidas Argyrocantharides set out from Smyrna on one of his prettiest ships, a vexatious little accident befell him by the way. The ship, which had taken in a cargo of tanned hides at Stambul, was overtaken, *en route*, by a tempest which drove her upon the coast of Seleucia. There, in the darkness of the night, she was thrown upon a sand-bank, from which she was unable to extricate herself till morning; and it was only when the land became visible in the early light of dawn that the merchant began to realize the awkward position into which his ship had got, despite Saint Procopius and Saint Demetrius, who were very beautifully painted on both sides of her prow. The vessel had heeled over on one side, and that side of her which lay above the waves was threatened every moment with destruction by the onset of the foaming surf which broke from time to time over the deck, making a pretty havoc of the masts and spars. The joints of the ship's timbers began to be loosened, creaking and shivering at each fresh shock of the waves. And if the fate of the ship on the sand-bank was sad enough, still sadder would it have been if she had broken loose therefrom; for right in front of her lay the rocks of the

Seleucian coast, whose steep crags were lashed so furiously by the raging sea that the crashing waves leaped fully a hundred fathoms up their sides. A nice place this would have been for any ship to play pitch-and-toss in!

The worthy merchant sorely lamented his fate, sorely lamented, also, his fine ship, which was painted in elaborate patterns with all the colors of the rainbow. He lamented his many beautiful goat-skins, not a single bundle of which he would allow to be cast into the sea for the purpose of lightening the ship; rather let them all go to the bottom together! He mourned over himself, too, condemned at the beginning of the best years of his life to be suffocated in the sea; but what he lamented far more than ship, goat-skins, or even life itself, were the two Circassian children, the precious, beautiful boy and girl, Thomar and Milieva, who were worth, at the current market prices of the day, ten thousand ducats apiece; Leonidas would have given his own skin for them any day!

Full of great hopes, he had embarked the two children at Stambul (the tanned hides were only a secondary consideration); and lo! now, just when he was reaching his goal, the curse of Kasi Mollah overtook him.

Two long-boats fully manned had made an attempt to reach the shore, in order that they might from thence haul the ship off the sand-bank, and both boats had been seized before his very eyes by the breakers, and dashed to pieces against the steep rocks; so there was nothing for it but to remain behind and perish on the sand-bank.

One wave after another drove the hulk deeper

and deeper down; those who still remained aboard wrung their hands and prayed or cursed, according as temperament or habit urged them.

As for Leonidas, he did both — he prayed and cursed at the same time; for it seemed quite clear to him that praying or cursing separately was of not the slightest use. The two children, meanwhile, holding each other tightly embraced, sat beside the broken stump of the mast and seemed to mock at the terrible tempest.

Not a sign of fear was visible on their faces. This roaring wind, these foam-churning waves, seemed to afford them a pleasant pastime. The black-and-white storm-birds sitting on the towering billows were swimming there all round the doomed ship, merrily flapping the water with their wings. Oh, those sea-swallows were having a fine time of it!

The two children had agreed between themselves, some time before, that if the ship went down, they would fling themselves into the water and swim ashore. That would be a mere trifle to them, of course.

Full of despair, the merchant rushed towards them, and embracing them with both his arms, he exclaimed, looking bitterly at the sky, "Merciful Heaven! ten thousand ducats!"

The children fancied that terror had made the merchant mad, and they tried to comfort him with kind words:

"Don't distress yourself, dear foster-father; we will not perish here, and we will not leave you to perish either. As soon as the ship goes down, we'll swim for the shore. We both of us know very well how to cleave the waves with our strong arms, and we will fasten you to our girdles and save you along with ourselves."

The merchant kissed the two dear children, and embraced them tenderly. An hour later the last planks of the fine ship broke away from each other, and the shipwrecked crew clung desperately to the floating spars that the waves tossed hither and thither. The greater part of the ship's company was ingulfed forthwith by the waves or dashed to pieces against the hard rocks; only three persons were saved—the merchant and the two children.

Leonidas, fast tied to their girdles, allowed himself to be cast among the waters. The first who rose on the crest of the foaming waves was Thomar. He perceived the rock on which a huge mountain of surf, rushing after him, threatened to dash him to pieces, and, watching his opportunity, grasped the long dangling roots of a tree which grew out of a cleft of the rocks and, with a tremendous effort, dragged all three of them up to it. The wave rolled right over them, burying them for an instant in deep water; but the next moment the surge rolled back again, and they were on the rocky coast.

The merchant was more dead than alive, so the children had to drag him with them for a long way inland, lest the returning surge should carry them back to sea again. They only ventured to rest when they had reached a rocky cavity where they could feel sure that they were safe. Even here the water, which shot up as high as a tower against the opposing rock, covered them every moment; but they did not feel its weight.

There they had to remain, crouching closely together, till the evening. Neither in front nor behind was there any place of refuge, and it was with a feeling of envy that they looked down upon the stormy petrels which towards evening began to sit down in long rows on the edge of the rocks, whither it was impossible for them to follow.

Gradually, however, the storm died away, the sea subsided and grew smooth, and the place where the shipwrecked group had taken refuge rose three ells above the surface of the water. Then they could venture to look around them. The whole shore was strewn with pieces of timber and mangled corpses. Wreckage and dead bodies were all that the sea had vomited forth of the rich cargo of the fine ship.

But the merchant did not despair. Making the two children kneel down beside him, he knelt down in their midst, and made them pray a prayer of gratitude to Heaven for their marvellous deliverance; and then, pressing them to his bosom, he sobbed, with the tears in his eyes, "What do I care, though my ship is lost and all my wares are submerged, so long as ye remain to me, my precious offspring? That is quite consolation enough for me."

And the worthy merchant told the truth, for as soon as ever he could reach Stambul he was sure of getting for these two children enough to enable him to buy two ships and twice as many wares as he had lost at the bottom of the sea.

But now the most difficult question arose—How were they to get away from that spot to any place inhabited by man? All ships gave this dangerous coast a wide berth; there was nothing to tempt them to the spot. Even fishermen did not venture as far in their barks, so that the unfortunate refugees who had escaped the waters saw starvation approaching them.

But suddenly, while they were meditating over the misery of their position, they fancied they heard human voices a little distance off — deep, manly voices, apparently engaged in a lively dispute.

The two children rejoiced, thinking that good men were hard by; but the merchant trembled, for, thought he, "What if they be robbers?"

Thomar now bade his sister remain with Leonidas while he went in the direction of the voices to discover who the speakers might be. The brave boy clambered from one cliff to another, made the circuit of the rock-chamber behind which they were sitting, and when he came to the opposite side of it a spacious empty cavern yawned blackly in front of him, half covered by whortleberry bushes. Probably the conversation came from thence, but neither near nor far was a human creature to be seen, nor were there any footprints of men on the ground; the front of the cavern was covered with thick green moss, on which footprints left no trace. Thomar shouted into the cave, and as not a word came back, he boldly entered, and slowly advanced forward. He went on and on as far as the light of the outside world extended, and then, as no one replied to his loud challenges, turned back again by the way he had come, and, making the circuit of the rock again, told the merchant that he had not come upon any human beings, but had only found a cavern which, at any rate, would make them good night quarters.

The conversation they thought they had heard must have been a delusion. Then they helped one another along the rocks and arrived at the mouth of the cavern.

Milieva had scarcely cast a glance into it when she exclaimed, full of joy: "Look, Thomar, here are two chests among the bushes!" And, indeed, there were two boxes made of boards, and Thomar wondered that he had not noticed them before. No doubt the sea had cast them up thither out of some ship that had been wrecked there before.

One of the boxes resembled those chests in which sailors keep their biscuits, but the shape of the other suggested that it was one of those hermetically sealed vessels used for holding good wines. Why should they not turn them to some account?

They were not long in forcing them open, and what was their astonishment when they perceived that the biscuits in the first box were not even mouldy, but quite dry and sound, as if they had only been brought thither quite recently; while in the second box not one of the scores of flasks there displayed was broken or cracked, but lay neatly stored away in layers of straw?

The refugees did not greatly concern themselves with the question, Who put these boxes here? and why? Nobody who, after being tossed about on the sea for three days with nothing to eat or drink all the time, and is then unexpectedly confronted with rich stores of bread and wine—nobody, I am sure, under such circumstances would think of consulting the Kuran as to whether a conscientious

Mussulman should eat and drink such things, but would fall to at once, and thank Allah for the chance.

The children forgot, in the twinkling of an eye, the dangers to which they had been exposed, and, after the first glass or two of wine, overcome by fatigue, lay down on the soft bed which Nature had made ready for them with her most fragrant moss. Leonidas, however, remained sitting where he was, considering it his bounden duty to taste all the wines which were here offered to him gratis, one after the other; in consequence whereof, when he *did* lie down at last, he chose a position in which his head was very low down while his feet were high in the air, and so they all three slumbered peacefully together.

Then the voices of men were heard once more far off in the cavern, and not long afterwards there emerged from its black mouth six gray-haired, pale-faced human beings. He who came first was the eldest. His white beard reached to his girdle, his mouth was hidden by his mustache, and his eyes were covered by his white eyebrows.

These men were fakirs of the Omarite Order, whose rule obliges them to endure the most terrible of all renunciations—abstention from all enjoyment of the light of day. Plunging themselves into eternal darkness for the glory of Allah, they make of life a long midnight, and the sun never beholds them on the face of the earth.

The night was well advanced when the six Omarites came forth to the sleepers, and while five of the fakirs stood round them in silence, the sixth—the one with the long flowing beard—bent over the children and examined their features attentively in the darkness of the night, which was only mitigated by the light of a few faint stars half hidden among errant clouds. At last he whispered to his comrades, "It is they." Then, turning the tips of his thumbs downwards, he laid them softly on Thomar's head. All five fakirs listened with rapt attention. The bosom of the sleeping lad began to heave tumultuously; he clinched his fists; his face grew hot; his lips swelled. The old man then seemed to breathe upon his forehead, as if he would whisper something, whereupon the sleeping lad exclaimed, in a strong, audible voice, "With swords, with guns, with arms!"

The old men shook their heads, showing thereby that they approved of his words.

Then the eldest old man bent over the other child and made passes over her face with his five fingers. The maiden's bosom expanded visibly, and when the old man stooped over and breathed upon her she cried out in an energetic, dictatorial manner, "Down on your knees before me!"

At this the Omarites all whispered together, and two of them lifting the lad, two the girl, and two the merchant, they carried them on their shoulders into the depths of the cavern.

The mouth of this cavern was the already mentioned tunnel whose farthest exit debouched upon the valley of Seleucia, half a league from the sea—that waste, barren, and savage valley.

The Omarites moved to and fro in the black cave without a torch, like the blind, who do not go astray in the turnings and windings of the streets, although they see them not. The sleepers had drunk a magic potion, which did not permit them to awake for some time, and the men carried them on their shoulders to the opposite entrance of the cavern and there laid them down on the moss, in a place where the sunlight was wont to penetrate.

It was already late in the day when the two children awoke. As soon as they had opened their eyes, their first care was to kiss and embrace each other. Then they aroused the merchant also and, rubbing sleep out of their eyes, began to tell him, in childish fashion, what they had been dreaming about.

"Ah! what a lovely dream I had!" cried Thomar, and even now his eyes sparkled. "I was standing beside the Sultan, who was leaning on my shoulder. Before me and around me howled a rebellious multitude, and the Sultan was pale and sad. Turning towards me he sighed, 'Wherewith shall I appease this raging sea?' For a long time I could find no answer. It was as if something were weighing me down, something as heavy as a mountain, when suddenly the words escaped from my lips, 'With swords, with guns, with weapons!' And then the Padishah girded his own sword upon me, and I rushed among the howling mob, and I cut and hacked away at them till they were all consumed, and at last a field that had been reaped lay before me, and it was covered with nothing but corpses."

"That is a foolish dream," said Leonidas. "Why did you eat so much last night?"

And now Milieva told her dream.

"I also must have been confused by the wine. Before me also a rebellious multitude appeared, and it then seemed to me as if I was not a girl but a boy. Furiously they rushed upon me from every side, but I feared them not, and when they were quite near to me I cried out to them, 'Down on your knees before me! I am the Sultan's daughter!' And everything was instantly quiet."

The merchant laughed till he choked at this dream. Who but children could dream such rubbish?

"But at home they used to say," observed Thomar, with a grave face, "that whatever any one dreams in a strange place where he has never slept before, he will see that dream accomplished."

"Well, I am much obliged to you," said the merchant, "for in my dream I was hanging up in Salonika by my feet, with my head downwards."

Then the merchant made the children leave the cavern.

"Come, my children," said he, "let us see if the sea has calmed down, and whether a ship is approaching from anywhere."

Thomar obeyed, quitted the cavern, and exclaimed, in astonishment:

"Look, my dear foster-father! How could a ship come here when the very sea has vanished, and only the bottom of it remains."

And indeed the district stretching out before them was quite bare and barren enough to be taken for the bottom of the sea.

Leonidas took the lad's words for a joke, and it was a joke he did not relish.

"Keep your witticisms for another time, my son," said he, "and rub your eyes that they may see the better."

But Milieva leaped after Thomar, and when she

had got up to him she clapped her hands together, and exclaimed, with naïve amazement:

"Why, the sea has run away from us!"

And now the merchant himself arose from his place, went out of the cavern, and could scarce believe his eyes when he saw before him the savage, rocky region, where not a drop of moisture could be seen, to say nothing of the sea!

"God has worked wonders for us," sighed the merchant. "It is plain that we are in quite a different place from that wherein we went to sleep."

"No doubt the peris of the mountains of Kâf have conveyed us hither," said Milieva.

"Peris, no doubt," observed Leonidas, absently, groping for his long reticule, and feeling whether his diamonds were still there. If it were not peris, they would certainly have searched him for his diamonds.

And now they had to find out where they were, and what was the best way to get out of the wilderness. The greatest anxiety had disappeared; they had no longer anything to fear from the sea. On dry land it would be much easier to find a place of refuge.

After a little searching they came upon footprints in the sand, and these footprints led them to the mouth of the valley. Whole forests of the large cochineal cactus grew among the rocks, and here and there they saw a light-footed kid grazing on the dry sward. Not very long afterwards they fell in with the goatherd. Leonidas was rather alarmed than delighted at the sight of the grim muscular figure, who, on perceiving them, came straight towards them, and addressed them in a gruff voice.

"Are ye those shipwrecked fugitives who slept at night in the Cavern of the *dzhin?*"

"*Dzhin!*" said Leonidas to himself. "Methinks it must have been a spirit of evil, then."

The children answered the goatherd boldly, and begged him to direct them to some inhabited region.

"Go straight along this gorge," said he; "you cannot mistake the path. On your right hand you will find a hut where dwells a fakir of the Erdbuhar Order, who will direct you farther. Salám alek!" And with that the goatherd quitted them, to the great amazement of Leonidas, who had expected nothing less of him than highway robbery.

Towards evening they had arrived at the hut of the Erdbuhar hermit.

"I have been expecting you," said the dervish, when they came up to him. "Have you not suffered shipwreck and slept all night with the *dzhin?*"

Evidently one marvel after another was in store for them.

The dervish gave them meat and drink, and washed their feet, and after they had enjoyed his hospitality he offered to conduct them all the way to the gates of Seleucia. The merchant would very much have liked to know something of his wondrous deliverers, but as the dervish answered all his questions with quotations from the Kuran, he learned very little that was definite from that holy man.

When Seleucia came in sight, the merchant began thanking the dervish for his good offices. "Do not weary thyself any further, worthy Mussulman," cried he; "I know not how to reward thy labors, but Allah will requite thee. I am a beggar. Thou dost see that I am as bare as one of my fingers. The ocean hath swallowed up my all."

And all the while his reticule was full of precious stones; but he would have considered it a very great act of folly not to have made capital out of his wretchedness, and paid the dervish with fine words.

But the dervish would not even accept his thanks. "It is but my duty," said he, "and I did it not for thy sake, but for the sake of others." And with that he quitted them, after giving a string of praying-beads to each of the children.

The children went on in front till they reached the gate of the city, talking in a low voice together; but when they found themselves in the populous streets they took Leonidas by the hand, and Thomar said, "All that was thine has been lost in the sea, and who will help us in the great strange city, where nobody knows us? Let us therefore sing in the market-place and before the houses of the great men, and they will give us money, and so we shall be able to go on farther."

The merchant was greatly affected by this naïve offer, and allowed the children to sing in the market-place and in the porch of the pasha's house, and in this way they gained enough money to enable them to go on to the next city.

Thus, at last, they got back to Smyrna. If they had been his own children Argyrocantharides could not have looked for greater and heartier affection from them. They fasted that he might feast, they shivered that he might be warmly clad, they denied themselves sleep that he might slumber all the more tranquilly, and lowered themselves to singing in the market-place that he might not be compelled to beg at the corners of the streets.

Good children! sweet children!

As soon as the merchant could get a new ship he took them with him to Stambul, and this time no misfortune happened to them by the way.

At Stambul he exhibited them to the Kizlar-Agasi, who, after examining their limbs and satisfying himself as to their capabilities, bought the pair of them from the merchant at his own price —the youth for the Sultan's corps of pages, the girl for the harem.

To the honor of the worthy merchant, however, it must be said that when he did hand the children over he sobbed bitterly. Good, worthy man!

CHAPTER XIII

A BALL IN THE SERAGLIO

It was the birthday of the Sultana Valideh. The Sultana, Mahmoud's mother, was, we may remember, a Frenchwoman, whose parents, natives of the Isle of Martinique, had sent her to Paris while still very young, and placed her, till she was sixteen, in a convent to be educated. Then the family sent word that she was to return to the beautiful island on the farther side of Africa; but during the voyage a tempest destroyed the ship, and the crew had to take to the boats. One of these boats, in which was the pretty French girl, was captured by Barbary corsairs, who sold her to the Sultan. The rest we know, of course—

"Elle eut beau dire : Je me meurs!
De nonne elle devient Sultane!"

Those poor flowers that are brought together from all the corners of the earth to stock the Grand Signior's harem, and who know nothing except how to love, paled before the radiant loveliness and the sparkling wit of this damsel, who had been brought up in the midst of European culture. She became the favorite wife of Selim, she bore him Mahmoud, and her son loved his mother much better than all his damsels put together.

A great surprise had been prepared for the Sultana Valideh. The Sultan had arranged the whole thing himself in secret. He was going to give a dance, after the European fashion, in the Seraglio.

Tailors were brought from Vienna who set to work upon dresses in the latest fashion for the odalisks; the eunuchs were taught the latest waltz music, a minuet, and two French square dances; and the girls were all taught how to dance these dances. The men who had admittance into the harem, the Kizlar-Agasi, the Anaktar Bey, the heir to the throne (Abdul Mejid), and the Sultan himself, wore brown European dress-suits, so that when the Sultana stepped into the magnificently illuminated porcelain chamber she stood rooted to the floor with astonishment. She imagined herself to be at a court ball at Paris, just as she had seen it at the Louvre when a child. A surging mob of hundreds and hundreds of young odalisks was proudly strutting to and fro in stylish dresses of the latest fashion, in long gloves and silk stockings. Instead of turbans, plumed hats and bouquets adorned the magnificent masses of their curled and frizzled locks. They moved about with bare shoulders and bosoms, in soft wavy dresses, with fans painted over with butterflies, freely laughing and jesting in this, to them, newest of worlds, and the only thing that differentiated this ball from our dancing entertainments was the absence of the darker portion of the show—the masculine element.

There were only four representatives of this *sombre nuance*—to wit, the Sultan, the heir to the throne, the Kizlar-Agasi, and the Anaktar Bey. Of these four, two were no longer and two were not yet men. All four were dressed in stiff Hungarian dolmans, long black pantaloons, and red fezes. The Sultan, with his thick-set figure, would have passed very well for a substantial Hungarian deputy-lord-lieutenant, with his tight-fitting, bulging dolman buttoned right up to his chin. The young prince's elegant figure, on the other hand, was brought into strong relief by his well-made suit; his hair was nicely curled on both sides, and his genteel white shirt was visible beneath his open dolman. The Kizlar-Agasi, on the contrary, cut a very amusing figure in his unwonted garb. He was constantly endeavoring to thrust his hand into his girdle, and only thus perceived that he had none, and he kept on holding down the tails of his coat, as if he felt ashamed that they might not reach low enough to cover him decently.

The Sultana Valideh was favorably surprised. The spectacle brought back to her her childish years, and she gratefully pressed her son to her bosom for this delicate attention, while he respectfully kissed his mother's hands. The Sultan scattered his love among a great many women, but his mother alone could boast of possessing his respect.

The odalisks surrounded the good Sultan, rejoicing and caressing him. He was never severe to any of them—nay, rather, he was the champion, the defender of them all, and those whom he loved might be quite sure that his affection would be constant.

Every one tried to please the Sultana Valideh by showing her their new garments, but none of them found such favor in her eyes as the new flower, which had only recently been introduced into the

Seraglio, and was now the foremost of them all, the beautiful Circassian damsel. Her light step, the dove-like droop of her neck, the charm of her full, round shoulders, and her lovely young bosom, were such that one was almost tempted to believe that she had been carried off bodily from some Parisian salon, where they know so well how to take the utmost advantage of all the resources of fashion. Her locks were dressed up *à la Vallière*, with negligently falling curls which gave a slightly masculine expression to her face—an additional charm in the eyes of a connoisseur. Yes, the Greek merchant was right; there was no spot on the earth worth anything except the place where Milieva lived and moved.

The Valideh kissed the odalisk on the forehead, and led her by the hand to the Sultan, who would not permit her to kiss his hand (who ever heard of a lady kissing the hand of a gentleman in evening dress?), but permitted the young heir to the throne to take Milieva on his arm and conduct her through the room. What a pretty pair of children they made! Abdul Mejid at this time was scarce twelve years of age, the girl perhaps was fourteen; but for the difference of their clothes, nobody could have said which was the boy and which the girl.

And now the tones of the hidden orchestra began to be heard, and a fresh surprise awaited the Sultana. She heard once more the pianoforte melodies which she had known long ago, and the height of her amazement was reached when the Sultan invited her to dance—a minuet.

What an absurd idea! The Sultana dowager to dance a minuet with her son, the Sultan, before all those laughing odalisks, who had never beheld such a thing before? Where was the second couple? Why here—the prince and Milieva, of course. They take their places opposite the imperial couple, and to slow, dreamy music, with great dignity they dance together the courteous and melancholy dance, bowing and courtesying to each other with as much majesty and *aplomb* as was ever displayed by the powdered cavaliers and beauty-plastered goddesses of the age of the *Œil de Bœuf*.

Never had such a spectacle been seen in the Seraglio.

The Sultana herself was amazed at the triumphant dexterity which Milieva displayed in the dance; she was a consummate maid of honor, with that princely smile for which Gabrielle D'Estrées was once so famous. The good Mahmoud so lost himself in the contemplation of the eyes of Milieva, his *vis-à-vis*, that towards the end of the dance he quite forgot his own part in it, folding Milieva to his breast in defiance of all rule and ceremony, and even kissing her face twice or thrice, although he ought not to have gone beyond kissing her hand—nay, he ought not to have kissed her hand at all, but the hand of his partner, the Sultana Valideh.

When the minuet was over the eunuch musicians played a waltz in which all the odalisks took part, clinging to one another in couples, and thus they danced the pretty *trois pas* dance, for the *deux pas* revolution was the invention of a later and more progressive age. Louder than the music was the joyous uproar of the dancers themselves. Here and there some of them tumbled on the slippery floor to which they were not accustomed, and the nymphs coming after them fell around them in heaps. Some disliked the dance or were weary, but their firier and more robust partners dragged them along, willy-nilly. The old Kizlar-Agasi and the bey stood in the midst of them to take care that no scandal took place. Suddenly the madcap odalisk army surrounded them, clung on to them in twos and threes, dragged them into the mad waltz, and twisted them round and round at a galloping pace, till the two good old gentlemen had no more breath left in them.

The Sultan and the Valideh, with the prince and Milieva, were sitting on a raised daïs, laughing and looking on at the merry spectacle. The pipers piped more briskly, the drummers drummed more furiously, the cymbals clashed more loudly than ever, while the odalisks dragged their prey about uproariously.

Ah! Listen! What didst thou hear, good Sultan? What noise is that outside which mingles with the hubbub within? Outside there also is to be heard the roll of drums, the flourish of trumpets, and the shouts of men.

Nonsense! 'Tis but imagination. Bring hither the glasses—not those tiny cups of sherbet, for this is the birthday of the Valideh. We will be Europeans to-night. Bring hither wine and glasses for a toast!

The Sultan had a particular fondness for Tokay and champagne, and the ambassadors of both these great Powers had the greatest influence with him.

The odalisks also had to be made to taste these wines; and after that the dance proceeded more merrily, and the boisterous music and singing grew madder and madder.

What was that?

The Sultan grew attentive. What uproar is that outside the Seraglio? What light is that which shines at the top of the round windows?

That uproar is no beating of drums; those shouts are not the shouts of revellers; that din is not the beating of cymbals; no, 'tis the clashing of swords, the thundering of cannons, the tumult of a siege, and that light is not the light of bonfires but of blazing rafters!

Up, up, Mahmoud, from thy sofa! Away with thy glass and out with thy sword! This is no night for revelry; death is abroad; insurrection is at thy very gate! They are besieging the Seraglio!

Twelve thousand Janissaries, joined with the rabble of Stambul, are attacking the gates at the very time when the orchestra is playing its liveliest airs in the illuminated hall.

"Do ye hear that?" exclaimed Kara Makan, the most famous orator of the Janissaries, who with his own hand had hung up the Metropolitan of Constantinople on the very threshold of the palace. "Do ye hear that music? Here they are rejoicing when the whole empire around them is in mourning. Do ye know what are the latest tidings this night? The Suliotes have captured Gaskho Bey, and annihilated our army before Janina. A woman has blown up the ship of the Kapudan Pasha, and the Shah has fallen upon Kermandzhan with an army! Destruction is drawing near to us, and treachery dwells in the Seraglio. Hearken! They dance, they sing, they bathe their lips in wine, and their blasphemies bring upon us the scourge of Allah! We shed our tears and our blood, and they make merry and mock at us! Shall not they also weep? Shall not their blood also be shed? So fare it with them as it has fared with our brethren whom they sent to the shambles!"

The furious mob answered these seditious words with an indescribable bellowing.

"If we traversed the whole empire we should not find a worse spot than this place."

"Set fire to the Seraglio!" cried one voice suddenly, and the others took up the cry.

"And if you escape from all other enemies, would you fall into the claws of the worst enemies of all?"

"Death to the Viziers! Death to the lords of the palace!" thundered the people; and one voice close to Kara Makan, rising above the others, exclaimed, "Death to the Sultan!"

Kara Makan turned in that direction and defended his master. "Hurt not the Sultan! The life of the Sultan is sacred. He and his children are the last survivors of the blood of Omar; and although he be not worthy to sit on the throne which the heroic Muhammad erected for his descendants, yet he is the last of his race, and, therefore, the head of the Sultan is sacred. But death upon the head of the Reis-Effendi, death to the Kizlar-Agasi and the Kapudan Pasha! They are the cause of our desolation. The chiefs of the Giaours pay them to destroy their country. Tear all these up by the roots, and if there be any children of their family, destroy them also, even to the very babes and sucklings, that the memory of them may perish utterly!"

The mob thundered angrily at the gates of the Seraglio, which were shut and fastened with chains. The Janissaries blew the horns of revolt, the drums rolled, and within there the Sultan was reposing his head on the bosom of a beautiful girl. Suddenly a loud report shook the whole Seraglio. An audacious ichoglan had fired his gun upon the mob as it rushed to attack the water-gate.

The Sultan, in dismay, quitted the harem, and hastened to the middle gate in order to address the mob. On his way through the corridor, his servants and his ministers threw themselves at his feet and implored him not to show himself to the people. Mahmoud did not listen to them. In the confusion of the moment, moreover, it never occurred to him that he was wearing a Frankish costume, which the people hated and execrated.

When he appeared on the balcony the light of the torches fell full upon him, and the Janissaries recognized him. Every one at once pointed their fingers at him, and immediately an angry and scornful howl arose.

"Look! that is the Sultan! Behold the Caliph—the Caliph, the Padishah of the Moslems—in the garb of the Giaours! That is Mahmoud, the ally of our enemies!"

The Sultan shrank before this furious uproar of the mob, and, involuntarily falling back, stammered, pale as death:

"With what shall we allay this tempest?"

His servants, with quivering lips, stood around him. At that moment they neither feared nor respected their master.

Suddenly a bold young ichoglan rushed towards

the Sultan, and answered his question in a courageous and confident voice:

"With swords, with guns, with weapons!"

It was Thomar.

The Sultan scrutinized the youth from head to foot, amazed at his audacity; then hastening back to his dressing-chamber, exchanged his ball dress for his royal robes, and, coming back from the inner apartments, descended into the court-yard.

The guns were already pointed at the gates, the topijis stood beside them, match in hand, impatiently awaiting the order to fire.

When the Sultan appeared in the court-yard he was at once surrounded by some hundreds of the ichoglanler, determined to defend him to the last drop of their blood. Mahmoud again recognized Thomar among them; he appeared to be the leading spirit of the band.

The Sultan beckoned to them to put back their swords in their sheaths. He commanded the topijis to extinguish their matches. Next he ordered that the gate of the Seraglio should be thrown open to the people. Then, having bidden every one to stand aside, he went alone towards the gate in his imperial robes, with a majestic bearing.

No sooner was the gate thrown open than the mob streamed into the court-yard with torches and flashing weapons in their hands, standing for a moment dumb with astonishment at the appearance of the Sultan. He was no longer ridiculous, as he had been in that foreign garb. The majestic bearing of the prince stilled the tumult for an instant, but for an instant only. The following moment a hand was extended from among the mob of rebels which tore the Sultan's caftan from his shoulder.

Mahmoud grew pale at this audacity, and this pallor was a fresh occasion of danger to him, for now he was suddenly seized from all sides. The Sultan turned, therefore, and perceiving Thomar, called to him, "Defend my harem!" and, at the same time freeing his sword-arm, he drew his sword, waved it above his hand, and, while his foes were waiting to see on whom the blow would fall, he threw the sword to Thomar, exclaiming, "Defend my son!"

The young ichoglan grasped Mahmoud's sword, and, while the captured Sultan disappeared in the mazes of the mob, he and his comrades returned to the inner court-yard, and, barricading the door, fiercely defended the position against the insurgents. He had now to show himself worthy of that sword, the sword of the Sultan.

Gradually two thousand ichoglanler and three thousand bostanjis gathered round the young hero. The Janissaries already lay in heaps before the door, which they riddled with bullets till it looked like a corn-sifter. But the youths of the Seraglio repelled every onset.

And why did not the Sultan remain with them? They would have defended him against all the world. Who knew now what had become of him? Perhaps they had killed him outright.

The Janissaries speedily perceived that they could not have done anything worse for themselves than to have brought torches with them, for thereby they were distinctly visible to the defenders of the Seraglio, and every shot that came from thence told.

"Put out the torches!" shouted Kara Makan, who was holding a huge concave buckler in front of him, and felt a third bullet pierce through the twofold layers of buffalo-hide and graze his body.

The torches went out one after another, whereupon the spacious court-yard was darkened; only the flash of firearms cast an occasional gleam of light upon the struggling mass.

It might have been two hours after midnight when suddenly there was a cessation of hostilities. Both sides were weary, and ceased firing; the Janissaries whispered amongst themselves, and at last, in the midst of a deep silence, Kara Makan's thunderous voice made itself heard:

"Listen, all of ye who are inside the Seraglio. Ye are good warriors, and we are good warriors also, and it is folly for the Faithful to destroy one another. We did not take up arms to slay you and plunder the Seraglio, neither do we wish to kill the Padishah nor the heir to the throne; but we would rescue them from the hands of the traitors who surround them, and we would also deliver the realm from faithless Viziers and counsellors. Give us, therefore, the prince, the Sultan's son. Of a truth no harm shall befall him, and we will thereupon quit the court-yard of the Seraglio and trouble nobody within these doors. If, however, you will not grant our request, then Allah be merciful to all who are within these beleaguered walls."

The Kizlar-Agasi conveyed this message into the Seraglio, and besiegers and besieged awaited with rapt attention the reply of the Valideh; for the decision lay with her—she was superior in rank to all four of the Asseki sultanas.

After the lapse of a quarter of an hour the Kizlar-Agasi returned, and signified to the besiegers that the prince would be handed over to them.

The Janissaries received this message with a howl of triumph, while the ichoglanler shrugged their shoulders.

"They are not all women in there for nothing," said Thomar, savagely, to the Kizlar-Agasi, and he remained standing in the gate, that he might, at any rate, kiss the young prince's hand and whisper to him not to go.

The Janissaries relit their torches and crowded towards the gate. Inside reigned a pitch-black darkness.

Not long afterwards footsteps were audible in the dark corridor, and, escorted by two torch-bearers, the prince descended the steps. He had on the same garment which he wore when he went on horseback to the Mosque of Sophia during the Feast of Bairam. How the people had then huzzahed before him! He wore pantaloons of rose-colored silk, yellow buskins with slender heels, a green caftan embroidered with gold flowers, and a handsome yellow silk vest buttoned up to his chin. His ribbons and buttons were made so as to represent brilliant fluttering butterflies incrusted with precious stones.

On reaching the gate he beckoned to the torch-bearers to stand still, sent back the Kizlar-Agasi, and, proceeding all alone to the gate, commanded that it should be flung open.

While this was being done Thomar pressed close up to him, and seizing the prince's hand, kissed it, at the same time whispering in his ear, "Go not; we will defend you if you remain here."

15

The prince pressed Thomar's hand and whispered back, "I must go; you keep on defending the Seraglio!" And with that he embraced the youth and kissed him twice with great fervor.

Thomar was somewhat startled by this burning, affectionate kiss, and wondered what it meant. The darkness did not allow him to distinguish the prince's features; and when he tried to detain him once more the prince hastily disengaged himself and stepped forth from under the dark vault among the Janissaries.

Thomar covered his eyes with his hands; he did not want to see the fate of the prince at that moment. It was quite possible that the bloodthirsty might cut him down on the spot in a sudden access of fury.

The prince stepped forth among the rebels.

At that moment a cry of unbridled joy, triumph, and blood-thirstiness burst from the Janissaries. It needed but one of them to raise his hand, and the next would speedily have completed the bloodiest deed of all.

But the prince stood before them haughtily and valiantly, and, with amazing audacity, cried to them, "Down on your knees before me, ye rebels!"

At these words Thomar, with a start of terror, looked at the prince. The full light of the torches fell upon his charming face. It was not Abdul Mejid, but — Milieva! They had dressed her inside the harem in garments suitable to the Feast of Bairam, and she had come out instead of the prince, courageously, as if she had been born to it. Who was likely to notice the change? The heart of this odalisk loved to play a manly part, and it was not merely the masculine garb she wore which transformed her, but the masculine soul within her.

The Janissaries, moreover, were dumfounded by this bold attitude. This graceful, noble figure stood face to face with them and domineered the mob with a commanding look, proudly, majestically, as became a born ruler. And yet death hovered over the head of him who dared to say, "I am the prince!"

Thomar, forgetting himself, seized his sword, and would have rushed to the defence of his sister but his comrades held him back. "What would you do, unhappy wretch? Trust to Fate!"

Kara Makan, in savage defiance, approached the false prince with a drawn sword in his hand.

"On your knees before me!" cried the odalisk, and indicating where he should kneel with an imperious gesture, she looked steadily into the eyes of the savage warrior.

The ferocious figure stood hesitatingly before her. The magic of her look held the wild beast in him spellbound for an instant. His bloodshot eyes slowly drooped, his hand, with its flashing sword, sank down by his side, his knees gave way beneath him, and, falling down at the feet of the young child, he submissively murmured a salaam, kissing her hand and laying his bloody sword at her feet.

Milieva pressed her right hand on the head of the subdued rebel, looked proudly and fearlessly upon the dumb-stricken rebels, and then, raising the sword and giving it back to Kara Makan, she cried, "Go before and open a way for me!"

As if in obedience to a magic word, the crowd

parted on both sides before her, and Kara Makan, with his sword over his shoulder, led the way along. The crowd, with an involuntary homage, made way for her everywhere from the Seraglio to the Seven Towers, and two torch-bearers walked by her side, between whom she marched as proudly as if she were making her triumphal progress. Nobody perceived the deception. The resemblance of the young face to that of the prince, the well-known festal raiment of the Feast of Bairam, her manly bearing, all combined to keep up the delusion, and amongst this *canaille* which held her in its power there was not a single dignitary who knew the prince intimately and might have detected the fraud.

The Sultan had just been thrust into the dungeon of the Seven Towers, that place of dismal memories for the Sultans and their families in general. In that octagonal chamber, whose round windows overlooked the sea, more than one mortal sigh had escaped from the lips of the descendants of Omar, whom a powerful faction or a triumphant rival had, sooner or later, condemned to death.

It was now morning, the uproar of the rebellion had died away outside, the Seraglio was no longer besieged. It was now that Kara Makan appeared before the Sultan.

The Padishah was sitting on the ground—on the bare ground. His royal robes were still upon him, a diamond aigrette sparkled in the turban of the Caliph, and there he sat upon the ground, and never took his eyes off it.

"Your majesty!" cried Kara Makan, addressing him.

The Padishah, as if he had not heard, looked apathetically in front of him, and not a muscle of his face changed.

"Sire, I stand before thee to speak to thee in the name of the Moslem people."

He might just as well have been speaking to a marble statue.

"Every storm proceeds from Allah, sire, and nothing which Allah does is done without cause. When the lightnings are scattered abroad from the hands of the angel Adramelech, is not the air beneath them heavy with curses? and when the living earth quakes beneath the towns that are upon it, shall not innocently spilled blood shake it still more? So also the Moslem people rising in rebellion is the instrument of Allah, and Allah knoweth the causes thereof. I will guard my tongue against telling these causes to thee; thou knowest them right well already, nor is it for me to reprove the anointed successor of the Prophet. But I beg thee, sire, to promise me and the people, in the name of Allah, that thou wilt do what it beseemeth the ruler of the Ottoman nation to do—promise to remedy our wrongs, and we will set thee again upon thy throne."

At these words Mahmoud fixed his eyes upon the speaker, and gazed long upon those dark features, as sinister as an eclipse of the sun. Then he arose, turned away, and replied in a low voice, hissing with contempt:

"The Sultan owes no reply to his servants."

Kara Makan's face was convulsed at these words. Scarce was he able to stifle his wrath, and he replied, in broken sentences:

"Sire, the lion is the king of the desert—but if he is in a cage—he listens to the voice of his keeper—thou knowest this hand, which hath fought for thee in many engagements—and thou knowest that whatever this hand seizeth it seizeth with a grasp of iron."

The Sultan pondered long. Then all at once he seemed to bethink him of something, for his face seemed to lose its severity, and he turned towards the Janissary leader with a mild, indulgent look.

"What, then, dost thou require?" This softened look concealed the genesis of the thought—the Janissaries must be wiped off the face of the earth. "What dost thou require?" said the Padishah, softly.

Kara Makan put on an important look, as of one who knows that the fate of empires is in his hands.

"Hearken to our desires. We are honest Mussulmans. We do not ask impossibilities. If thou canst convince us that our demands are unlawful, we renounce them; if thou canst not convince us, accomplish them."

Mahmoud's lips wore a bitter smile at this wise speech.

"I do not strive with you," he replied. "Ye command me. The Caliph of caliphs listens to his servants. Bring hither parchment and an inkhorn, and dictate to my pen what ye demand. The Sultan will be your scribe, great rebel!"

Kara Makan was not bright enough to penetrate the irony of these words; nay, rather, he felt himself flattered by the humility of the Sultan's speech. With haughty self-assurance he bared his bosom and drew forth a large roll of manuscript.

"I will save your majesty the trouble," said he to Mahmoud, smoothing out the document before him. "Behold, it is all ready. Thou hast only to write thy name beneath it."

"Will ye allow me to read it?" inquired the Sultan, with the same bitter smile; "or is it the wish of the people that I should sign it unread?"

"As your majesty pleases."

Mahmoud took up the documents one after another, and piled them up beside him as he read them.

"Ah! the appointment of a new seraskier! I will read no further. I agree, but I would know his name. Is he whom you desire fit for the post?"

"We want Kurshid," explained Kara Makan, perceiving that the Sultan had not read the document.

"And the Janissaries demand other rewards for themselves. 'Tis only natural: I grant them. They cannot be expected to storm the Seraglio for nothing. The chief treasurer will pay you whatever you require. This third article, too, I see, demands the capture of Janina. Be it so. I grant it. Most probably the whole Janissary host will want to go against Ali Pasha."

"So long as thou art at their head," said Kara Makan, somewhat disturbed. "The Janissaries are only bound to fight under the direct command of the Sultan."

"And all these other demands are equally reasonable, eh?" said the Sultan, just glancing at one or two of them.

He took up the last one, but when he had unfolded it his face darkened, and he suddenly leaped to his feet, his good-natured apathy changed into wrath and fierceness, and, striking the open document with his fist, he exclaimed, with an access of emotion:

"What's this? Are ye so bold as to expect me to sign this paper?"

Kara Makan was so well prepared for this outburst of anger on the Sultan's part that he was not in the least taken aback. With rustic stolidity he replied:

"We wish it, and we demand it."

"Do you know what is written in this document?"

"Yes; that thou must free the realm from foreigners; that thou must put the Russian ambassador Stroganov on board ship and send him home; refuse to admit French and English ships into the Bejkoz; send the Sultana Valideh far away to Damascus; and slay the Grand Vizier, the Kizlar-Aga, the Berber Pasha, and the Kapudan Pasha, and give their bodies to the people."

The Grand Signior contemptuously threw the document to the floor and trampled it beneath his feet.

"Shameless filibusterers," he cried; "not blood but money is what you want. Ye want permission not to deliver the realm, but to plunder it. And you expect the Padishah to sanction it! Did not you yourselves raise the Viziers to power? Were not you the cause of their not being able to make any use of that power? Whenever the arms of the Giaours were triumphant, were you not always the first to fly from the field of battle? And when the realm was sinking, were you not always the last to hasten to its assistance? You are no descendants, but the mere shadows of those glorious Janissaries whose names are written with letters of blood in the annals of foreign nations; but ye make but a poor and wretched figure therein. Kill me, then! I shall not be the first Sultan whom the Janissaries have murdered, but, in Allah's name I say it, I shall be the last. After me, either nobody will sit on the throne of Omar, or, if any one sits there, he will be your ruin."

The opposition of his august captive only restored the Janissary leader to his proper element. He felt much more at home with those wrathful eyes than with the previous contemptuous nonchalance. He could now give back like for like.

He picked up the crumpled document, in which were written the death-sentences of the Viziers, and, brushing off the dust, again presented it to the Sultan.

"Either sign this document or descend from the throne of the family of Omar, and we will seek us out from among the descendants of the Prophet another who shall reign in thy stead."

"Most abject of slaves! In thy pride thou knowest not what thou sayest! Death comes from Allah and none can avoid it; but who amongst the descendants of Omar would be powerful enough to seize the royal sceptre, and who would be senseless enough to desire it?"

"Look at me."

"I am looking. The sun does not soil itself by shining upon a swamp, and therefore I may look even at thee; but I see nothing in thee that would justify the adorning of thy head with a diadem so long as one of the descendants of Sulaiman the Magnificent is alive."

"Another word and thou shalt cease to live!" cried the desperado, haughtily throwing back his head before the Sultan. "Art thou aware that thy son Abdul Mejid is in our hands?"

The Sultan shuddered. His consternation at these words was written in every feature.

"My son, Abdul Mejid? Impossible!"

"So it is. The Sultana Valideh gave him up at our request."

"Oh, madness!" exclaimed the Sultan; and he began pacing to and fro.

Abdul Mejid was still a mere child. The shock of such a rebellion might easily make an epileptic of him. To deliver him into the hands of these rebels was as good as to sign his death-warrant. Even if they did not kill him outright, his nerves might suffer from their violence, and he might perish, as the two and twenty other children of Sultan Mahmoud had perished, every one of whom had died of epilepsy. Their delicate nervous constitutions had been shattered in their youth under the influence of that perpetual terror to which the children of the Caliph of caliphs had been exposed from time immemorial. What, then, might not happen to Abdul Mejid if he fell into the hands of this savage mob?

"Oh, ye are hell's own children! Ye are worse than the Giaours, worse than the Greeks, worse than the Muscovites! Ye do place your feet on the heads of your rulers!"

The despair of the Sultan emboldened the Janissary still further.

"Sign this document, or thy son shall die in our hands!"

"Miserable cowards!" moaned the Sultan. "And cowards they also who should have defended him! Did not even his mother defend him? Was it necessary to give him up?"

"He is in no danger," said Kara Makan; "nay, he is in a safe place. It rests with thee to receive him back into thy arms;" and he shoved towards him again the soiled and crumpled manuscript.

The Padishah, overcome by the shock of his own feelings, humiliated by the sense of his own soft-heartedness, tottered to the wall, and when his groping hands came in contact with the cold marble he collapsed altogether, and leaning against it, he pressed his burning temples to the cold stone. The Janissary might now say whatever he would, the Sultan neither listened to nor answered him.

At last the rough warrior, who had jumped so suddenly into power, shouted angrily to his comrades, who were cooling their heels outside, "Bring hither the prince!"

The Sultan heard the pattering of many footsteps in the corridor outside, and the clashing of swords mingled with the murmuring of voices, but he did not look in that direction.

"Behold!" cried Kara Makan, advancing towards him, "here is thy son! A drawn sword hovers above his head! Choose either to see thine own name at the foot of that paper or his head at thy feet!"

Mahmoud trembled, but he answered nothing, nor did he turn his head.

"Write, or thy son dies!" cried a number of the Janissaries, suddenly.

Then a musical, familiar voice responded amidst the wild uproar:

"My father! hearken not unto them! Let them slay me if they be valiant enough, but chaffer not with thy slaves!"

Mahmoud looked up in astonishment at this well-known voice, and saw before him a handsome figure in the prince's garments and with a proud and majestic countenance; but that face, though familiar to him and very dear, was not his son's face. Ah, it was Milieva!

The odalisk perceived that Mahmoud's features softened, that he looked tenderly upon her; and as if she feared that the Sultan might yield out of compassion towards her, she hastily turned her flaming face to the Janissaries and exclaimed:

"Ye blood-thirsty dogs of Samound! who bay down the sun from the heavens, accomplish your bloody work! Forward, ye valiant heroes, with whose backs alone the enemy is familiar, fall upon me in twos and threes, if any one of you has not the courage to plunge his steel single-handed into the heart of the last scion of Omar's stock! My death will not constrain the Sultan to bargain with you. Kill me while you have power over me, for if ever I have power over you I will not weep before you, as ye have seen Mahmoud and Selim weep; but I will so utterly destroy you that even he who wears a garment like unto yours, even he who shall mention your name, shall pronounce his own doom."

The infuriated rebels raised their flashing swords

above the head of the presumptuous child at these menacing words; another moment and she would have lain in the dust. But Mahmoud arose, spurned them aside from the prince, as they supposed him to be, and taking from the hands of Kara Makan the document and writing materials, signed his name beneath it. Milieva seized the Sultan's hand to prevent him from writing, but he tenderly kissed her on the forehead and gently whispered, "Rather would I lose the whole world than thee," and with that he placed in the hands of the Janissaries the subscribed death-warrants.

After obtaining these concessions, the rebels grew calmer, the Sultan proclaimed amnesty for all offenders, appointed the chief brawlers to high offices, and distributed money amongst them from the treasury.

Peace was thus restored. The Sultan and the sham prince returned to the Seraglio, accompanied all the way by a vast throng, and the whole square by the fountains of Ibrahim was filled by the well-known turbans of the Janissaries, who, in the joy of their insulting triumph, shouted long life to the humiliated Padishah.

Mahmoud surveyed the huzzaing throng, where, man to man, they stood so tightly squeezed together that nothing could be distinguished but a sea of heads. And the Sultan thought to himself, "What a fine thing it would be to sweep all those heads away at one stroke!"

CHAPTER XIV

KURSHID PASHA

GASKHO BEY, the incapable giant, was captured by the Suliotes in a night attack, his army was scattered beneath the walls of Janina, and Ali Pasha became once more the absolute master of Epirus.

Then, like lightning fallen from heaven, unexpectedly, unforeseen, a man came from Thessalonica whose name was shortly to ring through half the world. The name of this man was Kurshid Pasha.

He was a man of a puny, meagre frame, his features were widely divergent from the characteristic Ottoman type, for he had a delicate profile, a bright blond beard and mustache, and blue eyes with flexible eyebrows, all of which gave a peculiar character to his face, which showed unmistakable traces of a penetrating mind and cool courage.

Ten thousand warriors accompanied the new commander to Janina, which grew into thirty thousand at the very first battle. Kleon's and Ypsilanti's armies were routed, and Gaskho Bey's scattered squadrons rallied around the banners of the victor.

While Ali Pasha was defending Janina, the leaders of the Greek insurgents besieged the fortress of Arta, which Salikh Bey defended with a small garrison.

Kurshid's predecessor, Gaskho Bey, had committed the error of besieging Janina and endeavoring to relieve Arta at the same time, and thus he came to grief at both places. The new commander acted on a different plan. He knew well that not a head amongst all the Greek rebels was half so dangerous as Ali Tepelenti's; so, leaving Salikh Pasha to his fate, he directed all his energies against Janina.

A man indeed hath come against thee, O Ali Pasha! A man as valiant, as crafty as thou; if thou be a fox, he is an eagle of the rocks, that pounces down on the fox; and if thou be a tiger, he is the boa-constrictor which infolds and crushes the tiger.

Ali urged Kleon and Artemis to hasten to his assistance. His messengers did not return to the fortress. The Greek leaders gave no reply to his summons. Anybody else would have found some consolatory explanation of their remissness, but Ali divined things better. The Greeks said amongst themselves, "Let the old monster tremble in his ditch; let them close him in and hold him tight. He will be constrained to make a life-and-death struggle to save his old beard. When we have captured Arta, and when our detested ally" (for they did detest him in spite of his being their good friend) "is at the very last gasp, then we will go to the rescue, relieve him, and let him live a little longer."

Tepelenti was well aware that they spoke of him in this way. He knew well that they hated him, and would gladly leave him to perish. The only reason the Greeks had for allying themselves with Ali was that his fortress was filled with an enormous store of treasure, arms, and muniments of war; his gray head was the pivot of the whole rebellion.

If the fortress were taken, they would be deprived of this strong pivot, those treasures, that gray head!

One day the Suliotes encamped before Arta heard the terrible tidings that Kurshid Pasha had captured Lithanizza and La Gulia, the two outlying forts of the stronghold of Janina, and had driven Ali back into the fortress. The tidings filled them with consternation. If Janina were lost, the whole Greek insurrection would lose the source of its supplies. The treasures which Ali had scattered amongst the Greeks with a prodigal hand would at once fall into the hands of the Sultan, and then he would be able to secure Epirus at a single blow.

A Greek army under Marco Bozzari immediately set out from Arta to relieve Janina. Ali knew of it beforehand. Bozzari's spies had crept through Kurshid's camp into Janina, and signified to Ali that their leaders were on their way to "The Five Wells," and that he should send forth an army to meet them.

"There is no necessity for it," replied Ali, with a cold smile. "I am quite capable of defending myself in Janina for three months against any force that may be brought against me. It is much more necessary to capture Arta. Go back, therefore, and say to Marco Bozzari, 'Come not to Janina, but go against Salikh Pasha. Tepelenti is sufficient for himself in Janina.'"

Bozzari understood the old lion's hint. He did not wish the Greek forces to get into Janina, he preferred to defend himself to the very last bastion. All the forces he had consisted of four hundred and thirty Albanians, but this number was quite sufficient to serve the guns. Even if but a tenth of this force remained to him, that would be amply sufficient to defend the red tower, and if the worst came to the worst, Ali alone would be sufficient to blow the place into the air.

Here Ali had accumulated all his treasures, all his arms, his garments, his correspondence with the princes of half the universe, his young damsels. In the cellar below the tower were piled up a thousand barrels of gunpowder, a long match reached from one of these barrels to Ali's chamber, and there a couple of torches were always burning by his side.

Whoever wanted Ali's head had better come for it!

So Bozzari returned to Arta, and not very long afterward the Greek army took the place by storm. In the whole fortress they did not find powder enough to fill a hole in the barrel; the Turkish army had, in fact, fired away its very last cartridge.

Ali had once more the satisfaction of seeing one of his enemies, Salikh Pasha, prostrate. Hitherto all who had fought against him had been his furious haters, personal enemies, enviers of his fortune; and, bitter hater as he was, it was with a strong feeling of satisfaction that Tepelenti saw them all bite the dust; but this Kurshid was quite indifferent to him, and knew nothing either of his fury or his intrigues. He had never been Ali's enemy, and had no reason for hating him. This thought made Ali uneasy.

It had often been Ali's experience that when any one who greatly hated him came during a siege or a battle within shooting distance of him, and he then pointed a gun at him, the ball so fired seemed to fly on the wings of his own savage fury, and would hit its man even at a thousand paces; but Kurshid often took a walk near the trenches, and though they fired at him one gun after another, not a bullet went near him.

"Let him alone," said Ali; "we shall never be able to kill this man." And his old energy left him as if he had suddenly become crippled.

He invited Kurshid Pasha to intercede for him with the Sultan, that he might be restored to favor, offering in such case to place his treasures at the disposal of the Grand Signior, and turn his arms against the Greeks. Kurshid demanded an assurance to this effect in writing, and when Ali complied, Kurshid sent the document, not to the Sultan at Stambul but to the Suliotes at Arta, that they might see how ready Ali was to betray them. The Greeks, in disgust, abandoned Ali. This last treachery dismayed them at the very zenith of their triumph; they perceived that a mighty antagonist had risen against them in Kurshid Pasha, who was magnanimous enough not to make use of traitors, but spurn them with contempt. This intellectual superiority guaranteed the success of Kurshid's arms. The Turkish commander had been acute enough to extend the hand of reconciliation, not to Ali, but to the Suliotes.

Tepelenti waited in vain in the tower of Janina for the arrival of the army of deliverance. The Suliotes returned to their villages, and Artemis reflected with secret joy that in the very red tower in which Ali had decapitated her plighted lover, he himself now sat in his despair, environed by foes, waiting with the foolish hope that the embittered Suliotes would hasten to deliver him.

The Epirote rebellion was already subdued by Kurshid Pasha, and only one point in the whole empire now glowed with a dangerous fire—the haughty Janina.

CHAPTER XV

CARETTO

Ali had now only about room enough to cover his head. His enemies had twenty times as much, and they besieged him night and day. The fortress on the hill of Lithanizza and the Isle of La Gulia were in Kurshid's power already.

Still the old warrior did not surrender. The bombs thrown into the fortress levelled his palaces with the ground. His marble halls were reduced to rubbish heaps, his kiosks were smoking ruins, and his splendid gardens lay buried, obliterated. Yet, for all that, Ali Pasha vomited back his wrath upon the besiegers out of eighty guns, and it happened more than once that hidden mines exploded beneath the more forward advanced of the enemy's batteries, blowing guns and gunners into the air.

The defence was conducted by an Italian engineer whom Ali had enticed into his service in his luckier days with the promise of enormous treasures and detained ever since. This Italian's name was Caretto. It was his science that had made Janina so strong. The clumsy valor of the Turkish gunners fell to dust before the strategy of the Italian engineer. Of late Caretto was much exercised by the thought that he might be discharged without a farthing, but discharge was now out of the question. If Caretto were outside the gates of Janina, then the fate of Janina would be in his hands, for every bastion, every subterranean mine, every corner of the fortress was known to him.

Now at home in Palermo was Caretto's betrothed, who, as the daughter of a wealthy family, could only be his if he also had the command of riches; and that was the chief reason why the youth had accepted the offer of the tyrant of Epirus. And now tidings reached him from Sicily that the parents of his bride were dead, and that she was awaiting him with open arms; let him only come to her, poor fellow, even if he brought nothing with him but the beggar's staff. And go he could not, for Ali Pasha held him fast. He had to point the guns, and send forth hissing bullets amongst the besiegers, and defend the fortress to the last, while his beloved bride awaited him at home.

One day, as Caretto was directing the guns, a grenade fired from the heights of Lithanizza burst over his head and struck out his left eye. Caretto asked himself bitterly whether his bride would be able to love him with a face so disfigured. Henceforth he went about constantly with a black bandage about his wounded face, and the besiegers called him "the one-eyed Giaour."

One fine morning in February Kurshid Pasha again directed a fierce fire against the fortress. The siege guns had now arrived which the army had used against Cassandra, and after a three hours' cannonade, the destructive effect of the new battery was patent, for the tower of the northern bastion lay in ruins. Ali Pasha galloped furiously up and down the bastions, stimulating and threatening the gunners with a drawn sword in his hand. Whoever quitted his place instantly fell a victim beneath Ali's own hand. Caretto was standing nonchalantly beside a gabion, whence he directed the fire of the most powerful of all the batteries, each gun of which was a thirty-six pounder. The guns of this battery discharged thirty balls each every hour.

All at once the battery stopped firing.

Transported with rage, Ali Pasha at once came galloping up to Caretto.

"Why don't you go on firing?" he cried.

"Because it is impossible," replied the engineer, coolly folding his arms.

"Why is it impossible," thundered the pasha, his whole body convulsed with rage, which the coolness of the Italian raised to fever heat.

"Because the guns are red-hot from incessant firing."

"Then throw water upon them!" cried Ali, and with that he dismounted from his horse.

Caretto, for the life of him, could not help laughing at this senseless command. Whereupon Tepelenti suddenly leaped upon him and struck him in the face, so that his cap flew far away, right off the bastion. He had struck Caretto on the very spot where Kurshid Pasha's grenade had lacerated his face a few weeks before.

The Italian readjusted over his eye the bandage, which had been knocked all awry by the blow, and observed, with a cold affectation of mirth:

"You did well, sir, to strike my face on the spot where one eye had been knocked out already, for if you had struck me on the other side you might have knocked out the other eye also, and then how could I have pointed your guns?"

Ali, however, pretended to take no notice, but directed that the guns should be douched with cold water and then reloaded; he himself fired the first. The cannon the same instant burst in two and smashed the leg of a cannonier standing close to it.

"It does not matter," cried Ali; "load the others, too."

When the second cannon also burst he dashed the match to the ground, threw himself on his horse, and galloped off, quivering in every nerve as if shaken by an ague.

The Italian, however, with the utmost *sang-froid*, ordered that the exploded cannons should be removed and fresh ones fetched from the arsenal and put in their places, and set them in position amidst a shower of bullets from the besiegers. When the battery was ready the enemy withdrew their siege guns, and till the next day not another shot was fired against Janina.

Tepelenti was well aware that he had mortally offended Caretto, and he had learned to know men (especially Italians) only too well to imagine for an instant that Caretto, for all his jocoseness on the occasion, would ever forget that cowardly and ungrateful blow. For, indeed, it was an act of the vilest ingratitude. What! to strike the wound which the man had received on his account! To strike a European officer in the face! Ali was well aware that such a thing could never be pardoned.

The same night he sent for two gunners and ordered them not to lose sight of Caretto for an instant, and if he attempted to escape to shoot him down there and then.

Next day Caretto was unusually good-humored. Early in the morning he went out upon the ramparts, which were then covered with freshly fallen snow. The winter seemed to be pouring forth its last venom, and the large flakes fell so thickly that one could not see twenty paces in advance.

"This is just the weather for an assault," said Caretto in a loud voice to the Turks standing around him; "in such wild weather one cannot see the enemy till he stands beneath the very ramparts. I will be so bold as to maintain that Kurshid's bands are likely to steal upon us under cover of this thick snow-storm. I should like to fire a random shot from the ramparts to let them know we are awake."

Many thought his anxiety just. Ali Pasha was also there, and he said nothing either for or against the proposal.

Caretto hoisted a cannon to the level of the ramparts of Lithanizza and fastened a long chain to the gun whereby his group of Albanians could raise and lower it.

"Leave the chain upon it," said Caretto, "for we may have to turn it in another direction."

Nevertheless it was in a good position already. Caretto calculated his distances with his astrolabe, then pointed the gun and ordered it to be loaded.

The two gunners whom Ali had set to watch him never took their eyes off the Italian; both of them had loaded pistols in their hands. Caretto did not seem to observe that they were watching him; he might have thought that they were there to help him.

The gun had to be turned now to the right and

now to the left. Caretto himself took aim, but the clumsy Albanians kept on pushing the heavy laffette either a little too much on this side or a little too much on that, till at last he cried to the two watchers behind him:

"Just lend a hand and help these blockheads!" They stooped mechanically to raise the laffette. "Enough!" cried the Italian, and with that he put his hand on the touch-hole. "Now fire!" he cried to the artilleryman, at the same time removing his hand.

The match descended, there was a thunderous report, and the same instant Caretto seized the chain wound round the wheel of the cannon, and, lowering himself from the ramparts, glided down the chain.

The watchers, with the double velocity of rage and fear, rushed to the breastwork of the ramparts. Caretto had got to the end of the chain and was grasping it with both hands; below him yawned a depth of thirty feet. The chian was not long enough, and there he was suspended between two deaths.

"Come back," cried the watchers, aiming their pistols at his head, "or we will shoot you through and through!"

Caretto cast a wild glance upward, the bandage fell from his bloody eye, and he looked at them with the dying fury of a desperately wounded wild beast. Then suddenly he kicked himself clear of the wall by a sharp movement of his foot, and describing the arc of a circle, he plunged into the depth beneath him like a rebounding bullet. The Albanians fired after him, but neither of them hit him. Below, at the foot of the bastion, the daring Italian lay motionless for a moment, but then he quickly rose to his feet and began to clamber up the other side of the ditch. He could only make use of one arm, for the other had been dislocated in his fall. Straining all his might, he struggled up; a whole shower of bullets pursued him and whistled about his head, but not one of them hit him, for the heavy snowfall made it difficult to take aim. At last he reached the top of the opposite side of the trench, and then he turned round and shook his fist at the devastating fortress, and disappeared in a heavy snow-drift. The gunners kept on firing after him at random for some time.

Ali Pasha turned pale and almost fell from his horse when the tidings reached him that Caretto had escaped.

"It is all over now!" cried he in despair, broke his sword in two, and shut himself up in the red tower. In the outer court-yard they saw him no more.

Ali knew for certain that with the departure of Caretto the last remains of his power had vanished; his stronghold and its resources were hopelessly ruined if any one revealed their secrets to his enemies outside. Caretto knew everything, and "the one-eyed Giaour" was received with great triumph in the camp of Kurshid Pasha. The next day Ali Pasha had bitter experience of the fact that the hand which had hitherto defended him was now turned against him. Within nine hours a battery, constructed by Caretto, had made a breach thirty fathoms wide in the outworks of Janina; the other cannons of the besiegers were set up in places whither Ali's mines did not extend, and when he made new ones they were immediately rendered inoperative by countermining, and at last Caretto discovered the net-work of hidden tunnels at the head of the bridge, although they had been carefully buried, and after a savage struggle forced his way through them into the fortress. The Albanians fought desperately, but Ali's enemies, who could afford to shed their blood freely, forced their way through and planted their scaling-ladders against the side of the fortress opposite the island, and where the *débris* of the battered-down wall filled up the ditch they crossed over and occupied the breach. In the evening, after a fierce combat in the courtyard, Tepelenti's forces were cut to pieces one by one, and he himself, with seventy survivors, took refuge in the red tower.

So only the red tower now remained to him.

CHAPTER XVI

EMINAH

THE vanquished lion was shut up within a space six yards square; a narrow tower into all four windows of which his enemies were peeping was now his sole possession! There he sits in that octagonal chamber, in which he had passed so many memorable moments. Perhaps now, as he leaned his heavy head upon his hand, the remembrance of those moments passed before his mind's eye like a procession of melancholy shadows. Around him lay his treasures in shining piles; heaps of gold and silver, massive gold plate, the spoils of sanctuaries, sparkling gems, lay scattered about the floor higgledy-piggledy, like so much sand or gravel.

Of all his kinsfolk, of all his warriors, not one was present with him; all had fallen on the battlefield, fighting either with him or against him. Of the seventy warriors who had taken refuge with him in the tower, sixty-four had deserted him. Kurshid had promised a pardon to the renegades, and only six remained with Ali. Why did these six remain? Ali had not told them not to leave him.

These faithful ones were keeping guard in his antechamber, and for some little time they had been whispering together.

At last they went in to Ali.

Tepelenti looked them every one through and through. He could read what they wanted in their confused looks and their unsteady eyes. He did not wait for them to speak, but said, with a wave of his hand:

"Go! leave me; you are the last. Go where the others have gone; save yourselves. Life is sweet; live long and happily. I will remain here. Tepelenti can die alone."

Sighing deeply, the soldiers turned away. They durst not raise their eyes to the face of the gray-haired veteran. Noiselessly, without a word, on the tips of their toes, five of them withdrew. But the sixth remained there still, and, after casting about for a word for some time, said, at last, to Ali:

"Oh, sir, cast the fulness of pride from thy heart, suffer not thy name to perish! The Sultan is merciful; bow thy head before him and he will still be gracious to thee!"

The soldier had scarce uttered the last word of this recommendation when Ali softly drew a pistol from his girdle and shot him through the head, so that he spun round and fell backward across the threshold. This was all the reward he got for advising Ali to ask for mercy.

And now Ali is alone. His doors, his gates stand wide open; anybody who so pleases can go in and out. Why, then, does nobody come to seize the solitary veteran? why do they fear to cross the threshold of the vanquished foe?

But hearken! fresh footsteps are resounding on the staircase, and through the open door, guarded by the corpse of the last soldier whom Ali slew, a strange man entered, dressed in an unusual, new-fangled uniform; he was Kurshid Pasha's silihdar.

Tepelenti allowed him to approach within five paces of where he sat, and then beckoned him to stop.

"Speak; what dost thou want?"

"Ali Tepelenti," said the silihdar, "surrender. Thou hast nothing left in the world and nobody to aid thee. My master, the seraskier, Kurshid Pasha, hath sent me to thee that I might receive thy sword and escort thee to his camp."

Tepelenti, with the utmost *sang-froid*, drew forth from the folds of his caftan a magnificent gold watch in an enamelled case set with diamonds.

"Hearken!" said he, in a low, soft voice. "It is now twenty minutes past ten; take this watch and keep it as a souvenir of me. Greet Kurshid Pasha from me, and point out to him that it was twenty minutes past ten when you spoke with me, and let him take notice that if after twenty minutes past eleven I can see from the windows of this tower a single hostile soldier in the court-yard of the fortress, then—I swear it by the mercies of Allah!—I will blow the fortress into the air, with every living soul within it. Inform Kurshid Pasha of this when you give him my salutation."

The silihdar hastened off, and at a quarter to eleven not a soul was to be seen in the court-yard of the fortress of Janina. Alive in his citadel sits Ali Tepelenti, the tyrant of Epirus, mighty even in his fall, who has nothing and nobody left, save only his indomitable heart.

Night descended upon the fortress of Janina, but sleep did not descend upon the eyes of Ali.

He sat in that red tower where he had perpetrated his crimes, in that chamber where his victims had breathed forth the last sighs of their tortured lives, and all round about glittering treasures looked upon Ali as if with eyes of fire—all of it the price of robbery, fraud, treason. What if these things could speak?

Everything was silent, night lay black before the eyes of men, only Ali saw shadows moving about therein, phantoms with pale, phantoms with bloody faces, who rose from the tomb to visit their persecutor and announce to him the hour of his death.

Ali trembled not before them; he had seen them at other times also. He had slept face to face with the severed head that spoke to him, he had listened to the enigmatical words of the *dzhin* of Seleucia, and he called them to mind again now. Calmly he looked back upon the current of his past life, from which so many horrible shapes arose and glared at him with cold, stony eyes. He recked them not, Allah had so ordered it. The hare nibbles the root, the vulture devours the hare, the hunter shoots the vulture, the lion fells the hunter, and the worm eats the lion. What, after all, is Ali? Naught but a greater worm than the rest. He has devoured much, and now a stronger than he devours him, and a still greater worm will devour this stronger one also.

Everything was fulfilled which had been prophesied concerning him. His own sons, his own wife, his own arms had fought against him. If only his wife had not done this he could have borne the rest.

"One, two," the decapitated head had said, and

the last moments of the two years were just passing away. "The hand which wipes out the deeds of the mighty shall at last blot out thy deeds also, and thou shalt be not a hero whom the world admires, but a slave whom it curses. Those whom thou didst love will bless the hour of thy death, and thy enemies will weep, and God will order it so to avert the ruin of thy nation."

So it is, so it has chanced; the hazard of the die has gone against him, and he has nothing left.

If only his wife had not betrayed him!

At other times also Ali had seen these phantoms of the night arise. He had seen them rise from the tomb pale and bloody; but in his heart there had always been a sweet refuge, the charming young damsel whose childlike face and angelic eyes had robbed the evil sorcery of all its power. When Tepelenti covered his gray head with her long, thick, flowing locks, he reposed behind them as in the shade of Paradise, whither those heart-tormenting memories could not pursue him. Why should he have lost her? She was the first of all, and the dearest; but Fate at the last would not even leave him her.

Even now his thoughts went back to her. The pale light of that face, that memory, lightened his solitary, darkened soul, which was as desolate as the night outside.

But lo! it is as if the night grew brighter; a sort of errant light glides along the walls and a gleam of sunshine breaks unexpectedly through the open door of the room.

The pasha looked in that direction with amazement. Who could his visitor be at that hour? Who is coming to drive the phantoms of darkness from his room and from his heart?

A pale female form, with a smile upon her face and tears in her eyes, appears before him. She comes right up to the spot where Tepelenti is sitting on the ground. She places her torch in an iron sconce in the wall and stands there before the pasha.

Ali looked at her sadly. He fancied that this also was only a dream shape, only one of those apparitions created by a fevered mind, like those which walked beside him headless and bloody. It was Eminah, at whose word the devastating tempest had been unchained against the mightiest of despots.

Tepelenti believed neither his eyes nor his heart when he saw her thus before him. The damsel took the old man by the hand and called him by his name, and even now the pasha believed that the warmth of that hand and the sweetness of that voice were only part of a dream.

"Wherefore hast thou come?" he inquired in a whisper, or perchance he did not ask but only dreamed that he asked.

Yet the gracious, childlike damsel was sitting there at his feet as at other times, and she had pillowed his gray head upon her breast and covered his face with the tent of her long tresses, as she had done long, long ago in the happy times that were gone.

Oh, how sweet it would be to still live!

"Oh, Ali Tepelenti, let go the hand of Death from thy hand and grasp my hand instead! See how warm it is! Oh, Ali Tepelenti, rise up from among these barrels of gunpowder, and rather lay thy head upon my breast; hearken how it beats! Oh, Ali Tepelenti, ask mercy from the Sultan! See, now, how lovely life is!"

Only at these words did Ali recover himself. His enemies had sought out this woman, the only being that he loved, and sent her to him to soothe away the rage of his soul and soften his heart with her caresses. Oh, how well they understood his heart!

"Kurshid Pasha swore to me that he would obtain the Sultan's favor for thee," said Eminah, in a tone of conviction. "He wrote a letter under his seal that thou shouldst never die beneath the hands of the executioner; that thy death should not be a violent one, unless it were in an honorable duel or on the field of battle. Behold, here is the letter!"

If at that moment Ali had listened to his heart, he must have extended the hand of submission without any letter of amnesty, but, like an escutcheon above a crown, pride was perched higher than his heart and spurned the offer.

"Allah may humble Ali, but Ali will never humble himself."

"Then thou wilt not live with me?" asked Eminah, fixing her piteously entreating eyes upon her husband.

Ali shook his head in silence.

"Then I will die with thee!" cried the damsel, with a determined voice.

The pasha regarded her in amazement.

"I swear," cried Eminah, "that I will either go back with thee or die with thee here! Dost thou hear that noise? They are slamming to the iron gates from the outside. At this moment every exit is closed, so that even if I wished to escape from hence I could not. These doors can only open at a word from Ali, and they will only open once more. Either thou wilt go with me from hence or I will remain here with thee."

Ali pressed the damsel to his bosom. She lay clinging there like a tender blossom. He pressed his lips to that pale brow, and covering her gently and gradually with his silken caftan, he whispered in a scarcely audible voice :

"Be it so ! be it so ! Here we will die together !"

Early next morning a flourish of trumpets awoke the Lord of Janina, the Lord of the last tower of Janina. The herald of Kurshid Pasha was standing beneath the round windows, and delivered in a loud voice the general's message to Ali Pasha, whereby he summoned Tepelenti to surrender voluntarily on the strength of the solemn assurance confirmed by oath to his wife.

Tepelenti appeared at the window with Eminah reclining on his bosom.

"Go back to your master," he cried to the messenger, "and tell him that Ali and his wife have resolved to die here together. The moment an armed host enters the court-yard of this fortress I will immediately blow up the tower."

In half an hour the messenger returned and again summoned Ali to the window.

"Kurshid Pasha sends thee this message," cried he. "If thou dost surrender, it is well, and if thou dost not surrender, it is well also. Thou hast still half an hour wherein thou mayest choose betwixt life and death. After that thou mayest, if thou wilt, throw thy torch into thy powder barrels and blow the fortress into the air. As to thyself, Kurshid Pasha troubles himself but little. As to thy treasures they will not remain in the air, and when they come to the ground it will be easy to pick them up. If, however, thou dost delay thy resolution beyond the half-hour, then Kurshid Pasha himself will help thee in the matter, and will blow up thy tower for thee, to save thee the trouble of blowing it up thyself. Do as thou wilt, then, and hoist either the white or the red flag as seemeth best to thee, for in half an hour the fortress of Janina shall see thee no more."

Ali listened solemnly to this ultimatum, and let the messenger depart without an answer.

Eminah lay down on a sofa in a corner, all trembling. Ali paced the vast chamber to and fro with long strides; but his strides became more and more uncertain. If only this woman were not here! If only he might be spared seeing her before him; might be spared half an hour's deliberation as to what he was to do! Nevertheless minute after minute sped away, and still Tepelenti could not make up his mind. Twice his hand seized the burning torch; he had but to bend over the nearest barrel of powder and all would be over; but on each occasion his eye fell upon the trembling woman who lay there looking at him without a word, and the death-bearing match fell from his hand. No, no; he was incapable of doing the terrible deed. And now the hour struck; the time had passed. Ali felt a pressure about his heart. Would Kurshid accomplish his dreadful threat?

At that instant a report sounded outside the fortress, and half a moment later a red-hot steel bullet burst through the metal roof and the massive vault of the tower with a violent crash. Falling heavily on the marble floor, it rebounded thence, and, passing between the powder-barrels, describing a wide semicircle as it went, ricocheted once more and struck the wall opposite, in which it bored a deep hole, whence it flashed and gleamed with a strong red glare, forcing blue sparks from the nitrous humidity of the walls.

Ali was now convinced that the enemy was quite capable of keeping his promise.

The scared woman, mad with terror, flung herself at his feet, and snatching the white veil from her head, forced it into the pasha's hand.

Tepelenti hastily seized the veil, and; hanging it on the point of a lance, hoisted it out of the round window.

Outside the besiegers set up a shout of triumph. Eminah, kissing Ali's hands, sank down at his feet. Tepelenti had given her more than manhood can bear to give : for her sake he had humbled his pride to the dust. If only he could have died as he had lived!

"Go, now," he said to the woman, with a sigh ; "go and tell my enemies that they may come for me. I am theirs!"

CHAPTER XVII

THE SILVER PEDESTAL IN FRONT OF THE SERAGLIO

The emissaries of Kurshid Pasha received the veteran warrior with great respect in the gates of the fortress, whither he went to meet them; they showed him all the honor due to his rank; they allowed him to retain his sword and all his other weapons. At the same time they confirmed by word of mouth the promise which Kurshid Pasha had given to Eminah in writing—that the executioner should never lay his hand on Ali's head, and that he should not die a violent death, except it were in an honorable duel or on the battle-field, which is a delight to a true Mussulman.

A former pleasure-house, a kiosk on the island of La Gulia, was assigned to him as a residence for the future. There they conveyed his favorite horses, his favorite slaves and birds, and took abundant care of his personal comfort.

Ali allowed them to do with him as they would. Neither threatening nor pleasant faces made any impression upon him; he merely looked from time to time at his wife, who had seized his hand, and never left him for an instant. At such times softer, gentler feelings were legible in his face; but at other times he would gaze steadily before him into the distance, into infinity. Perhaps he was now thinking within himself, "When shall I stand in front of the Seraglio on a silver pedestal?"

The *dzhin* of Seleucia had prophesied this termination to his career. All the other prophecies had been strictly fulfilled; this only remained to be accomplished.

A Mussulman's promise is stronger than his oath. Who does not remember the story of the Moorish chieftain in whose house a Christian soldier had taken refuge, and who begged for his protection? The Moor promised the man his protection. Subsequently the pursuers informed the Moor that this Christian soldier had killed his son, and still the father would not give up the fugitive, but assisted him to escape, because of his promise.

"A great lord is the sea," says the Kuran; "a great lord is the storm and the pestilence; but a greater lord still is a man's given word, from which there is no escape."

The Mussulman keeps his word, but beware of a play upon words, for therein lies death. If he has sworn by the sun, avoid the moon, and if he has promised to love thee as a brother, discover first whether he hath not slain his brother.

When Sulaiman adopted Ibrahim as a son, he swore that so long as he lived no harm should befall Ibrahim. Later on, when Ibrahim fell into disgrace, the wise Ulemas discovered a text in the Kuran according to which he who sleeps is not alive, and they slew Ibrahim while Sulaiman slept.

Kurshid had given his word and a written assurance that Ali should not die at the hand of the executioner; the document he had given to Ali's wife, his word he had given in the presence of his whole army; and he had escorted Ali Pasha with all due honor to the island kiosk, permitting him to retain his weapons and the jewelled sword with which he had won so many victories, with which he had so many times turned the tide of the battle; nay, more, they had selected fifty of Ali's own warriors, the bravest and the most faithful, to serve him as a guard of honor.

Nevertheless, a courier despatched in hot haste to Stambul announced there, from Kurshid Pasha, that the treasures of Ali Tepelenti of Janina were in his hands, and that a Tartar horseman would follow in three days with the head of the old pasha. And yet at this very moment Tepelenti's head stood firmly on his shoulders, and who would dare to say that that head was promised away while his good sword was by his side, and good comrades in arms were around him, and the sworn assurance of the seraskier rested upon him?

Eminah never quitted him for a moment. She was always with him. She sat beside him, with her head on his breast, or at his feet, and in her hand she carried the amnesty of the seraskier, so that if any one should approach Ali with dangerous designs she might hold it before his eyes like a magic buckler, and ward off the axe of the executioner from his head.

But there was nothing to guard against; the executioner did not approach Ali. He received, indeed, a great many visitors, but these were all worthy, honorable men, musirs, effendis, officers of the army, who treated him with all respect, and sipped their sherbet-cups most politely, and smoked their fragrant chibooks, exchanging a word or two now and then, perhaps, and on taking their leave saluted him in a manner befitting grave Mussulmans.

He was allowed free access to every part of the island, and never encountered anybody there but his own warriors.

At such times great ideas would occur to him. Perchance with these fifty men he might win back everything once more? And then he would hug himself with the thought of the silver pedestal in front of the Seraglio, where he was one day to stand, amidst the joyful plaudits of the people; and then the night before him was not altogether dark, for here and there he saw a gleam of hope.

It was only Eminah who trembled. God has created woman for this very purpose; she has the faculty of fearing instead of man, and can foresee the danger that threatens him.

Whence will this danger come, and in what shape? Perchance in the dagger of the assassin? The woman's bosom stood between it and the heart of Ali; the assassin will not be able to pierce it. In a poisoned cup, perhaps? Eminah herself tastes of every dish, of every glass, before they reach the hands of Ali; the power of the poison would reach her first.

And yet danger is near.

One day they told Ali that an illustrious visitor was coming to see him; Mehemet Pasha, the sub-seraskier and governor of the Morea, wished to pay his respects to him.

This was a great honor for the fallen general. Ali began to be sensible that even his enemies respected him. Who knows? he might find good friends amongst his very enemies, who would not think him too old for use and employment even in his last remaining years.

On the day of the visit, the kiosk was swept and garnished. Tepelenti put on his most costly caftan, his warriors were marshalled in front of his dwelling, and he himself went out on horseback to meet the seraskier when he arrived, with an escort of one hundred mounted spahis.

Mehemet Pasha was a tall, powerful man, the hero of many a fight and many a duel. He had often given proof of his dexterity, when the hostile armies stood face to face, by galloping betwixt them and challenging the bravest warriors on the other side to single combat, and the fact that he was alive at the present moment was the best possible proof that he had been always victorious.

The two heroes exchanged greetings when they met, and returned together to the pleasure-house. Ali conducted the sub-seraskier into the inner apartments; the attendants remained outside.

A richly spread table awaited them, and they were waited upon by a group of young odalisks, the handmaidens of Eminah, who sat at Ali's feet on the left-hand side, and, as usual, tasted of every dish and cup before she gave it to Ali.

Pleasant conversation filled the intervals of the repast, and at the end of it a mess of preserved pistachios was brought in and presented to Mehemet Pasha.

"I thank thee," said he, "and, indeed, I am very fond of them, but piquant, hot-spiced meats always awaken within me sinful desires and a longing for wine which is forbidden by the Prophet, and, as a good Mussulman, I would rather avoid the occasion of sinning than suffer the affliction of a late repentance."

Ali laughed aloud.

"Eat and be of good cheer, valiant seraskier," said he, "and set thy mind at rest. What I give thee shall be wine and yet not wine—the juice of the grape, yet still unfermented; 'tis an invention of the Franks. This the Prophet does not forbid.* I have still got a case of bottles thereof, which Bunaberdi† formerly sent me, and we will now break it open in thy honor. Truly fizz is not wine, but only the juice of the grape which they bottle before it becomes wine. It is as harmless as milk."

Mehemet shook his head and laughed, from which one could see that the proposition was not displeasing to him, whereupon Ali beckoned to the odalisks to fetch the bottles from the cellar.

Eminah, all trembling, bent over him and whispered, imploringly, "Oh, put not wine on thy table; it will be dangerous to thee!"

Ali smiled, and stroked his wife's head. He thought that only religious scruples made her dissuade him from drinking the wine, so he drew her upon his bosom and began to reassure her.

"Say now, my one and only flower, is not Moses a prophet, like unto Muhammad?"

"Of a truth he is. His tent stands beside the tent of Muhammad in the Paradise of the true Believers."

"And yet Moses said: Give wine to them that be

---

* The Moslems do not include French "fizz" amongst the canonically forbidden drinks.

† Bonaparte.

sorrowful! Leave the matter then to the two prophets up above there; surely, what passes through our lips does not make us sin?"

But that was not the reason why Eminah feared the wine.

They brought the bottles, and the liberated corks popped merrily. At first Mehemet Pasha hesitated, but they filled his glass with fizz and, to prevent the sparkling foam from running over, he sipped a little of it, and quickly drained the glass, maintaining afterwards, with a smile, that it was a similar drink to wine, but much more pleasant.

Ali filled once more the glass of the seraskier, while Eminah tremulously watched his features, which gradually grew darker as he drank. Drink has this effect on some men.

Suddenly the sub-seraskier dashed his glass upon the table and exclaimed, with a furious expression of countenance:

"I'll drink no more! I'll drink no more! Thou art a villain, Ali! Thou hast made me drink wine and hast lied to me, saying it was not wine; but it is wine, a frightful, burning drink, which has made my head whirl."

"Come, come, Mehemet," said Ali, in the coaxing tone one uses to drunken men, "be not so wrathful."

"Speak not to me, thou dog!" thundered the other, striking the table with his fist. "I might have known when I dismounted at thy door with whom I had to do, thou sly, treacherous fox, thou godless renegade!"

Ali leaped from his seat with flashing eyes, and clapped his hand on the hilt of his sword at these words; but Eminah seized his hand, and said to him, in a terrified whisper:

"Draw not thy sword, Ali; show no weapons here! Dost thou not perceive that he only came hither to fasten a quarrel upon thee?"

Ali instantly recovered himself at these words. He saw now the snare that had been laid for him, and calmly sat down in his place again, crossing his legs beneath him, and, quietly taking up his chibook, began to smoke with an air of unconcern.

Meanwhile, Mehemet played his drunken *rôle* still further.

"I might have known beforehand, when I sat down at table with thee, that I was sitting down with an accursed wretch, thou blood-thirsty dog, who hath lapped up the blood of thy kinsfolk; but I never ventured to imagine that thou wouldst be audacious enough to make me drink that abominable liquid—may its sinfulness fall back again on thine accursed head!"

With these words Mehemet caught up the half full glass and pitched all the wine that was in it straight between Ali's eyes, so that it trickled down the full length of his long white beard.

Ali, with the utmost *sang-froid*, beckoned to the attendant odalisks to place before him a bowl of fresh water, in which he washed his face and beard. He did not answer the sub-seraskier a single word.

Mehemet planted himself in front of him with a contemptuous expression.

"Wretched worm! that can wipe away such an insult so tamely! Thou wert never valiant, thy heroic deeds were so many murders. Those whom thou didst slay, thou didst butcher as doth a headsman. Thou couldst surprise like a thief, but to fight like a man was never thy way, and the blood that stains thee is the blood of fettered slaves. Thou abominable thing! The very victory is abominable which we have gained over such a writhing worm as thou art. I should pity my sword if it ever came into contact with thine. Let others say if they will that they have conquered Ali, I will only say that I have struck Ali Tepelenti in the face."

"By Allah, the one true God, that thou shall never say!" thundered Ali, leaping from his seat; and quickly drawing his sword, he whirled it like a glittering circle through the air.

Mehemet retreated a step backward, and drew his Damascus blade with a satisfied air.

"Fight not, Ali; go inside!" exclaimed Eminah, violently seizing Ali by the sword-arm.

Tepelenti shook her off and, with his sword flashing above his head, fell upon the sub-seraskier. Mehemet parried the stroke with his sword, and the next instant a huge jet of blood leaped into the air from Ali's shoulder.

Eminah, full of despair, flung herself between the combatants. She saw that Ali was bleeding profusely, and throwing one arm around his knee, with the other hand she held up before the seraskier the amnesty of Kurshid Pasha.

"Look at that! The general swore that Tepelenti should not be slain."

"Not by the executioner," replied Mehemet; "but he did not guarantee him against the sword of a warrior. Come, thou coward! or wilt thou hide behind the petticoat of thy wife?"

Eminah stretched out her arms towards Ali, but

the old man thrust her aside and rushed upon Mehemet Pasha once more; but before he could reach him another thrust pierced him through the heart. Without a sob he collapsed at the feet of his foe.

The terrified odalisks rushed shrieking into the camp, whilst outside a bloody combat began between the warriors of Mehemet and the warriors of Ali. The former were numerous, so it was not long before Tepelenti's guards were cut down, and Mehemet, with a contented countenance, returned to camp. A silken-net bag was hanging to his saddle-bow, and in it was the head of Ali.

Kurshid Pasha washed his hand when the head was placed before him.

"I was not the cause of thy death!" he cried. "I guaranteed thee against the headsman, but not against the sword of warriors. Why didst thou provoke the lion?"

On the day fixed, beforehand, the Tartar horseman arrived in Stambul with the head of Ali. The hours of his life had been calculated exactly. An astronomer who determines the distances between constellation and constellation is not more accurate in his calculations than was Kurshid in determining the date of his enemy's death.

On that day the Sultan held high festival.

The Tsirogan palace, the Seraglio, all the fountains were illuminated, and Ali's head was carried through the principal streets of the town in triumphal procession, and finally exhibited on a silver salver in front of the middle gate of the Seraglio in the sight of all the people.

So there he stood at last, on a silver pedestal in

front of the Seraglio. And the prophecy was fulfilled which had said, "A time will come when thou shalt be in two places at once, in Stambul and in Janina!" So it was.

Ali's dead body was buried at Janina, and his head, at the same time, was standing in front of the Seraglio. At Janina, a single mourning woman was weeping over the headless corpse; at Stambul, a hundred thousand inquisitive idlers were shouting around the bodyless head.

At that gate where the head of Ali was exhibited the throng was so great that many people were crushed to death by the gaping sight-seers, who had all come hither to stare at the gray-bearded face, before whose wrathful look a whole realm had trembled.

At last, on the evening of the third day, when the well-feasted mob had stared their fill and begun to disperse, there drew nigh to the gate of the Seraglio an old yellow-faced fakir who, from the appearance of his eyes, was evidently blind. His clothing consisted of a simple sackcloth mantle, girded lightly round the waist by a cotton girdle, from which hung a long roll of manuscript; on his head he wore a high mortar-shaped hat, the distinguishing mark of the Omarites.

All the people standing about respectfully made way for him as, with downcast eyes and hands stretched forth, he groped his way along, and, without any one guiding him, made his way straight up to Tepelenti's head.

There he stood and laid his right hand on the severed head, none preventing him.

And lo! it seemed to those who stood round as if

the severed head slowly opened its eyes and looked upon the new-comer with cold, stony, stiff, dim eyeballs. This only lasted for a moment, and then the Omarite took his hand off the head and the eyes closed again. Perhaps it was but an illusion, after all!

Then the dervish spoke. His deep, grave voice sank into the hearts of all who heard him: "Go to Mahmoud, and tell him that I have bought from him the head of Ali Pasha and the heads of his three sons, Sulaiman, Vely, and Mukhtar, and a whole empire is the price I pay him therefor."

"What empire art thou able to give?" inquired the captain of the ciauses who were guarding the head.

"That which is the fairest of all, that which is nearest to his heart, that which he had the least hope of—his own empire."

These bold words were reported to the Sultan, and the Grand Signior summoned the Omarite dervish to the palace, and shut himself up alone with him till late at night. When the muezzin intoned the fifth namazat, towards midnight, Mahmoud dismissed the dervish. What they said to each other remained a secret known only to themselves. The fakir, on emerging from the Sultan's dressing-room, plucked a piece of coal from a censer, and wrote on the white alabaster wall this sentence, "Rather be a head without a hand than a hand without a head," and nobody but the Sultan understood that saying.

Mahmoud commanded that nine purses of gold should be given to the dervish; he gave him also the heads of Ali and of Ali's three sons.

The dervish left the Seraglio with the four heads

and the nine purses. With the nine purses he bought an empty field in front of the Selembrian gate and planted it with cypress-trees, and at the foot of every cypress he set up a white turbaned tombstone—there were hundreds and hundreds side-by-side without inscriptions. He said, too, that it would not be long before the owners of these tombs arrived. In the middle of this cemetery, moreover, he dug a wide grave, and in it he buried the heads of Ali's three sons, with their father's head in the middle. He erected four turbaned tombstones over them, two at the head and two at the foot of the grave, and on the largest of these tombstones was written: "Here lies the valiant Ali Tepelenti, Pasha of Janina, leaving behind him many other warriors who deserve death just as much as he."

The people murmured because of what was written on the tomb, but who durst obliterate what is inscribed on the dwellings of the dead?

There the mysterious inscription remained on the tomb for four years, and in the fourth year its meaning was revealed.

Now this dervish was the *dzhin* of Seleucia.

CHAPTER XVIII

THE BROKEN SWORDS

"Allah Kerim!
Allah akbar!
Great is God and mighty!"

WHAT avails prayer if there be no longer any to hearken? What avails the bright sword if there be none to wield it? What avails the open book if there be none to understand what is written therein?

Ye nations of the half-moon! now is the time when the song of the dervishes, and the scimitar, and the dirk, and the Kuran, can help no more! From the west and from the north strange people are coming, armed warriors in serried ranks, like a wall of steel, who are set in motion, brought to a stand-still, expanded into an endless line, contracted into a solid mass by a single brief word of command. Before the charge of their bayonets the ranks of the Janissaries scatter and disperse like chaff before the wind, and before their fire-vomiting brazen tubes the flowers of Begtash's garden fall like grass before the mower. Wise men are with them, who go about in simple black coats, who know much that ye do not know; each one of whom is capable of directing a state, and who are equally triumphant on the battle-field and in the council-chamber.

In vain ye call upon the name of the Prophet, in vain do ye knock at the gate of Paradise. It is closed. Muhammad·slumbers, and the other prophets no longer trouble themselves about earthly affairs. Paradise is full already. There they look askance now at new-comers, who reach the shadow of the tuba-tree without the rumor of victory. The eternally young houris, from beyond the Bridge of Alsiroth, no longer smile upon those who fall in battle, for battle has now lost its glory. Ye must be born again, or die forever.

Look now! the more far-seeing ones among you know what to do. They send their children far, far away, to the dominions of the Giaours, there to learn worldly wisdom, and prepare to make great changes in the empire.

The old dervishes, the friends of the Turks, are excluded from the Seraglio; they do but creep stealthily up and peep through the guarded gates, and compare notes with one another, "Behold! within there, they are doing the work of the stranger, they are teaching the true-believing warriors to leap to and fro at a word of command, and twirl their weapons. They have abandoned the jiridé, that ever-victorious weapon, and have stuck darts at the ends of their muskets, as do the unbelievers, who dare not come within sword-distance of the enemy. It is all over, all over with the faith of Osman."

Most jealous of all these innovations were the priests of Begtash. One could every moment see them in their ragged, dirty mantles, lounging about in front of the gates of the Seraglio, impudently looking in the faces of all who go in and out ; and if an imam passed them, or one of those wise men who favored the innovations, they would spit after him, and exclaim in a loud voice, "Death to every one who proclaims the forbidden word !"

Now this forbidden word was the name "Neshandchi." The mob of Stambul had murdered Mahmoud's father because of this name, which designated a new order of soldiers, and his successor had been compelled to order that whoever pronounced this name should be put to death.

The mob would often follow the Grand Vizier all the way to the palace, reviling him all the way, and shouting up at the windows, "Remember the end of Bajraktar !"

Bajraktar had been the Sultan's Grand Vizier fourteen years before, who had wished to reform the Turkish army, on which account a riot broke out at Stambul, which lasted till the partisans of Bajraktar were removed from office. As for Bajraktar himself, he was burned to death in one of his palaces, together with his wife and children. Every one who took part in these mysterious and accursed deliberations in the Seraglio, from the lowliest soldier to the sacred and sublime Sultan himself, carried his life in his hands.

It had long been rumored that some great movement was on foot, and the priests of Begtash went from town to town through all the Turkish domains fanning the fanaticism of their beloved children, the Janissaries, and gradually collecting them in Stambul. In those days there were more than twenty thousand Janissaries within the walls of the capital, not including the corporation of water-carriers who generally made common cause with them in times of uproar. When their lordships, the Janissaries, set the place on fire, it was the duty of the water-carriers to put out the flames, whereupon they plundered comfortably together; hence the ancient understanding between them.

With the exception of the Ulemas, only the blind fakirs of the Omarite order were admitted into the council of the Divan, and their chief, Behram, often took counsel with the Sultan for hours together when he was alone.

On the 23d May, 1826, at the invitation of the chief mufti, all the Ulemas assembled in the Seraglio and decided unanimously that, in accordance with the words of the Kuran, it was lawful to fight the enemy with his own weapons.

Six days later they reassembled, and then the Sheik-ul-Islam laid before them a fetva, by which it was proclaimed that a standing army was to be raised for the defence of the realm. In order, however, that nobody might pronounce the accursed name of Neshandchi, three names were given to the corps of the army to be raised. The first was akinji, or "rushers," these were the young conscripts; the second was taalimlüaske, "practised men," these were selected from the soldiers of the Seraglio; the third name was khankiar begerdi, and designated the corps to be chosen from amongst the Janissaries. This name meant "the will of the emperor," yet the word "khankiar" means, in Turkish, by itself, "effusion of blood."

When the fetva came to be signed, very few of

the leaders of the Janissaries were present, but amongst those who were was the Janissary Aga, or colonel, and his name stood there alongside the name of the Sheik-ul-Islam, the Grand Vizier, and Najib Effendi.

Early next morning the people of Stambul read the fetva, which was posted up at every corner. The decisive word had been spoken which was to evoke the bloody spectre to whom so many crowned heads had been sacrificed.

The first day a fearful expectation prevailed. Every one awaited the tempest, and prepared for it. The Sultan was passing the time at his summer palace, Bekshishtash, so, at least, it was said. An anxious, tormenting, and bloody pastime it proved to be.

In one wing of his palace were the damsels of the harem, in the others the chief Ulemas and councillors. Mahmoud paced from one room to another, and found peace nowhere.

Hundreds of times he sat in a row with his wise men, and caused the annals of the Ottoman Empire by his favorite historian, Ezaad Effendi, to be read aloud to him, and yet it was a terror to him to listen. The whole history from beginning to end was written in blood! The same principles always produced the same fruits! How many Grand Viziers, how many Padishahs, had not fallen? Their blood had flowed in streams from the throne, which had never tottered as it now tottered beneath him. And when he returned to the harem, and the charming odalisks appeared before him with their music and dances, and Milieva amongst them, the loveliest of them all, to whom in an hour of rapture he had given the rose-garden of his realm, Damascus, he bethought him that perchance to-morrow, or even that very night, those sweetly smiling heads might all be cut off, seized by their flowing locks and cast in heaps, while their dear and tender bodies might be sent swimming in the cold waves of the Bosphorus, to serve as food for the monsters of the deep. Who knows how many hours, who knows how many moments, they have still to live?

Every hour, every moment, the tidings arrive from Stambul that the Janissaries are assembling in menacing crowds, and now the conflagrations begin; every day fires break out in three or four parts of the town, but the heavy rains prevented any great damage from being done. This was always the way in which the riots began in Stambul.

The priests of Begtash stirred up the fanaticism of the masses in front of the mosques and in the public squares, incited the mob which had joined the ranks of the Janissaries to acts of outrage against the Sultan's officials and those of the Ulemas, softas, and Omarite fakirs who were in favor of the reforms.

On July 14th a rumor spread that a company of Janissaries, actuated by strong suspicion, had surrounded the cemetery which had been laid out and enclosed by the Omarite fakir, and cut down all the dervishes they found there, and amongst them their chief, Behram. They found upon him a bundle of papers which plainly revealed that a secret understanding existed between him and the great men of the Seraglio. They also found in his girdle a metal plate, on which was the following inscription:

"I am Behram, the son of Halil Patrona, the

strong man, and of Gül-Bejáze,* the prophetess. My father in his lifetime began a great work, which after his death I continued. This work will only be accomplished and confirmed when I am dead and there is no further need of me. Blessed be he who knoweth the hours of his life and of his death."

Those who were acquainted with the life and the end of Halil Patrona knew right well what this great work was thus mentioned by Behram, who had lived one hundred and eight years after his father's death, and had striven all that time to develop and mature the ideas which the former had vainly attempted to carry out at the point of the sword.

The mob tore the dervish to pieces and distributed his bleeding limbs as trophies, and then, like wild beasts who have scented blood, they attacked the castles of the great men. Whom should they fall upon first? That was the only question.

Suddenly one of the priests of Begtash tore down from the corner of the street a copy of the fetva which proclaimed the reform and showed it to the mob. "Behold!" cried he, "here, foremost amongst the names of the destroyers of the Faith stands the name of the Janissary Aga! The leader of the Janissaries has himself betrayed his own children. Death to him!"

"Death to him!" howled the mob, and, seizing their torches, they rushed towards the palace of the Janissary Aga.

The Janissary Aga heard the tumult, and, quick-

---

* The heroine of Jókai's *White Rose*.

ly dressing a slave in his robes, mingled with the crowd, and, without being noticed, reached the palace of the Grand Vizier in safety.

The Grand Vizier was sitting down to supper when the Janissary Aga rushed in and informed him of his danger. He lost no time in barricading the gates, and, slipping through his garden with his servants and his family, escaped across the Bosphorus to the Jali Kiosk, on the other side of the water. The besieging mob, therefore, only found empty walls upon which to wreak their fury, and these they levelled with the ground.

But the Janissary Aga had left his wives and children in his palace, and these the rioters seized and murdered with the most excruciating tortures. In the evening twilight the Aga, from his place of safety on the other side of the water, could see the flames of his palace shooting up towards the sky, and heard perchance the agonized death-cries of those he loved best.

A few moments later they were joined by Nedjib Effendi, the representative of the Viceroy of Egypt, who also took refuge with them and brought the tidings that the insurgents were in possession of the whole of Stambul, and had wreaked their savage fury on the families of the refugee magnates.

The Sultan was standing on the roof of his palace, whence he could view far away the spreading scarlet glow of the conflagration which lit up the night with a terrifying glare, whose fiery columns were reflected in the black Bosphorus.

Panic-stricken fugitives spread the report that the Seraglio itself was in flames, and indeed it looked in the distance as if the fiery waves had reached its cupolaed towers.

Mahmoud spent the whole night in prayer. Two hours after midnight a horseman arrived who had forced his way through Stambul, his good steed collapsing as it reached the cypress grove of Bekshishtash. The horseman himself demanded an audience of the Sultan, and was instantly admitted.

A bright momentary ray of hope was visible on the face of Mahmoud as he recognized the horseman. It was Thomar, now the Akinji Feriki, the bravest warrior in the three continents of the Ottoman Empire.

When Mahmoud had quitted the Seraglio he had picked out sixteen young horsemen from amongst his retinue, and left them behind in the palace, with the injunction that if a rebellion should break out in Stambul, which was pretty certainly to be anticipated, they were to cut their way through the enemy and bring him word thereof. Thomar alone had arrived—the other fifteen had been killed by the rebels; he had cut out a road for himself and contrived to reach Bekshishtash.

"The dragon has raised all his twelve heads, my master," said he to the Sultan; "now is the time to cut them all off, or it will devour thy empire."

The Sultan, who greatly loved the youth, wiped the sweat from his face with his own handkerchief, and bade him await him below in the banqueting-chamber.

And with that he resumed his devotions.

Towards five o'clock, when the sun rose from behind the blue hills of Asia in all its glory, the Sultan descended from the roof of his palace and commanded his servants and men-at-arms to form in rank in front of the palace. All the fighting-men he had with him were a thousand akinjis and about as many horsemen, silchidars, and bostanjis. He himself first went to take leave of his womenkind.

Those who had seen his face but an hour ago were amazed at the change that had come over it. Its generally mild and peaceful expression had given place to a proud resentment and a death-defying audacity. He embraced his wife and the Sultana Asseki, and finally his son, the heir to the throne. Not a tear was visible on his face as he embraced his beloved ones. They all noticed a new vigor flashing from his eyes; he looked as if he were inspired. He had no need now for any to encourage him.

As he held one arm round his wife and the other round his child, he said to them, "And now I go. My path leads me into Stambul; whether it will lead me back again I know not. But I swear that if I do return it will be as the veritable ruler of my realm. What will ye do if I perish?"

The face of Milieva glowed at this question. She led Mahmoud aside into the back part of the room. There the Sultan perceived a large heap of pillows and cushions.

"If Mahmoud perishes," said the Circassian girl, enthusiastically, "those who loved him will discover a way of following him; yea, thine enemies, when they look for us, will only find our ashes here."

Mahmoud kissed the girl on the forehead; she was indeed worthy to sit at the foot of the throne.

With that he descended into the court-yard, and they led his good steed in front of the arched door.

The Sultan beckoned to Thomar to hold the reins while he mounted, then he detached an agate from the heron plume that waved above his turban, and fastened it on the fez of the youth as he knelt before him.

"I name thee leader of the akinjis; and now whoever has a sword, let him show that he is worthy of our ancestors!"

With these words the Padishah drew his scimitar, and, galloping to the front of his horsemen, took the place of command. A moment later the little host was already on its way to Stambul. In front marched the akinjis with glittering bayonets; in the centre was the Sultan with his suite; the rear was brought up by the horsemen and the gardeners. Every one of them was resolved to die honorably and gloriously.

On reaching the city the bold band met at first with but little opposition, for they came unawares. The rebels were weary from the exertions of the previous night. After putting out the conflagration the mob had set to work plundering, and towards morning the greater part of it had dispersed amongst the coffee-houses and other places of amusement.

Mahmoud and his aggressive band met with no opposition right up to the Seraglio. The streets indeed were thronged by a noisy mob, but it made way at once before the serried ranks of the akinjis. None insulted the Sultan by so much as an offensive word; on the contrary, cries of admiration were audible here and there. Men were astounded when they beheld the Padishah appear with a handful of armed men amidst the raging tempest, and permitted him to enter the gates of the Seraglio in peace.

The shout bursting through all the doors, which resounded for some minutes from the inside of the place, announced to those outside what courage the appearance of the Sultan had instilled into the hearts of those of his warriors who were shut up in the Seraglio.

Kara Makan, full of amazement, withdrew the bulk of the rebels from the Grand Signior's palace and massed the Janissaries near the Etmeidan, where banners were hoisted side by side with the subverted kettles. At the corners of the streets the wild priests of Begtash continued to incite the agitated mob with hoarse cries, and from the summits of the minarets the horns of the rebels sounded continuously, only ceasing at such times as the imams summoned the people of Osman to glorify Allah, about the fifth hour of the day. At the sound of the namazat even the furious popular tempest abated, only beginning again when the last notes of the call to prayer ceased to resound.

Stambul was literally turned upsidedown, and the dregs were swimming on the surface. The confraternity of porters, the water-carriers, the boatmen, all stood by the Janissaries and swelled enormously the bulk of the rebels. Every mosque, every barrack, was in their power; even the towers of the Dardanelles had opened their gates to the Jamaki, who were in alliance with the Janissaries. The Sultan was shut up in his own palace.

The Janissaries intended to carry the edifice of the Sublime Porte by assault, and had, therefore, sent forth criers to the jebejis, or camp-blacksmiths, who were encamped with the heavy cannons on the grounds of the Mosque of Sophia, to invite them to begin the siege.

The emissaries of the Janissaries, in brief, savage harangues, called upon the jebejis to put their hands to the bloody work. The latter listened to them, but for a long time hesitated. Suddenly a shot fired from amongst the crowd struck one of the speakers, who fell down dead, whereupon the other jebejis rushed upon the envoys of the Janissaries, cut them down, and, flinging their severed heads into a heap, shouted, "Long live the Sultan!" and with that they proceeded in force to the Seraglio, took up their positions in front of it, and turned their guns against the rebels.

Towards mid-day, amidst strains of martial music, the Kapudan Pasha Ibrahim, whose nickname was "The Infernal," arrived with four thousand marines and fourteen guns. A quarter of an hour later were to be seen in the proximity of the Jali Kiosk the overwhelming forces of the Grand Vizier Muhammad, who, under the protection of the night, had got together the hosts of Asia, which had always been opposed to the Janissaries. The Janissary Aga was there, too, with the Komparajis from Tophana. The concentrating masses welcomed one another with blood-thirsty greeting. It was evident, from the faces of their leaders, that they were determined not to retreat a step on the path they had taken. The last hour of the Janissaries, or of the Ottoman Empire, had struck.

And now the gates of the Seraglio were thrown open, and, escorted by the high officers of state and the Ulemas, the Sultan came forth.

The Ulemas, the imams, and the officers of the army stood in a semicircle round the gate. The Sultan remained standing on the highest step. There he stood in the full regalia of the padishahs, holding in one hand the banner of the Prophet and in the other a drawn sword.

"What do the rebels desire," exclaimed, with a loud, penetrating voice, the Sheik-ul-Islam, "who rise up against Allah and against the Head of the Faith, the Padishah?"

The chief mufti replied with unction: "It is written in the Kuran, 'If the infidels rise against their brethren, let them die the death!'"

"Then swear by the banner of the Prophet that ye will root out them who have risen up against me!"

The viziers kissed the holy flag and took the oath to defend it to the last drop of their blood.

"And now close the gates!" commanded the Sultan; and immediately he sent orders to the warders of all the gates of Stambul to let nobody either out or in. One of the opposing hosts was never to leave the city alive.

"Long life to the Sultan! Death to the Janissaries!" resounded from fifteen thousand lips in front of the Seraglio.

The Sultan would have led his army in person against the rebels, but his generals fell down on their knees and implored him in the name of the Prophet not to expose his life to danger. Let him at least give his sword to the Grand Vizier, that he might not soil it in the blood of rebels.

So the gates were shut. This circumstance filled the hearts of the rebels with terror. They foresaw that this day would not be followed by another; the hand of indulgence, of reconciliation, now grasped the weapons of war, of massacre.

They all assembled round the Etmeidan, pulled down the buildings in the street, and made barricades of them. 'Tis a bad sign for a rebellion when it has to look to its defence.

The forces of the Grand Vizier slowly approached amidst the roll of kettle-drums; the Derben Aga appeared in front of the barricades of the Janissaries, with the sanjak-i-sherif in his hand, and summoned the rebels to disperse and return to the allegiance of the sacred banner. The rebels drowned his speech in curses, and above the curses rose the thundering voice of Kara Makan hounding on the fanatical mob against the destroyers of the faith of Osman.

"Wipe out these new ordinances, give up the heads of the godless ones who signed their names below the khat-i-sherif—to wit the Janissary Aga, the Grand Vizier, the chief mufti, and Nedjib Effendi! This is what the ortas of the Janissaries demand and their honest confederates, the Jamaki, the Kayikjis, and the Hamaloks, who remain faithful to the God of the Moslemin."

Thrice did the Derben Aga summon the rebels to surrender, and thrice did he receive the same answer. They demanded the heads of the viziers.

Mahmoud's predecessor had, on a similar request, surrendered the heads of the viziers. Mahmoud broke his sword in two above their heads, and throwing the broken pieces in the dust, exclaimed:

"Just as I now break in two this sword and nobody shall weld it together again, so also shall ye be overthrown and none shall raise you up again."

The next moment the cannons of Ibraham the Infernal thundered forth their volleys from the Etmeidan. The bombs tore through the rickety wooden barriers, and through the breach thus made rushed Hussein Pasha at the head of the akinjis with Thomar Bey by his side.

The appearance of the detested new soldiers was greeted by the Janissaries with a furious howl, but the very first moment convinced them that the bayonet was a very much more powerful weapon than the dirk. Thomar Bey headed the charge in person, making a way for himself with his bayonet and clearing the ranks of the insurgents like a sharp wedge.

On this side there was no deliverance, so now, with the fury of despair, the insurgents flung themselves on the guns of Ibraham Pasha, three times charging his death-vomiting batteries, and, thrice recoiling, leaving the ground covered with their corpses, the terrible grape-shot mowing them down in heaps.

It was all, all over. The flowers of Begtash's garden, vanquished, humbled by the new soldiers, fled for refuge to the huge quadrangular barracks which occupied the ground at the rear of the Etmeidan.

Kara Makan did not live to experience that hour of humiliation; a cannon-ball took off his head so cleanly that his body could only be identified by his girdle.

Within the walls of the barracks the Janissaries made ready for their last desperate combat. It was now late. Ibrahim the Infernal began to bombard the barracks with red-hot bullets, and within an hour's time the whole of the enormous building was in flames. Those who were inside the gates remained there, for there they were doomed to perish together. Amidst the roaring of the flames their death-cries were audible, but the flames grew stronger every moment and the cry of their mortal anguish waxed fainter. The generals stood around the building, and tears glittered in more eyes than one; after all, it had been a valiant host!

Had been! Those words explain their doom.

On that day twenty thousand Janissaries fell by the command of the Padishah. Those whom the bullet and the sword did not reach perished by the axe and the bowstring. Their bodies were given to the Bosphorus, and for a long time afterwards the billows of distant seas cast their headless trunks on the shores of countries far away. These were the flowers of Begtash.

And so the name of the Janissaries was blotted out of the annals of Ottoman history.

The wearing of their uniforms and their insignia was forbidden under sentence of death. Their barracks were levelled with the ground, their banners were torn to bits, their kettles were smashed to pieces, their memory was made accursed.

The order of the Priests of Begtash was abolished forever, their religious homes were destroyed, their possessions confiscated.

Thus came to an end a soldiery which had existed for centuries, which the wise Chendereli founded, and which had won so many glorious triumphs for the Ottoman arms. It was now unlawful to mention its very name.

But when the bloody work was done, the Ottoman nation arose again full of fresh vigor, and it owed a new life, full of glorious days, to the hand which delivered the empire from its two greatest enemies—Tepelenti and the Janissaries.

GLOSSARY OF THE TURKISH WORDS USED IN THIS STORY

AGA—a military and aulic title.
AKINJI—a sort of irregular cavalry.
ANADOLI HISSAR—eastern castle.
AZAB—irregular infantry.
BAIRAM—the great Muhammadan ecclesiastical feast.
BAYADERE—a dancing-girl.
BEY—a dignitary next below a pasha.
BOSTANJI—originally the gardeners of the Seraglio, subsequently attendants, body-guards.
CHORBAJI—a Janissary officer.
CIAUS—palace officials employed as attendants, messengers, envoys.
DERBEND AGA—the chief of the street watchmen.
DIRHAM—a coin worth about $2\frac{1}{2}d$.
DIVAN—council of state.
DZHIN—a huge supernatural being.
EFFENDI—a title of honor.
ETMEIDAN—the headquarters of the Janissaries.
FETVA—the opinion or judgment of a mufti.
FIRAK—bodies of troops.
FIRMAN—a decree issued by the Sultan.
GIAOUR—an infidel.
ICHOGLANLER—pages of non-Muhammadan parentage brought up at the Sultan's palace.
IMAM—a priest who recites the canonical prayers.

JAMAK—the servant of a Janissary.
JANISSARIES—literally, "new soldiers" (jeni-cheri), originally captive children brought up to be soldiers. This corps was for centuries the flower of the Ottoman army.
JANISSARY AGA—the chief of the Janissaries.
JERID—a stick used as a dart in military exercises.
KADI—a judge.
KADUN-KEIT-KHUDA—guardian of the harem.
KAPU-AGASI—Lord Chamberlain.
KAPUDAN PASHA—Lord High Admiral.
KAPUJI—gate-keeper of the Seraglio.
KAPUJI PASHA—the introducer of the ambassadors.
KAPU-KIAJA—chief magistrate.
KHAT-I-SHERIF—a command either signed by the Sultan or issued directly through him.
KHUMBARAJI—a bombardier.
KIZLAR-AGASI—chief inspector of the harem.
MOLLAH—the title of the highest grade of Ulemas.
MUEZZIN—the caller to prayer.
MUFTIS—those of the Ulemas who publish or seal the fetvas or other public documents.
MURSHID—a spiritual guide.
NAMAZAT—the canonical prayer.
ODALISK—a concubine; literally, chambermaid.
ORTA—a company of Janissaries.
PALIKÁR—"strong youth," a name given to themselves by the Klephts, freebooters of Thessaly.
PARA—a farthing.
REIS-EFFENDI—Minister of Foreign Affairs.
SANDJAK-I-SHERIF—the sacred banner of the Prophet.
SERAGLIO } The Sultan's court.
SERAI
SERAI-AGASI—chief inspector of the Seraglio.
SERASKIER—a commander-in-chief.
SHEIK-UL-ISLAM—the chief of all the muftis and Ulemas.
SILCHIDARS—one of the six divisions of the mercenary cavalry, also the Sultan's armor-bearers.

SIPAHIS \} One of the six divisions of the mercenary cavalry.
SPAHIS /

SULIOTES—a warlike Hellenized race of Albanian origin in the Pachalik of Janina.

SULTANA-ASSEKI—The Sultan's consort.

SULTANA-VALIDEH—the Sultan's mother.

TIMARIOTES—Turkish feudal militia.

TOPORABAJI—gunners.

TOPIJIS—gunners.

ULEMAS—the learned men, including the muftis, the mollahs, the kadis—in short, all the legal and ecclesiastical functionaries.

THE END

www.ingramcontent.com/pod-product-compliance
Lightning Source LLC
Chambersburg PA
CBHW022116230426
43672CB00008B/1407